The History of American Education

GOLDENTREE BIBLIOGRAPHIES
IN AMERICAN HISTORY

under the series editorship of
ARTHUR S. LINK

AMERICAN COLONIES IN THE EIGHTEENTH CENTURY, THE, 1689-1763 •
Jack P. Greene

AMERICAN COLONIES IN THE SEVENTEENTH CENTURY, THE • Alden T. Vaughan

AMERICAN ECONOMIC HISTORY BEFORE 1860 • George Rogers Taylor

AMERICAN ECONOMIC HISTORY SINCE 1860 • Edward C. Kirkland

AMERICAN REVOLUTION, THE • John Shy

AMERICAN SOCIAL HISTORY BEFORE 1860 • Gerald N. Grob

AMERICAN SOCIAL HISTORY SINCE 1860 • Robert H. Bremner

GILDED AGE, THE, 1877-1896 • Vincent P. De Santis

HISTORY OF AMERICAN EDUCATION, THE • Jurgen Herbst

MANIFEST DESTINY AND THE COMING OF THE CIVIL WAR, 1841-1860 •
Don E. Fehrenbacher

NATION IN CRISIS, THE 1861-1877 • David Donald

PROGRESSIVE ERA AND THE GREAT WAR, THE, 1896-1920 • Arthur S. Link &
William M. Leary, Jr.

RELIGION IN AMERICAN LIFE • Nelson R. Burr

FORTHCOMING TITLES

AFRO-AMERICAN HISTORY

AMERICAN DIPLOMATIC HISTORY BEFORE 1890 • Norman A. Graebner

AMERICAN DIPLOMATIC HISTORY SINCE 1890 • W. B. Fowler

AMERICAN CONSTITUTIONAL DEVELOPMENT • Alpheus T. Mason

AMERICAN NATIONALISM AND SECTIONALISM, 1801-1841 • Edwin A. Miles

AMERICAN URBAN DEVELOPMENT • Seymour J. Mandelbaum

CONFEDERATION AND THE CONSTITUTION, THE, 1781-1801 • E. James Ferguson

FRONTIER AND THE AMERICAN WEST, THE • Rodman W. Paul

NEW SOUTH, THE • Paul M. Gaston

OLD SOUTH, THE • Fletcher M. Green

THE HISTORY OF AMERICAN EDUCATION

compiled by

Jurgen Herbst

The University of Wisconsin

AHM PUBLISHING CORPORATION
Northbrook, Illinois 60062

134559

016.37
H538

Copyright © 1973
AHM PUBLISHING CORPORATION

ISBN: 0-88295-531-4

Library of Congress Card Number: 76-178293

PRINTED IN THE UNITED STATES OF AMERICA

713-1

Editor's Foreword

GOLDENTREE BIBLIOGRAPHIES IN AMERICAN HISTORY are designed to provide students, teachers, and librarians with ready and reliable guides to the literature of American history in all its remarkable scope and variety. Volumes in the series cover comprehensively the major periods in American history, while additional volumes are devoted to all important subjects.

Goldentree Bibliographies attempt to steer a middle course between the brief list of references provided in the average textbook and the long bibliography in which significant items are often lost in the sheer number of titles listed. Each bibliography is, therefore, selective, with the sole criterion for choice being the significance—and not the age—of any particular work. The result is bibliographies of all works, including journal articles and doctoral dissertations, that are still useful, without bias in favor of any particular historiographical school.

Each compiler is a scholar long associated, both in research and teaching, with the period or subject of his volume. All compilers have not only striven to accomplish the objective of this series but have also cheerfully adhered to a general style and format. However, each compiler has been free to define his field, make his own selections, and work out internal organization as the unique demands of his period or subject have seemed to dictate.

The single great objective of *Goldentree Bibliographies in American History* will have been achieved if these volumes help researchers and students to find their way to the significant literature of American history.

Arthur S. Link

Preface

This bibliography has grown out of my teaching a course in the history of American education. It is my hope that with its help students will be encouraged to investigate a great variety of subjects on their own. Graduate students may find the bibliography useful when preparing for comprehensive examinations.

The bibliography's subject matter has suggested a classification of general works in areas frequently touched on in a course on educational history as well as an arrangement by historical periods of books and essays of limited chronological coverage. As titles have been listed only once, readers searching for material on a given subject should look under the relevant headings in both the "General Works" category and the chronologically arranged categories. They should also consult the references given at the end of most sections, which will direct attention to related titles elsewhere in the collection.

While an alphabetical listing by authors' last names is common practice in this and other bibliographies of the series, titles in sections 12, 15B and 15C have been arranged alphabetically by state or name of institution, respectively. The bibliography does not include unpublished dissertations.

J. H.

Abbreviations

Ag Hist	Agricultural History
Ala Rev	Alabama Review
ACLS Newsletter	American Council of Learned Societies Newsletter
Am Hist Rev	American Historical Review
Am J Ed	American Journal of Education
Am J Psy	American Journal of Psychiatry
Am Lit	American Literature
Am Q	American Quarterly
Am Sch	American Scholar
Am Soc Rev	American Sociological Review
Ann Assn Am Geog	Annals, Association of American Geographers
Ann Iowa	Annals of Iowa
Ann Rep Am Hist Assn	Annual Report, American Historical Association
Ark Hist Q	Arkansas Historical Quarterly
Brit J Ed Stud	British Journal of Educational Studies
Brit J Socio	British Journal of Sociology
Bull Am Assn Univ Prof	Bulletin, American Association of University Professors
Bull Assn Am Col	Bulletin, Association of American Colleges
Bull Atomic Scientists	Bulletin of the Atomic Scientists
Bull Conn Hist Soc	Bulletin, Connecticut Historical Society
Bull School Ed (Ind)	Bulletin, School of Education, Indiana University
Bur Ed Res Col Ed (Ill)	Bureau of Educational Research, College of Education (University of Illinois)
Cal Law Rev	California Law Review
Cam Hist J	Cambridge Historical Journal
Cath Hist Rev	Catholic Historical Review
Church Hist	Church History
Coll R I Hist Soc	Collections, Rhode Island Historical Society
Colum U Q	Columbia University Quarterly
Conn Q	Connecticut Quarterly
Contrib Philos Psy Ed (Colum)	Columbia University Contributions to Philosophy, Psychology, and Education
Del Hist	Delaware History
Econ Hist Rev	Economic History Review

Ed Forum	Educational Forum
Ed Rec	Educational Record
Ed Res Bull	Educational Research Bulletin (Ohio State University)
Ed Rev	Educational Review
Ed Theory	Educational Theory
El School J	Elementary School Journal
El School Tchr	Elementary School Teacher
Fil Club	Filson Club
Fla Hist Q	Florida Historical Quarterly
Ga Hist Q	Georgia Historical Quarterly
Grad J	Graduate Journal
Har Al Bull	Harvard Alumni Bulletin
Har Ed Rev	Harvard Educational Review
Har Grad Mag	Harvard Graduates Magazine
Har Law Rev	Harvard Law Review
Historian	The Historian
Hist Ed J	History of Education Journal
Hist Ed Q	History of Education Quarterly
Hist Mag P E Church	Historical Magazine of the Protestant Episcopal Church
Hunt Lib Q	Huntington Library Quarterly
Ind Mag Hist	Indiana Magazine of History
Int J Ethics	The International Journal of Ethics
Iowa J Hist	Iowa Journal of History
J Am Hist	Journal of American History
J Am St	Journal of American Studies
J Chem Ed	Journal of Chemical Education
J Cont Hist	Journal of Contemporary History
J Econ Hist	Journal of Economic History
J Ed Res	Journal of Educational Research
J Gen Ed	Journal of General Education
J High Ed	Journal of Higher Education
J Hist Ideas	Journal of the History of Ideas
J Ill State Hist Soc	Journal of the Illinois State Historical Society
J Miss Hist	Journal of Mississippi History
J Mod Hist	Journal of Modern History
J Neg Ed	Journal of Negro Education
J Neg Hist	Journal of Negro History
J Presb Hist Soc	Journal of the Presbyterian Historical Society
J S Hist	Journal of Southern History
J Soc Iss	Journal of Social Issues
J Tchr Ed	Journal of Teacher Education
Kan Hist Q	Kansas Historical Quarterly
La Hist Q	Louisiana Historical Quarterly
Lib Ed	Liberal Education
Libr Q	Library Quarterly
Md Hist Mag	Maryland Historical Magazine
Mich Hist	Michigan History
Minn Hist	Minnesota History

Miss Val Hist Rev	Mississippi Valley Historical Review
Neb Hist Mag	Nebraska History Magazine
N Eng Q	New England Quarterly
N J Hist	New Jersey History
N Y Hist Soc Q	New York Historical Society Quarterly
N Y Hist	New York History
N C Hist Rev	North Carolina Historical Review
NW Ohio Q	Northwest Ohio Quarterly
Ohio Hist Q	Ohio Historical Quarterly
Ore Hist Soc Q	Oregon Historical Society Quarterly
Pac Hist Rev	Pacific Historical Review
Pae Hist	Paedagogica Historica
Pap Am Hist Assn	Papers, American Historical Association
Pap New Haven Colony Hist Soc	Papers, New Haven Colony Historical Society
P and P	Past and Present
Peabody J Ed	Peabody Journal of Education
Pa Hist	Pennsylvania History
Pa Mag Hist Bio	Pennsylvania Magazine of History and Biography
Philos Rev	Philosophical Review
Proc Am Ant Soc	Proceedings, American Antiquarian Society
Proc Am Philos Soc	Proceedings, American Philosophical Society
Proc Miss Val Hist Assn	Proceedings, Mississippi Valley Historical Association
Proc Vt Hist Soc	Proceedings, Vermont Historical Society
Prog Ed	Progressive Education
Pub Am Jew Hist Soc	Publications, American Jewish Historical Society
Pub Clark Univ Lib	Publications, Clark University Library
Pub Colonial Soc Mass	Publications, Colonial Society of Massachusetts
PMLA	Publications, Modern Language Association
Rec Am Cath Hist Soc Phil	Records, American Catholic Historical Society of Philadelphia
Rev Ed Res	Review of Educational Research
Rev Pol	Review of Politics
R I Hist	Rhode Island History
School Rev	School Review
School Soc	School and Society
Smith Inst, Ann Rep	Smithsonian Institution, Annual Report
S Atl Q	South Atlantic Quarterly
S C Hist Mag	South Carolina Historical Magazine
SW Hist Q	Southwestern Historical Quarterly
Tchr Col Rec	Teachers College Record
Tenn Hist Q	Tennessee Historical Quarterly
U S Bur Ed Bull	United States Bureau of Education Bulletin

U S Bur Ed, Circ Info	United States Bureau of Education, Circular of Information
U S Bur Ed, Rep Comm	United States Bureau of Education, Report of the Commissioner
U S Off Ed Bull	United States Office of Education Bulletin
U S Off Ed Pam	United States Office of Education Pamphlet
U S D A Misc Pub	United States Department of Agriculture, Miscellaneous Publication
U S Dept HEW Bull	United States Department of Health, Education, and Welfare Bulletin
Va Mag Hist Bio	Virginia Magazine of History and Biography
Wash Hist Q	Washington Historical Quarterly
W Pa Hist Mag	Western Pennsylvania Historical Magazine
Wm Mar Col Q Hist Mag	William and Mary College Quarterly Historical Magazine
Wm Mar Q	William and Mary Quarterly
Wis J Ed	Wisconsin Journal of Education
Wis Mag Hist	Wisconsin Magazine of History
Yale Rev	Yale Review
Yale Univ Lib Gaz	Yale University Library Gazette
Yrbk Nat Soc Stud Ed	Yearbook, National Society for the Study of Education

NOTE:

Cross-references are to page and item number. Items marked by a dagger (†) are available in paperback edition at the time this bibliography goes to press. The publisher and compiler invite suggestions for additions to future editions of the bibliography.

Contents

I. General Works

1. Bibliography

1 ALTBACH, Philip G. *Student Politics and Higher Education in the United States: A Select Bibliography.* St. Louis, 1968.

2 *Bibliography of Industrial, Vocational, and Trade Education.* US Bur Ed Bull 1913, no. 22. Washington, D.C., 1913.

3 *Bibliography of the Relation of Secondary Schools to Higher Education.* US Bur Ed Bull 1914, no. 32. Washington, D.C., 1914.

4 BLESSING, James H. *Graduate Education: An Annotated Bibliography.* US Off Ed Bull 1961, no. 26. Washington, D.C., 1961.

5 BRICKMAN, William W. *A Guide to Research in Educational History.* New York, 1949.

6 BROWN, Elmer E. "The History of Secondary Education in the United States—Bibliography." *School Rev,* V (1897), 59-66, 139-147.

7 BUTLER, Nicholas M., ed. *Educational Review: Analytical Index to Volumes 26-50, June, 1903, to December, 1915.* Easton, Pa., 1916.

8 CHAMBERS, Merritt M. "A Brief Bibliography of Higher Education in the Middle Nineteen Sixties." *Bull School Ed* (Ind), XLII (1966), 1-52.

9 CORDASCO, Francesco. "Poor Children and Schools: A Bibliography." *Choice,* VII (1970), 202-212, 355-356.

10 Educational Policies Commission. *A Bibliography on Education in the Depression.* Washington, D.C., 1937.

11 EELLS, Walter C. *Bibliography on Junior Colleges.* U S Off Ed Bull, no. 2. Washington, D.C., 1930.

12 EELLS, Walter C., and Ernest V. HOLLIS. *The College Presidency, 1900-1960: An Annotated Bibliography.* Washington, D.C., 1961.

13 GOUGHER, Ronald L. "Comparison of English and American Views of the German University, 1840-1865: A Bibliography." *Hist Ed Q,* IX (1969), 477-491.

14 GRAY, Ruth A., comp. *Bibliography of Research Studies in Education.* US Off Ed Bull 1928, no. 2. Washington, D.C., 1928. (Continued annually under various editors; contains section on educational history.)

15 *Index to the Reports of the Commissioner of Education: 1867-1907.* U S Bur Ed Bull 1909, no. 7. Washington, D.C., 1909.

16 JORGENSON, Lloyd P. "Materials on the History of Education in State Historical Journals." *Hist Ed Q,* VII (1967), 234-254, 369-389; VIII (1968), 510-527; IX (1969), 73-87.

2

1 *List of Publications of the United States Bureau of Education, 1867-1910.* U S Bur Ed Bull 1910, no. 3. Washington, D.C., 1910.

2 *List of Publications of the United States Office of Education, 1910-1936, Including Those of the Former Federal Board for Vocational Education from 1919 to 1933.* US Off Ed Bull 1937, no. 22. Washington, D.C., 1937.

3 MANN, B. Pickman. "Bibliography of Horace Mann." *U S Bur Ed, Rep Comm 1896-1897.* Vol. I. Washington, D.C., 1898, pp. 897-927.

4 MEETH, L. Richard, ed. *Selected Issues in Higher Education: An Annotated Bibliography.* New York, 1965.†

5 MENEFEE, Louis A., and Merritt M. CHAMBERS. *American Youth: An Annotated Bibliography.* Washington, D.C., 1938.

6 MONROE, Walter S., and Ollie ASHER. *A Bibliography of Bibliographies.* Bur Ed Res Col Ed (Ill), Bull no. 36. Urbana, Ill., 1927.

7 MONROE, Will S. *Bibliography of Education.* New York, 1897, 1968. (For works printed before 1900.)

8 NELSON, C., ed. *Educational Review: Analytical Index to Volumes 1-25, January, 1891 to May, 1903.* Easton, Pa., 1904.

9 NELSON, Martha F., comp. *Index by Authors, Titles, and Subjects to the Publications of the National Education Association for Its First Fifty Years, 1857 to 1906.* Winona, Minn., 1907.

10 PARK, Joe. *The Rise of American Education: An Annotated Bibliography.* Evanston, Ill., 1965.†

11 POLITELLA, Joseph. *Religion in Education: An Annotated Bibliography.* Oneonta, N.Y., 1956.

12 PORTER, Dorothy B., and Ethel M. ELLIS, comps. *The Journal of Negro Education: Index to Volumes 1-31, 1932-1962.* Washington, D.C., 1963.

13 PROCTOR, William M., comp. *Annotated Bibliography on Adult Education.* New York, 1934.

14 THOMAS, Milton H. *John Dewey: A Centennial Bibliography.* Chicago, 1962.

15 United States, Bureau of Education. *Analytical Index to Barnard's American Journal of Education.* Washington, D.C., 1892.

16 WILSON, Louis N. *Bibliography of Child Study for the Years 1908-1909.* U S Bur Ed Bull 1911, no. 11. Washington, D.C., 1911. (See also several annual continuations.)

17 WRIGHT, Edith A., and Mary S. PHILLIPS. *Bulletins of the Bureau of Education, 1906-1927.* U S Bur Ed Bull 1928, no. 17. Washington, D.C., 1928.

18 WYER, James I., Jr., and Martha L. PHELPS. *Bibliography of Education for 1907.* U S Bur Ed Bull 1908, no. 3. Washington, D.C., 1908. (See also subsequent annual volumes.)

See also 44.5, 92.9.

2. Historiography

19 BAILYN, Bernard. "Education as a Discipline: Some Historical Notes." *The Discipline of Education.* Ed. J. Walton. Madison, 1963.

1   BAILYN, Bernard. *Education in the Forming of American Society.* Chapel Hill, 1960.†

2   BRICKMAN, William W. "Conant, Koerner, and the History of Education." *School Soc*, XCII (1964), 135-139.

3   BRICKMAN, William W. "Educational Literature Review: Educational History of the United States." *School Soc*, LXXII (1950), 436-444.

4   BRICKMAN, William W. "An Historical Survey of Foreign Writings on American Educational History." *Pae Hist*, II (1962), 5-21.

5   BRICKMAN, William W. "Revisionism and the Study of the History of Education." *Hist Ed Q*, IV (1964), 209-223.

6   BUCK, Paul H., et al. *Education and American History.* New York, 1965.† (Published by the Committee on the Role of Education in American History —The Fund for the Advancement of Education.)

7   CREMIN, Lawrence A. *The Wonderful World of Ellwood Patterson Cubberley.* New York, 1965.†

8   CREMIN, Lawrence A., et al. "The Role of the History of Education in the Professional Preparation of Teachers." *Hist Ed J*, VII (1955-1956).

9   GOOD, Harry G. "The Approach to the History of Education." *School Soc*, XX (1924), 231-237.

10 HANSEN, Allen O. "Integrative Anthropological Method in History of Culture and Education." *Ed Forum*, I (1937), 361-378.

11 HENDRICK, Irving G. "History of Education and Teacher Preparation: A Cautious Analysis." *J Tchr Ed*, XVII (1966), 71-76.

12 KALISCH, Philip, and Harry HUTTON. "Davidson's Influence on Educational Historiography." *Hist Ed Q*, VI (1966), 79-87.

13 LILGE, Frederic. "The Functionalist Fallacy and the History of Education." *School Soc*, LXV (1947), 241-243.

14 MAYHEW, Lewis B. "The Literature of Higher Education." *Ed Rec*, XLVI (1965), 5-32.

15 RANDEL, William P. *Edward Eggleston.* New York, 1963.†

16 ROUCEK, Joseph. "The 'Foreign' Roots of American Educational History." *Ed Forum*, XXVII (1962), 47-57.

17 SMITH, Wilson. "The New Historian of American Education." *Har Ed Rev*, XXXI (1961), 136-143.

18 SPINDLER, George D. *Education and Culture: Anthropological Approaches.* New York, 1963.

19 STOUTEMEYER, J. H. "The Teaching of the History of Education in Normal Schools." *School Soc*, VII (1918), 571-580.

20 SWIFT, Fletcher H. "The Specific Objectives of a Professional Course in the History of Education." *Tchr Col Rec*, XXIII (1922), 12-18.

21 TYACK, David B. "The History of Education and the Preparation of Teachers: A Reappraisal." *J Tchr Ed*, XVI (1965), 427-431.

22 VEYSEY, Laurence R. "Toward a New Direction in Educational History: Prospect and Retrospect." *Hist Ed Q*, IX (1969), 343-359.

1 WESLEY, Edgar B. "Lo, the Poor History of Education." *Hist Ed Q*, IX (1969), 329-342.

See also 98.13, 99.2.

3. College Texts: General Surveys and Essays

2 BOONE, Richard G. *Education in the United States: Its History from the Earliest Settlements.* New York, 1889.

3 BORROWMAN, Merle, and Charles BURGESS. *History of American Education: The Clash of Ideologies.* Glenview, Ill., 1969.

4 BURGESS, Charles, and Merle L. BORROWMAN. *What Doctrines to Embrace: Studies in the History of American Education.* Glenview, Ill., 1969.†

5 BUTTS, R. Freeman, and Lawrence A. CREMIN. *A History of Education in American Culture.* New York, 1953.

6 CUBBERLEY, Ellwood P. *Public Education in the United States: A Study and Interpretation of American Educational History.* 2d ed. Boston, 1962.

7 CURTI, Merle E. *The Social Ideas of American Educators.* Paterson, N.J., 1959.†

8 DABNEY, Charles W. *Universal Education in the South.* 2 vols. Chapel Hill, 1936.

9 DAVIDSON, Thomas. *A History of Education.* New York, 1900.

10 DEXTER, Edwin G. *A History of Education in the United States.* New York, 1904.

11 EBY, Frederick. *The Development of American Education in Theory, Organization, and Practice.* 2d ed. New York, 1952.

12 EDWARDS, Newton, and Herman G. RICHEY. *The School in the American Social Order.* 2d ed. Boston, 1963.

13 FRENCH, William M. *America's Educational Tradition: An Interpretive History.* Boston, 1964.

14 GOOD, Harry G. *A History of American Education.* 2d ed. New York, 1962.

15 GUTEK, Gerald. *An Historical Introduction to American Education.* New York, 1970.

16 KARIER, Clarence J. *Man, Society, and Education: A History of American Educational Ideas.* Glenview, Ill., 1967.†

17 KNIGHT, Edgar W. *Education in the United States.* 3d rev. ed. Boston, 1951.

18 KNIGHT, Edgar W. *Public Education in the South.* Boston, 1922.

19 KRUG, Edward A. *Salient Dates in American Education: 1635-1964.* New York, 1966.†

20 MEYER, Adolphe E. *An Educational History of the American People.* 2d ed. New York, 1967.

21 MONROE, Paul. *Founding of the American Public School System.* 2 vols. New York, 1940. (2d vol. on Microfilm.)

1 MOORE, Ernest C. *Fifty Years of American Education: A Sketch of the Progress of Education in the United States from 1867 to 1917.* Boston, 1917.

2 NOBLE, Stuart G. *A History of American Education.* 2d ed. New York, 1954.

3 REISNER, Edward H. *Nationalism and Education Since 1789: A Social and Political History of Modern Education.* New York, 1922.

4 RIPPA, S. Alexander. *Education in a Free Society: An American History.* New York, 1967.†

5 THAYER, Vivian T. *Formative Ideas in American Education: From the Colonial Period to the Present.* New York, 1965.†

6 THWING, Charles F. *A History of Education in the United States Since the Civil War.* Boston, 1910.

7 WELTER, Rush. *Popular Education and Democratic Thought in America.* New York, 1962.†

8 WIEBE, Robert H. "The Social Functions of Public Education." *Am Q*, XXI (1969), 147-164.

9 WIGGIN, Gladys A. *Education and Nationalism: An Historical Interpretation of American Education.* New York, 1962.

See also 10.9, 10.12, 10.13, 10.14, 26.17, 86.12, 87.13-14, 87.17, 88.4

4. Anthologies of Documents and Readings

10 BEST, John H., and Robert T. SIDWELL, eds. *The American Legacy of Learning: Readings in the History of Education.* Philadelphia, 1967.†

11 CALHOUN, Daniel. *The Educating of Americans: A Documentary History.* Boston, 1969.†

12 COWLEY, Elizabeth B. *Free Learning.* Boston, 1941.

13 CUBBERLEY, Ellwood. *Readings in Public Education in the United States.* Boston, 1934.

14 EHLERS, Henry J., and Gordon C. LEE, eds. *Crucial Issues in Education: An Anthology.* Rev. Ed. New York, 1959.†

15 GROSS, Carl H., and Charles C. CHANDLER, eds. *The History of American Education Through Readings.* Boston, 1964.

16 HILLWAY, Tyrus, ed. *American Education, an Introduction Through Readings: A Collection of Basic Documents and Literature on the American School System.* Boston, 1964.†

17 HINSDALE, Burke A. "Documents Illustrative of American Educational History." *U S Bur Ed, Rep Comm 1892-1893.* Vol. II. Washington, D.C., 1895, pp. 1225-1414.

18 KNIGHT, Edgar W., ed. *A Documentary History of Education in the South Before 1860.* 5 vols. Chapel Hill, 1949-1953.

1   KNIGHT, Edgar W., and Clifton L. HALL, eds. *Readings in American Educational History*. New York, 1951.

2   RIPPA, S. Alexander, ed. *Educational Ideas in America: A Documentary History*. New York, 1969.†

3   TYACK, David B., ed. *Turning Points in American Educational History*. Waltham, Mass., 1967.†

4   VASSAR, Rena L., ed. *Social History of American Education*. 2 vols. Chicago, 1965.†

    See also 14.11-12, 14.19, 15.6, 16.8, 20.10, 24.6, 30.13, 74.2, 74.3, 75.9.

5. Books and Essays on Special Subjects

A. SCHOOLBOOKS

5   BARNARD, Henry. "American Textbooks." *Am J Ed*, XIII (1863), 202-222, 401-408, 626-640; XIV (1864), 751-757; XV (1865), 639-675.

6   BLACK, Marian W. "The Battle over Uniformity of Textbooks in Florida, 1868-1963." *Hist Ed Q*, IV (1964), 106-118.

7   BROWN, Ralph H. "The American Geographies of Jedidiah Morse." *Ann Assn Am Geog*, XXXI (1941), 145-217.

8   CARPENTER, Charles. *History of American Schoolbooks*. Philadelphia, 1963.

9   DONNALLY, Williams. "The Haymarket Riot in Secondary School Textbooks." *Har Ed Rev*, VIII (1938), 205-216.

10   ELSON, Ruth M. "American Schoolbooks and 'Culture' in the Nineteenth Century." *Miss Val Hist Rev*, XLVI (1959-1960), 411-435.

11   ELSON, Ruth M. *Guardians of Tradition: American Schoolbooks of the Nineteenth Century*. Lincoln, Neb., 1964.

12   ENGLAND, J. Merton. "The Democratic Faith in American Schoolbooks of the Republic, 1783-1861." *Am Q*, XV (1963), 191-199. (See also author's essay in *University of Birmingham Historical Journal*, IX (1963), 92-111.)

13   FELL, Marie L. *The Foundations of Nativism in American Textbooks, 1783-1860*. Washington, D.C., 1941.

14   FORD, Paul L., ed. *The New England Primer*. New York, 1962.†

15   GARFINKLE, Norton. "Conservatism in American Textbooks, 1800-1860." *N Y Hist*, XXXV (1954), 49-63.

16   JOHNSON, Clifton. *Old Time Schools and Schoolbooks*. New York, 1925.†

1   MARTIN, Helen. *Nationalism in Children's Literature.* Chicago, 1936.

2   MOSIER, Richard D. *Making the American Mind: Social and Moral Ideas in the McGuffey Readers.* Rev. ed. New York, 1965.

3   NIETZ, John A. *The Evolution of American Secondary School Textbooks.* Rutland, Vt., 1966.

4   NIETZ, John A. *Old Textbooks: Spelling, Grammar, Reading, Arithmetic, Geography, American History, Civil Government, Physiology, Penmanship, Art, Music—As Taught in the Common Schools From Colonial Days to 1900.* Pittsburgh, 1961.

5   NIETZ, John A. "Why the Longevity of the McGuffey Readers?" *Hist Ed Q*, IV (1964), 119-125.

6   RUGGLES, Alice M. *The Story of the McGuffeys.* New York, 1950.

7   SHANKLAND, Rebecca H. "The McGuffey Readers and Moral Education." *Har Ed Rev*, XXXI (1961), 60-72.

8   SPIESEKE, Alice W. *The First Textbooks in American History and Their Compiler John McCulloch.* New York, 1938.

9   VAIL, Henry H. *A History of the McGuffey Readers.* Rev. ed. Cleveland, 1911.

10 YOUNKER, Donna L. "The Moral Philosophy of William Holmes McGuffey." *Ed Forum*, XXVIII (1963), 71-77.

See also 15.1, 20.9, 42.14, 52.1, 52.13, 56.17, 106.4, 108.7.

B. *CURRICULUM*

11 BAGSTER-COLLINS, E. E. "History of Modern Language Teaching in the United States." *Studies in Modern Language Teaching.* Ed. W. W. Bager-Collins et al. New York, 1930, pp. 3-96.

12 BONSER, Frederick G. *Elementary School Curriculum.* New York, 1922.

13 CAJORI, Florian. *The Teaching and History of Mathematics in the United States.* U S Bur Ed, Circ Info, no. 3. Washington, D.C., 1890.

14 DOUGHERTY, Mary L. "History of the Teaching of Handwriting in America." *El School J*, XVIII (1917), 280-286.

15 GOODLAD, John I. *The Changing School Curriculum.* New York, 1966.

16 HANDSCHIN, Charles H. *The Teaching of Modern Languages in the United States.* U S Bur Ed Bull 1913, no. 3. Washington, D.C., 1913.

17 LAWSON, Douglas E. *Curriculum Development in City School Systems.* Chicago, 1940. (Concerns period from 1836 to 1936.)

18 LYMAN, Rollo L. *English Grammar in American Schools Before 1850.* U S Bur Ed Bull 1921, no. 12. Washington, D.C., 1922.

1 MEYERS, Ira B. "The Evolution of Aims and Methods in the Teaching of Nature—Study in the Common Schools of the United States." *El School Tchr*, XI (1910), 205-213, 237-248.

2 MEYERS, Ira B. "A History of the Teaching of Nature in the Elementary and Secondary Schools of the United States." *El School Tchr*, VI (1906), 258-264.

3 MONROE, Walter S. *The Development of Arithmetic as a School Subject.* Boston, 1917.

4 OSGOOD, Edith W. "The Development of Historical Study in the Secondary Schools of the United States." *School Rev*, XXII (1914), 444-454, 511-526.

5 PIERCE, Bessie L. *Public Opinion and the Teaching of History in the United States.* New York, 1926, 1970.

6 SUNDERMAN, Lloyd F. "History of Public School Music in the United States, 1830 to 1890." *Ed Rec*, XXII (1941), 205-211.

7 THURSFIELD, Richard E., ed. *The Study and Teaching of American History.* Washington, D.C., 1946.

8 WHEAT, Harry G. "Changes and Trends in Arithmetic Since 1910." *El School J*, XLVII (1946), 134-144.

9 WHITFORD, W. G. "Brief History of Art Education in the United States." *El School J*, XXIV (1923), 109-115.

See also 26.15, 27.5, 27.12, 27.17, 28.7, 29.10, 29.18, 29.21, 43.6, 52.12, 52.15, 57.2, 66.2, 68.13, 91.14, 91.16, 97.4, 98.6, 98.8, 106.11.

C. TEACHERS AND TEACHING

10 BARZUN, Jacques. *Teacher in America.* Boston, 1945.†

11 BEALE, Howard K. *A History of Freedom of Teaching in American Schools.* New York, 1936.

12 ELSBREE, Willard S. *The American Teacher, Evolution of a Profession in a Democracy.* New York, 1939.

13 JEWETT, James P. "The Fight Against Corporal Punishment in American Schools." *Hist Ed J*, IV (1952), 1-10.

14 WALL, James H. "Psychiatric Disorders in Fifty School Teachers." *Am J Psy*, XCVI (1939), 137-145.

See also 53.12, 54.4, 54.10, 55.3, 55.7, 56.4, 56.6, 56.14, 57.4, 57.9, 57.14.

D. SCHOOL ADMINISTRATION

15 BUCHNER, Edward F. *Educational Surveys.* U S Bur Ed Bull 1918, no. 45. Washington, D.C., 1919.

16 CUBBERLEY, Ellwood P., and Edward C. ELLIOTT. *State and County School Administration.* Vol. II: "Source Book." New York, 1915.

1 GILLAND, Thomas M. *The Origin and Development of the Power and Duties of the City School Superintendent.* Chicago, 1935.

2 MANN, Carleton H. *How Schools Use Their Time; Allotment Practice in 444 Cities Including a Study of Trends from 1826 to 1926.* New York, 1926.

3 PIERCE, Paul R. *The Origin and Development of the Public School Principalship.* Chicago, 1935.

4 SHERMAN, Jay J. "History of the Office of County Superintendent of Schools in Iowa." *Iowa J Hist*, XXI (1923), 3-93.

5 SMITH, Henry L., and Charles H. JUDD. *Plans for Organizing School Surveys with a Summary of Typical School Surveys.* 13th Yrbk Nat Soc Stud Ed. P. II. Bloomington, Ill., 1914.

6 STRAYER, George D. "The Education of the Superintendent of Schools." *Tchr Col Rec*, XLVI (1944), 169-176.

7 SUZZALO, Henry. *The Rise of Local School Supervision in Massachusetts (The School Committee, 1635-1827).* New York, 1905.

8 WELLS, Guy F. "The First School Survey." *Ed Rev*, L (1915), 166-174. (Rhode Island in 1845.)

See also 18.15, 56.11, 72.17, 89.10.

E. KINDERGARTEN AND PRESCHOOL EDUCATION

9 BLOW, Susan E. "The History of the Kindergarten in the United States." *Outlook*, LV (1897), 932-938.

10 "Early History of the Kindergarten in St. Louis, Mo." *U S Bur Ed, Rep Comm 1896-1897.* Vol. I. Washington, D.C., 1898, pp. 899-922.

11 International Kindergarten Union. *Pioneers of the Kindergarten in America.* New York, 1924. (Committee of Nineteen.)

12 JENKINS, Elizabeth. "How the Kindergarten Found Its Way to America." *Wis Mag Hist*, XIV (1930-1931), 48-62.

13 PEABODY, Elizabeth P. "Kindergarten Culture." *U S Bur Ed, Rep Comm 1870.* Washington, D.C., 1870, pp. 354-359.

14 PEABODY, Elizabeth P. "The Objects of the Kindergarten." *U S Bur Ed, Rep Comm 1871.* Washington, D.C., 1872, pp. 529-534.

15 WEBER, Evelyn. *The Kindergarten: Its Encounter with Educational Thought in America.* New York, 1969.

See also 72.8.

F. THE FAMILY AND CHILDHOOD

16 ABBOTT, Grace, ed. *The Child and the State.* 2 vols. Chicago, 1938.

17 BRONFENBRENNER, Urie, and John C. CONDRY, Jr. *Two Worlds of Childhood: U.S. and U.S.S.R.* New York, 1970.

18 CALHOUN, Arthur. *A Social History of the American Family from Colonial Times to the Present.* 3 vols. Cleveland, 1917-1919.

1 FLEMING, Sandford. *Children and Puritanism: The Place of Children in the Life and Thought of the New England Churches, 1620-1847.* New Haven, 1933.

2 GOODSELL, Willystine. *A History of the Family as a Social and Educational Institution.* New York, 1915.

3 KIEFER, Monica M. *American Children Through Their Books, 1700-1835.* Philadelphia, 1948.

4 KUHN, Anne L. *The Mother's Role in Childhood Education: New England Concepts, 1830-1860.* New Haven, 1947.

5 SAVETH, Edward N. "The Problem of American Family History." *Am Q,* XXI (1969), 311-329.

6 SIRJAMAKI, John. *The American Family in the Twentieth Century.* Cambridge, Mass., 1953.

7 SUNLEY, Robert. "Early Nineteenth Century American Literature on Child Rearing." *Childhood in Contemporary Culture.* Ed. Margaret Mead and M. Wolfenstein. Chicago, 1955.

8 WISHY, Bernard W. *The Child and the Republic: The Dawn of Modern American Child Nurture.* Philadelphia, 1967.

See also 1.9, 51.7, 51.9, 52.5, 52.6, 52.20, 54.6, 54.14, 55.9, 56.21, 91.13, 91.19, 109.12.

G. EDUCATION AND CULTURE

9 CREMIN, Lawrence A. *The Genius of American Education.* Pittsburgh, 1965.†

10 DITZION, Sidney H. *Arsenals of a Democratic Culture.* Chicago, 1947. (Concerns public libraries, 1850-1900.)

11 ENDRES, Raymond J. "Elementary School Functions in the United States: An Historical Analysis." *Pae Hist,* VII (1967), 378-416.

12 GREENE, Maxine. *The Public School and the Private Vision: A Search for America in Education and Literature.* New York, 1965.†

13 HENDERSON, John C. *Our National System of Education: An Essay.* New York, 1877.

14 HOFSTADTER, Richard. *Anti-Intellectualism in American Life.* New York, 1962.†

15 KARIER, Clarence J. "Elite Views on American Education." *J Cont Hist,* II (1967), 149-163. (Also in *Education and Social Structure in the Twentieth Century.* Ed. Walter Laqueur and George L. Mosse. New York, 1968.)†

16 KAZAMIAS, Andreas. "Meritocracy and Isocracy in American Education: Retrospect and Prospect." *Ed Forum,* XXV (1961), 345-354.

17 MC CLUSKEY, Neil Gerard. *Public Schools and Moral Education: The Influence of Horace Mann, William Torrey Harris, and John Dewey.* New York, 1958.

18 RICE, Edwin W. *The Sunday School Movement, 1780-1917 and the American Sunday School Union, 1817-1917.* Philadelphia, 1917.

See also 4.5, 4.7, 6.10, 106.22, 109.25.

H. MILITARY EDUCATION

1 BISHOP, Ralph C. *A Study of the Educational Value of Military Instruction in Universities and Colleges.* U S Off Ed, Pam, no. 28. Washington, D.C., 1932.

2 CHAMBERS, Merritt M. *"Every Man a Brick." The Status of Military Training in American Universities.* Bloomington, Ill., 1927.

3 CLARK, Harold F., and Harold S. SLOAN. *Classrooms in the Military.* New York, 1964.

4 GIGNILLIAT, Leigh R. *Arms and the Boy: Military Training in the Schools.* Indianapolis, 1916.

5 MANN, C. R. "Education in the Army, 1919-1925." *Ed Rec*, Suppl no. 1 (1926), 1-62.

6 MASLAND, John, and Lawrence RADAWAY. *Soldiers and Scholars.* New York, 1957.

7 REEVES, Ira L. *Military Education in the United States.* Burlington, Vt., 1919.

8 SCHAFFER, Ronald. "The War Department's Defense of ROTC, 1920-1940." *Wis Mag Hist*, LII (1969-1970), 108-120.

9 SHELBURNE, James C., and Kenneth GROVES. *Education in the Armed Forces.* New York, 1965.

10 SIMONS, William E. *Liberal Education in the Service Academies.* New York, 1965.

11 WHITE, Bruce. "ABCs for the American Enlisted Man: The Army Post School System, 1866-1898." *Hist Ed Q*, VIII (1968), 479-496.

See also 39.1, 39.2, 39.6, 39.7, 39.8, 83.1, 84.8, 84.12, 84.14, 85.1.

6. *Transatlantic Relations*

12 AHLSTROM, Sydney E. "The Scottish Philosophy and American Theology." *Church Hist*, XXIV (1955), 257-272.

13 *American Journal of Education.* Ed. Henry Barnard. 32 vols. Hartford, 1855-1882.

14 ANDERSON, Lewis F. *Pestalozzi.* New York, 1931.

15 ARMYTAGE, W. H. G. "Alcott House: An Anglo-American Educational Experiment." *Ed Theory*, VIII (1958), 129-142.

16 ARMYTAGE, W. H. G. *The American Influence on English Education.* London, 1967.†

1 BACHE, Alexander D. *Report on Education in Europe, to the Trustees of Girard College for Orphans.* Philadelphia, 1839.

2 BALLOU, Richard B. "The Commonwealth Educators: Puritan Progressives." *Har Ed Rev*, XI (1941), 301-318.

3 BARNARD, Henry. *Pestalozzi and His Educational System.* Syracuse, 1902.

4 BASSET, John S. "The Round Hill School." *Proc Am Ant Soc*, XXVII (1917), 18-62.

5 BELL, Whitfield J., Jr. "Philadelphia Medical Students in Europe, 1750-1800." *Pa Mag Hist Bio*, LXVII (1943), 1-29.

6 BUTTERFIELD, Lyman H., ed. *John Witherspoon Comes to America.* Princeton, 1953.

7 CLIVE, John, and Bernard BAILYN. "England's Cultural Provinces: Scotland and America." *Wm Mar Q*, XI (1954), 200-213.

8 COWLEY, W. H. "European Influences upon American Higher Education." *Ed Rec*, XX (1939), 165-190.

9 DUNKEL, Harold B. *Herbart and Education.* New York, 1969.†

10 DUNKEL, Harold B. "Herbartianism Comes to America." *Hist Ed Q*, IX (1969), 202-233, 376-390.

11 EGGLESTON, Edward. *The Transit of Civilization from England to America in the Seventeenth Century.* New York, 1901.†

12 GARD, Willis. "European Influence on Early Western Education." *Ohio Hist Q*, XXV (1916), 23-36.

13 GUTEK, Gerald. *Pestalozzi and Education.* New York, 1968.†

14 HERBST, Jurgen. *The German Historical School in American Scholarship: A Study in the Transfer of Culture.* Ithaca, N.Y., 1965.

15 HILLARD, George S., ed. *Life, Letters, and Journals of George Ticknor.* 12th ed., 2 vols. Boston, 1900.

16 HINSDALE, Burke A. "Notes on the History of Foreign Influence upon Education in the United States." *U S Bur Ed, Rep Comm 1897-1898*. Vol. I. Washington, D.C., 1899, pp. 591-629.

17 JONES, Howard M. *America and French Culture.* London, 1927.

18 KNIGHT, Edgar W., ed. *Reports on European Education by John Griscom, Victor Cousin, Calvin E. Stowe.* New York, 1930.

19 KRAUS, Michael. *The Atlantic Civilization: Eighteenth Century Origins.* New York, 1949.†

20 LANCASTER, Joseph. *Improvements in Education, as It Respects the Industrious Classes of the Community, Containing Among Other Important Particulars, an Account of the Institution for the Education of One Thousand Poor Children.* 3d ed. London, 1805.

21 LANCASTER, Joseph. *The Lancasterian System of Education with Improvements.* Baltimore, 1821.

1 LONG, Orie W. *Literary Pioneers: Early American Explorers of European Culture.* Cambridge, Mass., 1935.

2 MACVANNEL, John A. "The Educational Theories of Herbart and Froebel." *Tchr Col Rec*, VI (1905), 1-114.

3 MC CADDEN, Joseph J. "Joseph Lancaster and the Philadelphia Schools." *Pa Hist*, III (1936), 225-239; IV (1937), 241-247.

4 MC GROARTY, W. B. "Alexandria's Lancasterian Schools." *Wm Mar Col Q Hist Mag*, XXI (1941), 111-118.

5 MONROE, Will S. *History of the Pestalozzian Movement in the United States.* Syracuse, 1907.

6 MOSIER, Richard D. "Hegelianism in American Education." *Ed Theory*, III (1953), 97-103.

7 NASH, Paul. "Innocents Abroad: American Students at British Universities in the Early Nineteenth Century." *Hist Ed Q*, I (1961), 32-44.

8 PAULSTON, Roland G. "French Influence in American Institutions of Higher Learning, 1784-1825." *Hist Ed Q*, VIII (1968), 229-245.

9 PINLOCHER, Auguste. *Pestalozzi and the Foundation of the Modern Elementary School.* New York, 1901.

10 Public School Society of New York. *Manual of the Lancasterian System of Teaching Reading, Writing, Arithmetic, and Needlework, as Practiced in the Schools of the Free-School Society of New York.* New York, 1820.

11 REIGART, John F. *The Lancastrian System of Instruction in the Schools of New York City.* New York, 1916.

12 SALMON, David. *Joseph Lancaster.* London, 1904.

13 SILBER, Kate. *Pestalozzi: The Man and His Work.* 2d ed. London, 1965.

14 THWING, Charles F. *The American and the German University: One Hundred Years of History.* New York, 1928.

15 TYACK, David B. *George Ticknor and the Boston Brahmins.* Cambridge, Mass., 1967.

16 WALCH, Sister Mary R. *Pestalozzi and the Pestalozzian Theory.* Washington, D.C., 1952.

17 WALZ, John A. *German Influence in American Education and Culture.* Philadelphia, 1936.

18 WICKENDEN, William E. *A Comparative Study of Engineering Education in the United States and in Europe.* Lancaster, Pa., 1929.

See also 1.13, 3.4, 3.16, 45.16, 49.10, 49.13, 52.1, 52.7, 52.17, 52.18, 53.7, 53.9, 53.15, 58.6, 58.9, 86.13, 87.16.

7. Religious Education

19 BAINTON, Roland H. *Yale and the Ministry: A History of Education for the Christian Ministry at Yale from the Founding in 1701.* New York, 1957.

1 BURNS, James A., and Bernard J. KOHLBRENNER. *A History of Catholic Education in the United States.* New York, 1937.

2 CASSIDY, Francis P. *Catholic College Foundations and Development in the United States (1677-1850).* Washington, D.C., 1924.

3 CROSS, Robert D. *The Emergence of Liberal Catholicism in America.* Cambridge, Mass., 1958.†

4 DEFERRARI, Roy J., ed. *Essays on Catholic Education in the United States.* Washington, D.C., 1942.

5 DUNLAP, William C. *Quaker Education in Baltimore and Virginia Yearly Meetings, With an Account of Certain Meetings of Delaware and the Eastern Shore Affiliated with Philadelphia.* Philadelphia, 1936.

6 GOEBEL, Edmund J. *A Study of Catholic Secondary Education During the Colonial Period up to the First Plenary Council of Baltimore, 1852.* New York, 1937.

7 HASSENGER, Robert. *The Shape of Catholic Higher Education.* Chicago, 1967.

8 HEFFERNAN, Arthur J. *A History of Catholic Education in Connecticut.* Washington, D.C., 1937.

9 HOGAN, Peter E. "Americanism and the Catholic University of America." *Cath Hist Rev*, XXXIII (1947), 158-190.

10 KAISER, Laurina. *Development of the Concept and Function of the Catholic Elementary School in the American Parish.* Washington, D.C., 1955.

11 KLAIN, Zora, ed. *Educational Activities of New England Quakers: A Source Book.* Philadelphia, 1928.

12 MC CLUSKEY, Neil G., ed. *Catholic Education in America: A Documentary History.* New York, 1964.†

13 MANIER, Edward, and John W. HOUCK, eds. *American Freedom in the Catholic University.* Notre Dame, 1967.

14 PATTILLO, Manning M., Jr., and Donald M. MACKENZIE. *Church-Sponsored Higher Education in the United States.* Washington, D.C., 1967.

15 POWER, Edward J. *A History of Catholic Higher Education in the United States.* Milwaukee, 1958.

16 QUINAN, Richard J. "Growth and Development of Catholic Education in the Archdiocese of Boston." *Cath Hist Rev*, XXII (1936), 27-41.

17 SANDERS, James W. "Catholic Elementary-School Enrollment: Chicago, 1925-65." *El School J*, LXVIII (1967), 88-96.

18 SHEEDY, Morgan M. "The Catholic Parochial Schools of the United States." *U S Bur Ed, Rep Comm 1903.* Vol. I. Washington, D.C., 1905, pp. 1079-1101.

19 WOODY, Thomas. *Quaker Education in the Colony and State of New Jersey: A Source Book.* Philadelphia, 1923.

See also 2.11, 10.18, 19.11, 28.12, 32.19, 33.6-9, 34.9, 34.17, 34.23, 35.20, 39.19, 52.17, 54.1, 55.2, 55.5, 55.8, 55.17, 56.1, 56.3, 56.9, 57.17, 58.8, 58.15, 67.4, 67.9, 80.11, 122.17.

8. Church, State, and Education

1 ALILUNOS, Leo J. "The Image of Public Schools in Roman Catholic American History Textbooks." *Hist Ed Q*, III (1963), 159-165.

2 BEGGS, David W., and R. Bruce MC QUIGG, eds. *America's Schools and Churches: Partners in Conflict.* Bloomington, 1965.

3 BELL, Sadie. *The Church, the State, and Education in Virginia.* Philadelphia, 1930.

4 BLANSHARD, Paul. *Religion and the Schools: The Great Controversy.* Boston, 1963.

5 BOLES, Donald E. *The Bible, Religion, and the Public Schools.* 3d ed. Ames, Iowa, 1965.

6 BOLES, Donald E. *The Two Swords: Commentaries and Cases in Religion and Education.* Ames, Iowa, 1967.

7 BRICKMAN, William W., and Stanley LEHRER, eds. *Religion, Government, and Education.* New York, 1961.

8 BROWN, Samuel W. *The Secularization of American Education as Shown by State Legislation, State Constitutional Provisions and State Supreme Court Decisions.* New York, 1912.

9 BRUBACHER, John S., et al. *The Public School and Spiritual Values.* New York, 1944. (7th Yearbook of the John Dewey Society.)

10 BUTTS, R. Freeman. *The American Tradition in Religion and Education.* Boston, 1950.

11 CHAPER, Jesse H. "Establishment Clause and Aid to Parochial Schools." *Cal Law Rev*, LVI (1958), 260-341.

12 CLEGG, Ambrose A., Jr. "Church Groups and Federal Aid to Education." *Hist Ed Q*, IV (1964), 137-154.

13 CONFREY, Burton. *Secularism in American Education: Its History.* Washington, D.C., 1931.

14 CURRAN, Francis A., S.J. *The Churches and the Schools: American Protestantism and Popular Elementary Education.* Chicago, 1954.

15 DRINAN, Robert F. *Religion, the Courts, and Public Policy.* New York, 1963.

16 DUKER, Sam. *The Public Schools and Religion: The Legal Context.* New York, 1966.†

17 DUNN, William K. *What Happened to Religious Education? The Decline of Religious Teaching in the Public Elementary School, 1776-1861.* Baltimore, 1958.

18 EVANS, John W. "Catholics and the Blair Education Bill." *Cath Hist Rev*, XLVI (1960), 273-298.

19 FREUND, Paul A. "Public Aid to Parochial Schools." *Har Law Rev*, LXXXII (1969), 1680-1692.

1 GOBBEL, Luther L. *Church-State Relationships in Education in North Carolina Since 1775.* Durham, N.C., 1938.

2 GRUBER, Frederick C. *Education and the State.* Philadelphia, 1960.

3 HALL, Arthur J. *Religious Education in the Public Schools of the State and City of New York.* Chicago, 1914.

4 HOLSINGER, M. Paul. "The Oregon School Bill Controversy, 1922-1925." *Pac Hist Rev*, XXXVII (1968), 327-341.

5 JOHNSON, Frederick E., ed. *American Education and Religion: The Problem of Religion in the Public Schools.* New York, 1952.

6 JORGENSON, Lloyd P. "The Oregon School Law of 1922: Passage and Sequel." *Cath Hist Rev*, LIV (1968), 455-466.

7 KERWIN, Jerome G. *The Catholic Viewpoint on Church and State.* Garden City, N.Y., 1960.

8 KLIEBARD, Herbert W. *Religion and Education in America: A Documentary History.* Scranton, Pa., 1969.

9 KOHLBRENNER, Bernard J. "Religion and Higher Education: An Historical Perspective." *Hist Ed Q*, I (1961), 45-56.

10 LA NOUE, George R. "Religious Schools and 'Secular' Subjects." *Har Ed Rev*, XXXII (1962), 255-291.

11 LAUBACH, John H. *School Prayers: Congress, the Courts, and the Public.* Washington, D.C., 1969.

12 MC AVOY, Thomas T. "Public Schools vs. Catholic Schools and James McMaster." *Rev Pol*, XXVIII (1966), 19-46.

13 MC CLUSKEY, Neil G. *The Catholic Viewpoint on Education.* Garden City, N.Y., 1959.

14 MITCHELL, Fredric, and James W. SKELTON. "The Church-State Conflict in Early Indian Education" *Hist Ed Q*, VI (1966), 41-51.

15 MOEHLMAN, Conrad H. *School and Church, the American Way: An Historical Approach to the Problem of Religious Instruction in Public Education.* New York, 1944.

16 MOEHLMAN, Conrad H. *The Wall of Separation Between Church and State: An Historical Study of Recent Criticism of the Religious Clause of the First Amendment.* Boston, 1951.

17 PERKINSON, Henry J. "The Role of Religion in American Education, an Historical Interpretation." *Pae Hist*, V (1965), 109-121.

18 PFEFFER, Leo. *Church, State and Freedom.* Rev. ed. Boston, 1967.

19 PRATT, John W. *Religion, Politics, and Diversity: The Church-State Theme in New York History.* Ithaca, N.Y., 1967.

20 ROSS, Earle D. "Religious Influences in the Development of State Colleges and Universities." *Ind Mag Hist*, XLVI (1950), 343-362.

21 SIEVERS, Harry J. "The Catholic Indian School Issue and the Presidential Election of 1892." *Cath Hist Rev*, XXXVIII (1952), 129-155.

1 SMITH, Sherman H. *The Relation of the State to Religious Education in Massachusetts.* Syracuse, 1926.

2 STALLO, Johann B., et al. *Bible in the Public Schools.* With a new introduction by Robert McCloskey. New York, 1870, 1967.

3 TYACK, David B. "The Perils of Pluralism: The Background of the Pierce Case." *Am Hist Rev*, LXXIV (1968), 74-98.

4 WALTER, Erich A., ed. *Religion and the State University.* Ann Arbor, 1958.†

   See also 2.11, 17.6, 31.11, 55.11, 68.17, 69.15, 71.6, 72.15, 72.19, 73.3, 73.4, 73.8, 73.11, 73.12, 79.6.

9. Government, the Courts, and Education

5 ALLEN, Hollis P. *The Federal Government and Education: The Original and Complete Study of Education for the Hoover Commission Task Force on Public Welfare.* New York, 1950.

6 BEACH, Fred F., and Robert F. WILL. *The State and Nonpublic Schools.* Washington, D.C., 1958.

7 BRUBACHER, John S. *The Judicial Power of the New York State Commissioner of Education: Its Growth and Present Status with A Digest of Decisions.* New York, 1927.

8 BUEHLER, Ezra C. *Federal Aid for Education.* New York, 1934.

9 BUFFUM, Hugh S. "Federal and State Aid to Education in Iowa." *Iowa J Hist*, IV (1906), 554-98; V (1907), 3-45, 147-192, 311-325.

10 BURRELL, B. Jeannette, and R. H. ECKELBERRY. "The High School Question Before the Courts in the Post-Civil War Period." *School Rev*, XLII (1934), 255-265.

11 BUTTS, R. Freeman. "States' Rights and Education." *Tchr Col Rec*, LVIII (1957), 189-197.

12 Congressional Quarterly. *The Federal Role in Education.* Washington, D.C., 1965.

13 COON, Charles L. "School Support and Our North Carolina Courts, 1868-1926." *N C Hist Rev*, III (1926), 399-438.

14 EDWARDS, Newton. *The Courts and the Public Schools: The Legal Basis of School Organization and Administration.* Rev. ed. Chicago, 1955.

15 ENSIGN, Forest C. *Compulsory School Attendance and Child Labor: A Study of the Historical Development of Regulations Compelling Attendance and Limiting the Labor of Children in a Selected Group of States.* Iowa City, 1921.

16 FELLMAN, David, ed. *The Supreme Court and Education.* New York, 1960.†

17 FLANDERS, Jesse K. *Legislative Control of the Elementary Curriculum.* New York, 1925.

1 GAUERKE, Warren E. "Organized Labor and Federal Aid to Education." *Hist Ed J*, IV (1953), 81-92.

2 KIZER, George A. "Federal Aid to Education, 1945-1963." *Hist Ed Q*, X (1970), 84-102.

3 KNIGHT, George W. "History and Management of Land Grants for Education in the Northwest Territory." *Pap Am Hist Assn*, I (1885), 79-247.

4 LEE, Gordon C. *The Struggle for Federal Aid, First Phase: A History of the Attempts to Obtain Federal Aid for the Common Schools, 1870-1890.* New York, 1949.

5 MAYO, Amory D. "Original Establishment of State School Funds." *U S Bur Ed, Rep Comm 1894-1895.* Vol. II. Washington, D.C., 1896, pp. 1505-1511.

6 MORT, Paul R. *Federal Support for Public Education: A Report of an Investigation of Educational Need and Relative Ability of States to Support Education as They Bear on Federal Aid to Education.* New York, 1936.

7 MUNGER, Frank J., and Richard F. FENNO. *National Politics and Federal Aid to Education.* Syracuse, 1962. (No. 3 in *The Economics and Politics of Public Education.*)

8 PETERSON, LeRoy J., Richard A. ROSSMILLER, and Marlin M. VOLZ. *The Law and Public School Operation.* New York, 1969.

9 PIERCE, Truman M. *Federal, State, and Local Government in Education.* Washington, D.C., 1964.

10 PITKIN, Royce S. *Public School Support in the United States During Periods of Economic Depression.* Brattleboro, Vt., 1933.

11 REISNER, Edward H. "Antecedents of the Federal Acts Concerning Education." *Ed Rec*, XI (1930), 196-207.

12 RUSSELL, John D. "The Evolution of the Present Relations of the Federal Government to Education in the United States." *J Neg Ed*, VII (1938), 244-255.

13 SCHAFER, Joseph. *The Origin of the System of Land Grants for Education.* Bulletin of the University of Wisconsin. Madison, 1902.

14 SPURLOCK, Clark. *Education and the Supreme Court.* Urbana, Ill., 1955.

15 STRAYER, George D., Jr. *Centralizing Tendencies in the Administration of Public Education: A Study of Legislation for Schools in North Carolina, Maryland, and New York Since 1900.* New York, 1934.

16 SUFRIN, Sidney. *Issues in Federal Aid to Education.* Syracuse, 1962. (No. 4 in *The Economics and Politics of Public Education.*)†

17 SWIFT, Fletcher H. *Federal Aid to Public Schools.* U S Bur Ed Bull 1922, no. 47. Washington, D.C., 1923.

18 SWIFT, Fletcher H. *Federal and State Policies in Public School Finance in the United States.* New York, 1931.

19 SWIFT, Fletcher H. *A History of Public Permanent Common School Funds in the United States, 1795-1905.* New York, 1911.

20 SWISHER, Jacob. "A Century of School Legislation in Iowa." *Iowa J Hist*, XLIV (1946), 174-205.

1 TAYLOR, Howard C. *The Educational Significance of the Early Federal Land Ordinances.* New York, 1922.

2 THUT, I. N. "Some Historical Factors Bearing upon the Authority of States in Education." *Ed Theory*, IX (1959), 193-202.

3 TIEDT, Sidney W. *The Role of the Federal Government in Education.* New York, 1966.†

4 TODD, Lewis P. *Wartime Relations of the Federal Government and the Public Schools, 1917-1918.* New York, 1945.

See also 19.7, 20.4, 22.2, 23.17, 25.12, 28.13, 29.12, 36.18, 46.6, 46.9, 47.13, 49.14, 52.3, 52.16, 56.16, 59.5, 59.13, 72.17, 77.14, 85.15, 102.2, 103.4, 103.5, 103.11, 103.15, 104.2, 104.7, 109.3.

10. Racial Minorities and Education

5 ALDERMAN, Edwin A., and Churchill G. ARMISTEAD. *J. L. M. Curry: A Biography.* New York, 1911.

6 ASHMORE, Harry S. *The Negro and the Schools.* Chapel Hill, 1954.†

7 BEATTY, Willard W. "The Federal Government and the Education of Indians and Eskimos." *J Neg Ed*, VII (1938), 267-272.

8 BOND, Horace M. *The Education of the Negro in the American Social Order.* Englewood Cliffs, N.J., 1934.

9 BULLOCK, Henry A. *A History of Negro Education in the South: From 1619 to the Present.* Cambridge, Mass., 1967.†

10 CARTER, Thomas P. *Mexican Americans in School: A History of Educational Neglect.* Princeton, 1970.

11 CLEMENT, Rufus E. "The Church School as a Factor in Negro Life." *J Neg Hist*, XII (1927), 5-12.

12 CLIFT, Virgil A., Archibald W. ANDERSON, and H. Gordon HULLFISH, eds. *Negro Education in America: Its Adequacy, Problems, and Needs.* New York, 1962. (16th Yearbook of the John Dewey Society.)

13 DE COSTA, Frank A. "The Relative Enrollment of Negroes in the Common Schools in the United States." *J Neg Ed*, XXII (1953), 416-431.

14 FUNKE, Loretta. "The Negro in Education." *J Neg Hist*, V (1920), 1-21.

15 "General Condition of Education Among the Indians." *U S Bur Ed, Rep Comm 1870.* Washington, D.C., 1870, pp. 339-354.

16 JACKSON, Reid E. "The Development and Character of Permissive and Partly Segregated Schools." *J Neg Ed*, XVI (1947), 301-310.

17 JOHNSON, Charles S. *The Negro College Graduate.* Chapel Hill, 1938.

18 JOHNSON, Charles S., and Horace M. BOND. "The Investigation of Racial Differences Prior to 1910." *J Neg Ed*, III (1934), 328-339.

19 JONES, Thomas J. *Negro Education.* 2 vols. U S Bur Ed Bull 1916, nos. 38 and 39. Washington, D.C., 1916.

1 KING, E. J. "Segregation and American Society." *Brit J Ed Stud*, V (1956), 3-14.

2 KNOX, Ellis O. "A Historical Sketch of Secondary Education for Negroes." *J Neg Ed*, IX (1940), 440-453.

3 KNOX, Ellis O. "The Origin and Development of the Negro Separate School." *J Neg Ed*, XVI (1947), 269-279.

4 LANE, David A., Jr. "The Development of the Present Relationship of the Federal Government to Negro Education." *J Neg Ed*, VII (1938), 273-281.

5 LEAVELL, Ullin W. *Philanthropy in Negro Education.* Nashville, 1930.

6 NEWBOLD, Nathan C. *Five North Carolina Negro Educators.* Chapel Hill, 1939. (Simon G. Atkins, James B. Dudley, Annie W. Hollard, Peter W. Moore, Ezekiel E. Smith.)

7 PRATT, Richard H. *Battlefield and Classroom: Four Decades with the American Indian, 1867-1904.* Ed. Robert M. Utley. New Haven, 1964.

8 REID, Ira De A. "The Development of Adult Education for Negroes in the United States." *J Neg Ed*, XIV (1945), 299-306.

9 SAHLI, John R. "The Slavery Issue in Early Geography Textbooks." *Hist Ed Q*, III (1963), 153-158.

10 WEINBERG, Meyer, ed. *Integrated Education: A Reader.* Beverly Hills, Calif., 1968.†

11 WOODSON, Carter G. *The Education of the Negro Prior to 1861: A History of the Education of the Colored People of the United States from the Beginning of Slavery to the Civil War.* New York, 1915.

12 WRIGHT, Marian. *The Education of Negroes in New Jersey.* New York, 1941. (Covers years 1776-1932.)

See also 2.12, 4.8, 4.18, 5.19, 16.14, 35.1, 36.11, 53.18, 54.1, 54.9, 58.7, 73.15, 74.8, 108.21, 109.8.

11. The Education of Women

13 BLANDIN, I. M. E. *History of Higher Education of Women in the South Prior to 1860.* Washington, D.C., 1909.

14 BOAS, Louise S. *Woman's Education Begins: The Rise of the Women's Colleges.* Norton, Mass., 1935.

15 CAPEN, Eliza P. "Zilpah Grant and the Art of Teaching; 1829." *N Eng Q*, XX (1947), 347-364. (Concerns teaching at Ipswich Female Academy in Massachusetts in days of Mary Lyon.)

16 CROSS, Barbara M., ed. *The Educated Woman in America: Selected Writings of Catharine Beecher, Margaret Fuller, and M. Carey Thomas.* New York, 1965.†

17 DEXTER, Elisabeth W. *Colonial Women of Affairs: Women in Business and the Professions in America Before 1776.* 2d ed., rev. Boston, 1931.

18 GILCHREST, Beth. *Life of Mary Lyon.* New York, 1910. (In re Mt. Holyoke College.)

1 GOODSELL, Willystine, ed. *Pioneers of Women's Education in the United States: Emma Willard, Catherine Beecher, Mary Lyon.* New York, 1931.

2 HARVESON, Mae E. *Catherine Ester Beecher: Pioneer Educator.* Philadelphia, 1932.

3 HUGHES, Robert M., and Joseph A. TURNER. "Notes on Higher Education of Women in Virginia." *Wm Mar Col Q Hist Mag*, IX (1929), 325-334.

4 LUTZ, Alma. *Emma Willard: Pioneer Educator of American Women.* Boston, 1964.

5 MC CLELLAND, Clarence P. "The Education of Females in Early Illinois." *J Ill State Hist Soc*, XXXVI (1943), 378-407.

6 MAC LEAR, Martha. *The History of Education of Girls in New York and New England, 1800-1870.* Washington, D.C., 1926.

7 NEWCOMER, Mabel. *A Century of Higher Education for American Women.* New York, 1959.

8 RICHARDSON, Eudora R. "The Case of the Women's Colleges in the South." *S Atl Q*, XXIX (1930), 126-139.

9 ROBINSON, Mabel L. *The Curriculum of the Woman's College.* U S Bur Ed Bull 1918, no. 6. Washington, D.C., 1918.

10 SACK, Saul. "The Higher Education of Women in Pennsylvania." *Pa Mag Hist Bio*, LXXXIII (1959), 29-73.

11 SHERZER, Jane. "The Higher Education of Women in the Ohio Valley Previous to 1840." *Ohio Hist Q*, XXV (1916), 1-26.

12 SMITH, Anna T. "Coeducation in the Schools and Colleges of the United States." *U S Bur Ed, Rep Comm 1903.* Vol. I. Washington, D.C., 1905, pp. 1047-1078.

13 SYKES, Fredrick H. "The Social Basis of the New Education for Women." *Tchr Col Rec*, XVIII (1917), 226-242.

14 TAYLOR, James M. *Before Vassar Opened: A Contribution to the History of the Higher Education of Women in America.* New York, 1915.

15 THOMPSON, Eleanor W. *Education for Ladies, 1830-1860.* New York, 1947.

16 THORNTON, Harrison J. "Coeducation at the State University of Iowa." *Iowa J Hist*, XLIV (1947), 380-412. (Concerns the 1840s and 1850s.)

17 WOODY, Thomas. *A History of Women's Education in the United States.* 2 vols. Lancaster, Pa., 1929.

See also 32.17, 32.18, 33.2, 34.6, 36.12, 37.13, 37.22, 38.21, 39.4, 46.18, 55.19, 79.11, 113.2, 121.3.

12.   Education in the Individual States (arranged by states in alphabetical order)

18 CLARK, Willis G. *The History of Education in Alabama.* U S Bur Ed, Circ Info 1889, no. 3. Washington, D.C., 1889.

1 WEEKS, Stephen B. *History of Public School Education in Alabama.* U S Bur Ed, Circ Info 1915, no. 12. Washington, D.C., 1915.

2 WEEKS, Stephen B. *History of Public School Education in Arizona.* U S Bur Ed Bull 1918, no. 17. Washington, D.C., 1918.

3 SHINN, Josiah H. *History of Education in Arkansas.* U S Bur Ed, Circ Info 1900, no. 1. Washington, D.C., 1900.

4 WEEKS, Stephen B. *History of Public School Education in Arkansas.* U S Bur Ed Bull 1912, no. 27. Washington, D.C., 1912.

5 FALK, Charles J. *The Development and Organization of Education in California.* New York, 1968.†

6 GRIFFIN, Orwin B. *Evolution of the Connecticut State School System.* New York, 1928.

7 STEINER, Bernard C. *The History of Education in Connecticut.* U S Bur Ed, Circ Info 1893, no. 2. Washington, D.C., 1893.

8 POWELL, Lyman P. *The History of Education in Delaware.* U S Bur Ed, Circ Info 1893, no. 3. Washington, D.C., 1893.

9 WEEKS, Stephen B. *History of Public School Education in Delaware.* U S Bur Ed Bull 1917, no. 18. Washington, D.C., 1917.

10 BUSH, George G. *History of Education in Florida.* U S Bur Ed, Circ Info 1888, no. 7. Washington, D.C., 1889.

11 COCHRAN, Thomas E. *History of Public School Education in Florida.* Lancaster, Pa., 1921.

12 ORR, Dorothy. *A History of Education in Georgia.* Chapel Hill, 1950.

13 WIST, Benjamin O. *A Century of Public Education in Hawaii.* Honolulu, 1940.

14 COOK, John W. *An Educational History of Illinois.* Chicago, 1912.

15 COTTON, Fassett A. *Education in Indiana, 1793-1934.* Bluffton, Ind., 1934.

16 AURNER, Clarence R. *History of Education in Iowa.* 5 vols. Iowa City, 1914-1920.

17 LIGON, Moses E. *A History of Public Education in Kentucky: A Study of the Development and Control of Public Education Based upon the Constitutional Provisions and the Legislative Acts of the General Assembly.* Lexington, Ky., 1942.

18 HILTON, C. W. et al. *The Development of Public Education in Louisiana.* Baton Rouge, 1965.

19 CHADBOURNE, Ava H. *A History of Education in Maine.* Bangor, Me., 1936.

20 CHADBOURNE, Ava H., comp. *Readings in the History of Education in Maine.* Bangor, Me., 1932.

21 STEINER, Bernard C. *History of Education in Maryland.* U S Bur Ed, Circ Info 1894, no. 2. Washington, D.C., 1894.

22 FITZGERALD, Raymond A. *A History of the Statutory Development of the Board of Education Since Its Inception, 1837-1964.* Boston, 1964.

23 MARTIN, George H. *The Evolution of the Massachusetts Public School System.* New York, 1894.

1 WICHERS, Wynand, ed. *History of Education in Michigan.* 4 vols. Detroit, 1963-1968.

2 GREER, John N. *The History of Education in Minnesota.* U S Bur Ed, Circ Info 1902, no. 2. Washington, D.C., 1902.

3 MAYES, E. *History of Education in Mississippi.* U S Bur Ed, Circ Info 1899, no. 2. Washington, D.C., 1899.

4 CARRINGTON, William T. *The History of Education in Missouri.* Jefferson City, Mo., 1931.

5 BUSH, George G. *History of Education in New Hampshire.* U S Bur Ed, Circ Info 1898, no. 3. Washington, D.C., 1898.

6 BISHOP, Eugene A. *The Development of a State School System: New Hampshire.* New York, 1930.

7 BURR, Nelson R. *Education in New Jersey, 1630-1871.* Princeton, 1942.

8 WEST, Roscoe L. *Elementary Education in New Jersey: A History.* Princeton, 1964.

9 WILEY, Tom. *Politics and Purse Strings in New Mexico Schools.* Albuquerque, 1968.

10 FINEGAN, Thomas E. *Free Schools: A Documentary History of the Free School Movement in New York State.* Albany, 1921.

11 GRIFFEY, Carl H. *The History of Local School Control in the State of New York.* New York, 1936.

12 HORNER, Harlan H., ed. *Education in New York State, 1784-1954.* Albany, 1954.

13 HOUGH, Franklin B., comp. *Historical and Statistical Record of the University of the State of New York During the Century from 1784-1884.* Albany, 1885.

14 PALMER, Archie E. *The New York Public School: Being A History of Free Education in the City of New York.* New York, 1905.

15 NOBLE, M. C. S. *A History of the Public Schools of North Carolina.* Chapel Hill, 1930.

16 SMITH, Charles L. *History of Education in North Carolina.* U S Bur Ed, Circ Info 1888, no. 2. Washington, D.C., 1888.

17 BOSSING, Nelson L. "The History of Educational Legislation in Ohio from 1851-1925." *N W Ohio Q*, XXXIX (1930), 78-219.

18 HINSDALE, Mary C. "A Legislative History of the Public School System of the State of Ohio." *U S Bur Ed, Rep Comm 1900-1901.* Vol. I. Washington, D.C., 1902, pp. 129-160.

19 WALSH, Louise G., and Matthew J. WALSH. *History and Organization of Education in Pennsylvania.* 2d ed. Indiana, Pa., 1928.

20 WICKERSHAM, James P. *A History of Education in Pennsylvania: Private and Public, Elementary and Higher, from the Time the Swedes Settled on the Delaware to the Present Day.* Lancaster, Pa., 1886.

1 CARROLL, Charles. *Public Education in Rhode Island.* Providence, 1918.

2 STOCKWELL, Thomas B. *A History of Public Education in Rhode Island, 1636 to 1876.* Providence, 1876.

3 THOMASON, John F. *The Foundations of the Public Schools of South Carolina.* Columbia, S.C., 1925.

4 HOLT, Andrew D. *The Struggle for a State System of Public Schools in Tennessee, 1903-1936.* New York, 1938.

5 EBY, Frederick. *The Development of Education in Texas.* New York, 1925.

6 EBY, Frederick, ed. *Education in Texas: Source Materials.* Austin, 1921.

7 MOFFITT, John C. *The History of Public Education in Utah.* Provo, Utah, 1946.

8 FUSSELL, Clyde G. "The Emergence of Public Education as a Function of the State in Vermont." *Proc Vt Hist Soc,* XXVIII (1960), 179-194, 268-278; XXIX (1961), 210-219.

9 STONE, Mason S. *History of Education: State of Vermont.* Montpelier, Vt., 1936.

10 HEATWOLE, Cornelius J. *A History of Education in Virginia.* New York, 1916.

11 BOLTON, Frederick E., and Thomas W. BIBB. *History of Education in Washington.* U S Off Ed Bull 1934, no. 9. Washington, D.C., 1935.

12 WILSON, J. Ormond. "Eighty Years of the Public Schools of Washington: 1805 to 1885." *U S Bur Ed, Rep Comm 1894-1895.* Vol. II. Washington, D.C., 1896, pp. 1673-1698.

13 AMBLER, Charles H. *A History of Education in West Virginia from Early Colonial Times to 1949.* Huntington, W. Va., 1951.

14 CLARK, James I. *Education in Wisconsin.* Madison, 1958.

15 DOUDNA, Edgar G. "The Making of Our Wisconsin Schools: 1848-1948." *Wis J Ed,* LXXX (1948), 219-250.

16 PATZER, Conrad. *Public Education in Wisconsin.* Madison, 1924.

See also 14.8, 15.3, 16.1, 16.3, 16.19, 17.1, 17.7, 18.15, 18.20, 20.12, 26.12, 27.18, 28.1, 28.10, 28.13, 29.7, 29.8, 29.9, 29.15, 30.2, 32.7, 47.13, 55.18, 67.12, 68.8, 72.17, 74.2, 74.3, 77.3.

13. Vocational Education and the World of Work

17 ALDRICH, F. R. "Industrial Education in the Early Nineteenth Century." *El School Tchr,* XIII (1913), 478-485.

18 ANDERSON, Lewis F. *History of Manual and Industrial School Education.* New York, 1926.

19 BENNETT, Charles A. *A History of Manual and Industrial Education up to 1870.* Peoria, Ill., 1926.

1 BENNETT, Charles A. *A History of Manual and Industrial Education, 1870-1917.* Peoria, Ill., 1937.

2 BREWER, John M., et al. *History of Vocational Guidance: Origins and Early Development.* New York, 1942.

3 CALHOUN, Daniel H. *The American Civil Engineer: Origins and Conflict.* Cambridge, Mass., 1960.

4 CALHOUN, Daniel H. *Professional Lives in America: Structure and Aspiration, 1750-1850.* Cambridge, Mass., 1965.

5 COATES, Charles P. *History of the Manual Training School of Washington University (St. Louis Manual Training School).* U S Bur Ed Bull 1923, no. 3. Washington, D.C., 1923.

6 CUROE, Philip R. V. *Educational Attitudes and Policies of Organized Labor in the United States.* New York, 1926.

7 DAVIDSON, Elizabeth H. "The Child-Labor Problem in North Carolina, 1883-1903." *N C Hist Rev*, XIII (1936), 105-121.

8 DAVIDSON, Elizabeth H. "Child-Labor Reformers in North Carolina Since 1903." *N C Hist Rev*, XIV (1937), 109-130.

9 DAVIDSON, Elizabeth H. "Early Development of Public Opinion Against Southern Child Labor." *N C Hist Rev*, XIV (1937), 230-250.

10 DOUGLAS, Paul H. *American Apprenticeship and Industrial Education.* New York, 1921.

11 FISHER, Berenice M. *Industrial Education: American Ideals and Institutions.* Madison, 1967.

12 HAWKINS, Layton S., Charles PROSSER, and John WRIGHT. *Development of Federal Legislation for Vocational Education.* Chicago, 1962.

13 JONES, Arthur J. *The Continuation School in the United States.* U S Bur Ed Bull 1907, no. 1. Washington, D.C., 1907.

14 KNEPPER, Edwin G. *History of Business Education in the United States.* Bowling Green, Ohio, 1941.

15 MANN, Charles R. *A Study of Engineering Education.* New York, 1918.

16 MAYS, Arthur B. *The Concept of Vocational Education in the Thinking of the General Educator, 1845 to 1945.* Urbana, Ill., 1946.

17 OBERMANN, Carl E. *A History of Vocational Rehabilitation in America.* Minneapolis, 1965.

18 PERRIN, John W. "Beginnings in Compulsory Education." *Ed Rev*, XXV (1903), 240-243.

19 PERRIN, John W. "Indirect Compulsory Education: The Factory Laws of Massachusetts and Connecticut." *Ed Rev*, XXXI (1906), 383-394.

20 POWELL, Burt E. *The Movement for Industrial Education and the Establishment of the University, 1840-1870.* Urbana, Ill., 1918. (Semicentennial History of the University of Illinois.)

21 ROZWENC, Edwin C. "Agricultural Education and Politics in Vermont." *Proc Vt Hist Soc*, XXVI (1958), 69-106.

1 SEARS, William. *The Roots of Vocational Education: A Survey of the Origins of Trade and Industrial Education Found in Industry, Education, Legislation and Social Progress.* New York, 1931.

2 SLAY, Ronald J. *The Development of the Teaching of Agriculture in Mississippi with Special Emphasis on Agriculture as a Part of School Curricula.* New York, 1928. (Concerns years from 1880 to 1921.)

3 STRUCK, F. Theodore. *Foundations of Industrial Education.* New York, 1930.

4 TRUE, Alfred C. *A History of Agricultural Education in the United States, 1785-1925.* U S D A Misc Pub, no. 36. Washington, D.C., 1929.

5 WOERDEHOFF, Frank J. "Dr. Charles McCarthy: Planner of the Wisconsin System of Vocational and Adult Education." *Wis Mag Hist*, XLI (1958), 270-274.

6 WOODWARD, Calvin M. *The Manual Training School: Comprising a Full Statement of Its Aims, Methods, and Results, with Figured Drawings of Shop Exercises in Woods and Metals.* Boston, 1887.

7 WRIGHT, Carroll D. *The Apprenticeship System in Its Relation to Industrial Education.* U S Bur Ed Bull 1908, no. 6. Washington, 1908.

See also 1.2, 2.2, 17.15, 18.1, 29.20, 44.17, 50.10, 50.11, 50.17, 50.18, 52.9, 53.2, 67.1, 67.8, 68.2, 74.15, 89.8, 89.20, 107.14.

14. Secondary Education

8 ANDERSON, Lewis F. "The System of Mutual Instruction and the Beginnings of the High School." *School Soc*, VIII (1918), 571-576.

9 ANDREWS, Edward D. "The County Grammar Schools and Academies of Vermont." *Proc Vt Hist Soc*, IV (1936), 117-211. (Covers years from 1724 to 1860.)

10 BOLE, Robert D. and Laurence B. JOHNSON. *The New Jersey High School: A History.* Princeton, 1964.

11 BOLTON, Frederick E. "High Schools in Territorial Washington." *Wash Hist Q*, XXIV (1933), 211-220, 271-281.

12 BOOGHER, Elbert W. G. *Secondary Education in Georgia, 1732-1858.* Philadelphia, 1933.

13 BOYD, W. W. "Secondary Education in Ohio Previous to the Year 1840." *Ohio Hist Q*, XXV (1916), 118-134.

14 BRIGGS, Thomas H. "Secondary Education in Our Times." *Tchr Col Rec*, XLVI (1944), 177-185.

15 BRIGGS, Thomas H. "The Secondary School Curriculum: Yesterday, Today, and Tomorrow." *Tchr Col Rec*, LII (1951), 399-448.

16 BRINK, William G. et al. *Adapting the Secondary School Program to the Needs of Youth.* 52nd Yrbk Nat Soc Stud Ed. Pt. I. Chicago, 1953.

17 BROWN, Elmer E. *The Making of Our Middle Schools: An Account of the Development of Secondary Education in the United States.* 3d ed. New York, 1907.

1 BUNKER, Frank F. *The Junior High School Movement: Its Beginnings.* Washington, D.C., 1935.

2 BURRELL, B. Jeannette, and R. H. ECKELBERRY. "The Free Public High School in the Post-Civil War Period." *School Rev*, XLII (1934), 606-614, 667-675.

3 BURRELL, B. Jeannette, and R. H. ECKELBERRY. "The High-School Controversy in the Post-Civil War Period: Times, Places, and Participants." *School Rev*, XLII (1934), 333-345.

4 BUTLER, Nicholas M. "The Reform of Secondary Education in the United States." *U S Bur Ed, Rep Comm 1892-1893*. Vol. II. Washington, D.C., 1895, pp. 1448-1456.

5 *Cardinal Principles of Secondary Education: A Report of the Commission on the Reorganization of Secondary Education, Appointed by the National Education Association.* U S Bur Ed Bull 1918, no. 35. Washington, D.C., 1918.

6 CHASE, Francis S., and Harold A. ANDERSON, eds. *The High School in a New Era.* Chicago, 1958.

7 CONANT, James B. *The American High School Today: A First Report to Interested Citizens.* New York, 1959.†

8 CONANT, James B. *The Comprehensive High School: A Second Report to Interested Citizens.* New York, 1967.†

9 COUNTS, George S. *Secondary Education and Industrialism.* Cambridge, Mass., 1929.

10 CREMIN, Lawrence A. "The Revolution in American Secondary Education 1893-1918." *Tchr Col Rec*, LVI (1955), 295-308.

11 CROSBIE, Laurence M. *The Phillips Exeter Academy: A History.* Norwood, Mass., 1924.

12 DAVIS, Calvin O. *Our Evolving High School Curriculum.* New York, 1927.

13 DAVIS, Thomas B. *Chronicles of Hopkins Grammar School, 1660-1935: Containing a Life of the Founder Together with School Records and Reminiscences Covering 275 Years.* New Haven, 1938.

14 DILLAWAY, Charles K. *A History of the Grammar School or "The Free Schoole of Roxburie."* Roxbury, Mass., 1860.

15 DOUGLASS, Aubrey A., et al. *The Junior High School.* 15th Yrbk Nat Soc Stud Ed. Pt. III. Bloomington, Ill., 1916.

16 DOUGLASS, Harl R. *Secondary Education for Youth in Modern America.* Washington, D.C., 1937.

17 DOUGLASS, Harl R., ed. *The High School Curriculum.* 3d ed. New York, 1964.

18 DRAPER, Andrew S. "The New York Secondary School System." *U S Bur Ed, Rep Comm 1905*. Vol I. Washington, D.C., 1907, pp. 143-154. (Concerns period from 1787 to 1904.)

19 ELIOT, Charles W., and Ernesto NELSON. *Needed Changes in Secondary Education.* U S Bur Ed Bull 1916, no. 10. Washington, D.C., 1916.

20 FUESS, Claude M. *An Old New England School: A History of Phillips Academy, Andover.* Boston, 1917.

1 GIFFORD, Walter J. *Historical Development of the New York State High School System.* Albany, 1922.

2 GRIZZELL, Emit D. *The Origin and Development of the High School in New England Before 1865.* New York, 1923.

3 HALE, Richard W. *Tercentenary History of the Roxbury Latin School, 1645-1945.* Cambridge, Mass., 1946.

4 HAMMOND, Charles A. "New England Academies and Classical Schools." *U S Bur Ed, Rep Comm 1867-1868.* Washington, D.C., 1868, pp. 403-429. (Concerns period from 1638-1833.)

5 HANEY, John L. "The First High School Diplomas." *School Rev*, XXXVIII (1930), 544-547.

6 HANUS, Paul H. "High-School Pioneering: Denver High School, District No. 2: 1886-1890." *School Rev*, XLV (1937), 417-428.

7 HARRIS, William T. "The Curriculum for Secondary Schools." *U S Bur Ed, Rep Comm 1892-1893.* Vol. II. Washington, D.C., 1895, pp. 1452-1464.

8 HARRIS, William T. "The Growth of the Public High-School System in the Southern States and a Study of Its Influence." *Ed Rev*, XXVII (1904), 259-269.

9 HERBST, Jurgen. "High School and Youth in America." *J Cont Hist*, II (1967), 165-182. (Also in *Education and Social Structure in the Twentieth Century.* Ed. Walter Laqueur and George L. Mosse. New York, 1968.)†

10 HERTZLER, Silas. *The Rise of the Public High School in Connecticut.* Baltimore, 1930.

11 HOLMES, Pauline. *The Tercentenary History of the Boston Public Latin School, 1635-1935.* Cambridge, Mass., 1935.

12 HOLTZ, Adrian A. *A Study of the Moral and Religious Elements in American Secondary Education up to 1800.* Menasha, Wis., 1917.

13 HOWARD, Charles A. "A History of High School Legislation in Oregon to 1910." *Ore Hist Soc Q*, XXIV (1923), 201-237. (Covers the years from 1878 to 1910.)

14 INGLIS, Alexander J. *The Rise of the High School in Massachusetts.* New York, 1911.

15 JUDD, Charles H. "Changing Conceptions of Secondary and Higher Education in America." *School Rev*, XLV (1937), 93-104.

16 JUDD, Charles H. "The Historical Development of Secondary Education in America." *School Rev*, XLIII (1935), 173-183.

17 KANDEL, Isaac L. *History of Secondary Education: A Study in the Development of Liberal Education.* Boston, 1930.

18 KNIGHT, Edgar W. *The Academy Movement in the South.* Chapel Hill, 1919.

19 KOOS, Leonard V. "The Rise of the People's College." *School Rev*, LV (1947), 138-149.

20 KOOS, Leonard V. *Trends in American Secondary Education.* Cambridge, Mass., 1926.

1 KRUG, Edward A. "Charles W. Eliot and the Secondary School." *Hist Ed Q*, I (1961), 4-21.

2 KRUG, Edward A. *The Shaping of the American High School.* 2 vols. New York, 1964, Madison, Wis., 1971.†

3 KRUG, Edward A., ed. *Charles W. Eliot and Popular Education.* New York, 1961.†

4 LENTZ, Donald W. "History and Development of the Junior High School." *Tchr Col Rec*, LVII (1956), 522-530.

5 MC LACHLAN, James. *American Boarding Schools: A Historical Study.* New York, 1970.

6 MARR, Harriet W. *The Old New England Academies Founded Before 1826.* New York, 1959.

7 MILLER, George F. *The Academy System of the State of New York.* Albany, 1922.

8 MOCK, Albert. *The Mid-Western Academy Movement: A Comprehensive Study of Indiana Academies, 1810-1900.* Indianapolis, 1949.

9 MULHERN, James. *A History of Secondary Education in Pennsylvania.* Lancaster, Pa., 1933.

10 NEUMANN, Henry. *Moral Values in Secondary Education: A Report of the Commission on the Reorganization of Secondary Education Appointed by the National Education Association.* U S Bur Ed Bull 1917, no. 51. Washington, D.C., 1918.

11 NEVILLE, Charles E. "Origin and Development of the Public High School in Philadelphia." *School Rev*, XXXV (1927), 363-375.

12 NEVINS, Archie P. "The Kalamazoo Case." *Mich Hist*, XLIV (1960), 91-100.

13 NORDSTROM, Carl, Edgar Z. FRIEDENBERG, and Hillary A. GOLD. *Society's Children: A Study of Ressentiment in Secondary School Education.* New York, 1967.†

14 RYAN, Will C., et al. *Secondary Education in the South.* Chapel Hill, 1946.

15 SCHAFER, Joseph. "Genesis of Wisconsin's Free High School System." *Wis Mag Hist*, X (1926), 123-149.

16 SIZER, Theodore R. *Secondary Schools at the Turn of the Century.* New Haven, 1964.

17 SIZER, Theodore R., ed. *The Age of the Academies.* New York, 1964.†

18 SNEDDEN, David. "Cardinal Principles of Secondary Education." *School Soc*, IX (1919), 517-527.

19 SPAULDING, Francis T. *High School and Life.* New York, 1938.

20 STOMBAUGH, Ray M. *A Survey of the Movements Culminating in Industrial Arts Education in Secondary Schools.* New York, 1936.

21 STOUT, John E. *The Development of High School Curricula in the North Central States from 1860 to 1918.* Chicago, 1921.

22 STUART, George. "The Raison d'Etre of the Public High School." *U S Bur Ed, Rep Comm 1886-1887.* Washington, D.C., 1888, pp. 1017-1022.

1 TILDSLEY, John L. *The Mounting Waste of the American Secondary School.* Cambridge, Mass., 1936.

2 WALKER, W. G. "The Development of the Free Public High School in Illinois During the Nineteenth Century." *Hist Ed Q,* IV (1964), 264-279.

3 WILLARD, H. K. "Contributions to the History of the Hopkins Grammar School, New Haven, Conn., 1660 to 1900." *U S Bur Ed, Rep Comm 1899-1900.* Vol. II. Washington, D.C., 1901, pp. 1281-1296.

See also 1.3, 1.6, 7.3, 8.4, 12.4, 14.6, 17.10, 20.2, 42.5, 46.12, 56.18, 57.10, 68.3, 68.13, 74.4, 75.2, 76.6, 76.15, 77.13, 89.20, 91.1, 98.21, 104.13, 107.3, 107.9, 107.14, 107.20, 107.25, 108.3, 110.8, 111.14.

15. Higher Education

A. TEXTS, ESSAYS, DOCUMENTS

4 BRICKMAN, William, and Stanley LEHRER, eds. *A Century of Higher Education.* New York, 1962.

5 BRUBACHER, John S., and Willis S. RUDY. *Higher Education in Transition: A History of American Colleges and Universities, 1636-1968.* Rev. ed. New York, 1968.

6 BUTTS, R. Freeman. *The College Charts Its Course: Historical Conceptions and Current Proposals.* New York, 1939.

7 CURTI, Merle, and Roderick NASH. *Philanthropy in the Shaping of American Higher Education.* New Brunswick, 1965.

8 EARNEST, Ernest. *Academic Procession: An Informal History of the American College, 1636-1953.* Indianapolis, 1953.

9 EELLS, Walter C., and Ernest V. HOLLIS. "The Origin and Development of the Public College in the United States." *J Neg Ed,* XXXI (1962), 221-229.

10 HOFSTADTER, Richard. *Academic Freedom in the Age of the College.* New York, 1961. (See also as part of *The Development of Academic Freedom in the United States.*)†

11 HOFSTADTER, Richard, and C. De Witt HARDY. *The Development and Scope of Higher Education in the United States.* New York, 1952.

12 HOFSTADTER, Richard, and Walter P. METZGER. *The Development of Academic Freedom in the United States.* New York, 1955. (See also publication in two volumes, separately under each author.)

13 HOFSTADTER, Richard, and Wilson SMITH, eds. *American Higher Education: A Documentary History.* 2 vols. Chicago, 1961.†

14 KELLY, Robert L. *The American Colleges and the Social Order.* New York, 1940.

15 MADSEN, David. *The National University: Enduring Dream of the USA.* Detroit, 1966.

1 METZGER, Walter P. *Academic Freedom in the Age of the University.* New York, 1961. (See also as part of Richard Hofstadter and Walter P. Metzger, *The Development of Academic Freedom in the United States.*)†

2 "Philanthropy in the History of American Higher Education." *Bull Am Assn Univ Prof*, IX (1923), 356-368.

3 PIERSON, George W. "American Universities in the Nineteenth Century: The Formative Period." *The Modern University.* Ed. Margaret Clapp. Ithaca, N.Y., 1950, pp. 59-94.

4 RUDOLPH, Frederick. *The American College and University: A History.* New York, 1962.†

5 SANFORD, Nevitt, ed. *The American College: A Psychological and Social Interpretation of the Higher Learning.* New York, 1962.†

6 SEARS, Jesse B. *Philanthropy in the History of American Higher Education.* U S Bur Ed Bull 1922, no. 26. Washington, D.C., 1922.

7 SNYDER, Henry N. "The Denominational College in Southern Education." *S Atl Q*, V (1906), 8-20.

8 STORR, Richard J. "Academic Culture and the History of American Higher Education." *J Gen Ed*, V (1950), 6-16.

9 STORR, Richard J. "The Education of History: Some Impressions." *Har Ed Rev*, XXXI (1961), 124-135.

10 THWING, Charles F. *A History of Higher Education in America.* New York, 1906.

11 UNDERWOOD, Kenneth, et al. *The Church, the University, and Social Policy.* 2 vols. Middletown, Conn., 1969.†

12 WESLEY, Edgar B. *Proposed: The University of the United States.* Minneapolis, 1936.

13 WILLS, Elbert V. *Growth of American Higher Education: Liberal, Professional, and Technical.* Philadelphia, 1936.

See also 1.1, 1.3, 2.4, 12.8, 13.14, 14.2, 14.7, 14.14, 14.15, 16.9, 20.13, 20.14, 21.7, 21.14, 48.4, 57.18, 81.5, 81.6, 81.20.

B. THE INDIVIDUAL STATES *(arranged by states in alphabetical order)*

14 MC GIFFERT, Michael. *The Higher Learning in Colorado: An Historical Study, 1860-1940.* Denver, 1964.

15 WOODBURN, James A. *Higher Education in Indiana.* U S Bur Ed, Circ Info 1891, no. 1. Washington, D.C., 1891.

16 BLACKMAR, Frank W. *Higher Education in Kansas.* U S Bur Ed, Circ Info 1900, no. 2. Washington, D.C., 1900.

17 LEWIS, Alvin F. *History of Higher Education in Kentucky.* U S Bur Ed, Circ Info 1899, no. 3. Washington, D.C., 1899.

18 HALL, E. W. *History of Higher Education in Maine.* U S Bur Ed, Circ Info 1903, no. 3. Washington, D.C., 1903.

32

1   BUSH, George G. *History of Higher Education in Massachusetts.* U S Bur Ed, Circ Info 1891, no. 6. Washington, D.C., 1891.

2   DUNBAR, Willis F. *The Michigan Record in Higher Education.* Detroit, 1963.

3   DUNBAR, Willis F. "Public Versus Private Control of Higher Education in Michigan." *Miss Val Hist Rev*, XXII (1935-1936), 385-407.

4   CARMICHAEL, Oliver C. "The Roots of Higher Education in Minnesota." *Minn Hist*, XXXIV (1954), 90-95.

5   SNOW, M. S. *Higher Education in Missouri.* U S Bur Ed, Circ Info 1898, no. 2. Washington, D.C., 1898.

6   CALDWELL, E. W. "An Introduction to the History of Higher Education in Nebraska." *Neb Hist Mag*, III (1892), 210-229.

7   SHERWOOD, Sidney. *The University of the State of New York: History of Higher Education in the State of New York.* U S Bur Ed, Circ Info 1900, no. 3. Washington, D.C., 1900.

8   KNIGHT, George W., and John R. COMMONS. *The History of Higher Education in Ohio.* U S Bur Ed, Circ Info 1891, no. 5. Washington, D.C., 1891.

9   SACK, Saul. *History of Higher Education in Pennsylvania.* 2 vols. Harrisburg, Pa., 1963.

10   TOLMAN, W. H. *History of Higher Education in Rhode Island.* U S Bur Ed, Circ Info 1894, no. 1. Washington, D.C., 1894.

11   MERIWETHER, Colyer. *History of Higher Education in South Carolina: With a Sketch of the Free School System.* U S Bur Ed, Circ Info 1888, no. 3. Washington, D.C., 1889.

12   MERRIAM, Lucius S. *Higher Education in Tennessee.* U S Bur Ed, Circ Info 1893, no. 5. Washington, D.C., 1893.

See also 21.3, 47.13, 58.1, 79.3.

C. INDIVIDUAL COLLEGES AND UNIVERSITIES (alphabetically arranged by institution)

13   KNEPPER, George W. *New Lamps for Old: One Hundred Years of Urban Higher Education at the University of Akron.* Akron, Ohio, 1970.

14   SELLERS, James B. *History of the University of Alabama, 1818-1902.* University, Ala., 1953.

15   FUESS, Claude M. *Amherst: The Story of a New England College.* Boston, 1935.

16   REYNOLDS, John H., and David Y. THOMAS. *History of the University of Arkansas.* Fayetteville, Ark., 1910.

17   WHITE, Marian C. *A History of Barnard College.* New York, 1954.

18   JONES, Barbara. *Bennington College: The Development of an Educational Idea.* New York, 1946.

19   DUNIGAN, David R. *A History of Boston College.* Milwaukee, 1947.

1   BRONSON, Walter C. *The History of Brown University, 1764-1914.* Providence, 1914.

2   MEIGS, Cornelia. *What Makes A College? A History of Bryn Mawr.* New York, 1956.

3   FERRIER, William W. *Origin and Development of the University of California.* Berkeley, 1930.

4   STADTMAN, Verne A. *The University of California, 1868-1968.* New York, 1970.

5   HEADLEY, Leal A., and Merrill E. JARCHOW. *Carleton: The First Century.* Northfield, Minn., 1966.

6   AHERN, Patrick H. *The Catholic University of America, 1887-1896.* Washington, D.C., 1948.

7   BARRY, Coleman J. *The Catholic University of America, 1903-1909: The Rectorship of Denis J. O'Connell.* Washington, D.C., 1950.

8   ELLIS, John T. *The Formative Years of the Catholic University of America.* Washington, D.C., 1946.

9   HOGAN, Peter E. *The Catholic University of America, 1896-1903.* Washington, D.C., 1949.

10 GOODSPEED, Thomas W. *A History of the University of Chicago, Founded by John D. Rockefeller: The First Quarter Century.* Chicago, 1916.

11 STORR, Richard J. *Harper's University: The Beginnings—A History of the University of Chicago.* Chicago, 1966.

12 MC GRANE, Reginald C. *The University of Cincinnati: A Success Story in Urban Higher Education.* New York, 1963.

13 SANFORD, Edmund C. *A Sketch of the History of Clark University.* Worcester, Mass., 1923.

14 ATWOOD, Wallace W. *The First Fifty Years of Clark University: An Administrative Report.* Worcester, Mass., 1937.

15 CREMIN, Lawrence A., David A. SHANNON, and Mary E. TOWNSEND. *A History of Teachers College, Columbia University.* New York, 1954.

16 HOXIE, R. Gordon, et al. *A History of the Faculty of Political Science, Columbia University.* New York, 1955.

17 KEPPEL, Frederick P. *Columbia.* New York, 1914.

18 RANDALL, John H., et al. *A History of the Faculty of Philosophy, Columbia University.* New York, 1957.

19 VAN AMRINGE, John H., et al. *A History of Columbia University, 1754-1904.* New York, 1904.

20 VAN METRE, Thurman W. *A History of the Graduate School of Business, Columbia University.* New York, 1954.

21 BECKER, Carl L. *Cornell University: Founders and the Founding.* Ithaca, N.Y., 1943.†

22 BISHOP, Morris. *A History of Cornell.* Ithaca, N.Y., 1962.

1 HEWETT, Waterman T. *Cornell University: A History.* Ithaca, N.Y., 1905.

2 CHASE, Frederick. *A History of Dartmouth College and the Town of Hanover, New Hampshire.* Ed. John K. Lord. 2d ed. 2 vols. Brattleboro, Vt., 1928.

3 RICHARDSON, Leon B. *History of Dartmouth College.* 2 vols. Hanover, N.H., 1932.

4 SWEET, William W. *Indiana Asbury-DePauw University, 1837-1937: A Hundred Years of Higher Education in the Middle West.* New York, 1937.

5 MORGAN, James H. *Dickinson College: The History of One Hundred and Fifty Years, 1783-1933.* Carlisle, Pa., 1933.

6 SCHMIDT, George P. *Douglass College: A History.* New Brunswick, 1968.

7 CHAFFIN, Nora C. *Trinity College, 1839-1892: The Beginnings of Duke University.* Durham, N.C., 1950.

8 PORTER, Earl W. *Trinity and Duke, 1892-1924: Foundations of Duke University.* Durham, N.C., 1964.

9 THORNBURG, Opal. *Earlham: The Story of the College, 1847-1962.* Richmond, Ind., 1963.

10 BARBER, W. Charles. *Elmira College: The First Hundred Years.* New York, 1955.

11 BULLOCK, Henry M. *A History of Emory University, 1836-1936.* Nashville, 1936.

12 ENGLISH, Thomas H. *Emory University, 1915-1965.* Atlanta, 1966.

13 KLEIN, Harry M. J. *A Century of Education at Mercersburg, 1836-1936.* Lancaster, Pa., 1936. (A history of Franklin and Marshall College.)

14 BROOKS, Robert D. *The University of Georgia Under Sixteen Administrations, 1785-1955.* Athens, Ga., 1956.

15 BRITTAIN, Marion L. *The Story of Georgia Tech.* Chapel Hill, 1948.

16 KNIPP, Anna H., and Thaddeus P. THOMAS. *The History of Goucher College.* Baltimore, 1938.

17 GILBERT, Dorothy L. *Guilford: A Quaker College.* Guilford, N.C., 1937.

18 PILKINGTON, Walter. *Hamilton College, 1812-1962.* Clinton, N.Y., 1962.

19 HARRINGTON, Thomas F. *The Harvard Medical School: A History Narrative and Documentary, 1782-1905.* Ed. James Gregory Mumford. New York, 1905.

20 MORISON, Samuel E. *Three Centuries of Harvard, 1636-1936.* Cambridge, Mass., 1936.

21 QUINCY, Josiah. *History of Harvard University.* 2 vols. Cambridge, Mass., 1840.

22 SUTHERLAND, Arthur E. *The Law at Harvard: A History of Ideas and Men.* Cambridge, Mass., 1967.

23 WILLIAMS, George H., ed. *The Harvard Divinity School.* Boston, 1954.

1 LOGAN, Rayford W. *Howard University: The First Hundred Years, 1867-1967*. New York, 1969.

2 PATTERSON, Samuel W. *Hunter College: Eighty-Five Years of Service*. New York, 1955.

3 RAMMELKAMP, Charles H. *Illinois College: A Centennial History, 1829-1929*. New Haven, 1928.

4 MARSHALL, Helen E. *Grandest of Enterprises: Illinois State Normal University, 1857-1957*. Normal, Ill., 1956.

5 MOORES, Richard G. *Fields of Rich Toil: The Development of the University of Illinois College of Agriculture*. Urbana, Ill., 1970.

6 NEVINS, Allan. *Illinois*. New York, 1917. (A history of the University of Illinois, 1867-1916.)

7 SOLBERG, Winton U. *The University of Illinois, 1867-1894: An Intellectual and Cultural History*. Urbana, Ill., 1968.

8 PLOCHMANN, George K. *The Ordeal of Southern Illinois University*. Carbondale, Ill., 1959.

9 MYERS, Burton D. *History of Indiana University, 1902-1937*. Bloomington, 1952.

10 WOODBURN, James A. *History of Indiana University, 1820-1902*. 2 vols. Bloomington, 1940, 1952.

11 PICKARD, J. L. "Historical Sketch of the State University of Iowa." *Ann Iowa*, IV (1899), 1-66.

12 FRENCH, John C. *A History of the University Founded by Johns Hopkins*. Baltimore, 1946.

13 HAWKINS, Hugh. *Pioneer: A History of the Johns Hopkins University, 1874-1889*. Ithaca, N.Y., 1960.

14 GOODSELL, Charles T., and Willis F. DUNBAR. *Centennial History of Kalamazoo College*. Kalamazoo, Mich., 1933.

15 WILLARD, Julius T. *History of the Kansas State College of Agriculture and Applied Sciences*. Manhattan, Kan., 1940.

16 CORRELL, Charles M. "The First Century of Kansas State University." *Kan Hist Q*, XXVIII (1962), 409-444.

17 HOPKINS, James F. *The University of Kentucky: Origins and Early Years*. Lexington, Ky., 1951.

18 BOWEN, Catherine D. *A History of Lehigh University*. South Bethlehem, Pa., 1924.

19 FERNALD, Merritt C. *History of the Maine State College and the University of Maine*. Orono, Me., 1916.

20 HAMILTON, Raphael N. *The Story of Marquette University: An Object Lesson in the Development of Catholic Higher Education*. Milwaukee, 1953.

21 CALLCOTT, George H. *A History of the University of Maryland*. Baltimore, 1966.

1 CARY, Harold W. *The University of Massachusetts: A History of One Hundred Years.* Amherst, 1962.

2 PRESCOTT, Samuel C. *When M.I.T. Was "Boston Tech," 1861-1916.* Cambridge, Mass., 1954.

3 HAVIGHURST, Walter. *The Miami Years: 1809-1969.* Rev. ed. New York, 1969. (Miami University.)

4 BEAL, William J. *History of the Michigan Agricultural College and Biographical Sketches of Trustees and Professors.* East Lansing, Mich., 1915.

5 HINSDALE, Burke A. *History of the University of Michigan.* Ann Arbor, 1906.

6 PECKHAM, Howard H. *The Making of the University of Michigan, 1817-1967.* Ann Arbor, 1967.

7 KUHN, Madison. *Michigan State: The First Hundred Years, 1855-1955.* Lansing, Mich., 1955.

8 GRAY, James. *The University of Minnesota: 1851-1951.* Minneapolis, 1951.

9 STEPHENS, Frank F. *A History of the University of Missouri.* Columbia, Mo., 1962.

10 VILES, Jonas, et al. *The University of Missouri: A Centennial History, 1839-1939.* Columbia, Mo., 1939.

11 BRAWLEY, Benjamin. *History of Morehouse College.* College Park, Md., 1917, 1970.

12 COLE, Arthur C. *A Hundred Years of Mount Holyoke College: The Evolution of an Educational Ideal.* New Haven, 1940.

13 MANLEY, Robert N. *Centennial History of the University of Nebraska.* Vol. I: "Frontier University, 1869-1919." Lincoln, Neb., 1969.

14 DOTEN, Samuel B. *An Illustrated History of the University of Nevada.* Carson City, Nev., 1924.

15 RUDY, S. Willis. *The College of the City of New York: A History, 1847-1947.* New York, 1949.

16 HUG, Elsie A. *Seventy-Five Years in Education: The Role of the School of Education, New York University, 1890-1965.* New York, 1965.

17 JONES, Theodore F., ed. *New York University, 1832-1932.* New York, 1933.

18 CARMICHAEL, Oliver C., Jr. *New York Establishes a State University: A Case Study in the Process of Policy Formation.* Nashville, 1955. (SUNY at Albany.)

19 CARRON, Malcolm. *The Contract Colleges of Cornell University: A Cooperative Educational Enterprise.* Ithaca, N.Y., 1958. (Concerns evolution of SUNY.)

20 BRUSH, Carey W. *In Honor and Good Faith: A History of the State University College at Oneonta, New York.* Oneonta, N.Y., 1965.

21 BATTLE, Kemp P. *History of the University of North Carolina.* 2 vols. Raleigh, 1907, 1912.

22 BOWLES, Elisabeth A. *A Good Beginning: The First Four Decades of the University of North Carolina at Greensboro.* Chapel Hill, 1967.

1   LOCKMILLER, David A. "The Establishment of the North Carolina College of Agriculture and Mechanic Arts." *N C Hist Rev*, XVI (1939), 273-295.

2   WILSON, Louis R. *The University of North Carolina, 1900-1930: The Making of a Modern University.* Chapel Hill, 1957.

3   GEIGER, Louis G. *University of Northern Plains: A History of the University of North Dakota, 1883-1958.* Grand Forks, N.D., 1958.

4   WARD, Estelle F. *The Story of Northwestern University.* New York, 1924.

5   ELLIS, William A. *Norwich University, 1819-1911.* Montpelier, Vt., 1911.

6   HOOVER, Thomas N. *The History of Ohio University.* Athens, Ohio, 1954.

7   MENDENHALL, Thomas C., ed. *History of the Ohio State University.* 5 vols. Columbus, Ohio, 1920-1941.

8   KINNISON, William A. *Building Sullivant's Pyramid: An Administrative History of the Ohio State University, 1870-1907.* Columbus, Ohio, 1970.

9   POLLARD, James E. *History of the Ohio State University: The Story of Its First Seventy-Five Years, 1873-1948.* Columbus, Ohio, 1952.

10 HUBBART, Henry C. *Ohio Wesleyan's First Hundred Years.* Delaware, Ohio, 1943.

11 GITTINGER, Roy. *The University of Oklahoma, 1892-1942.* Norman, Okla., 1942.

12 SHELDON, Henry D. *History of University of Oregon.* Portland, Ore., 1940.

13 HAWK, Grace E. *Pembroke College in Brown University: The First Seventy-Five Years, 1891-1966.* Providence, 1967.

14 CARSON, Joseph. *A History of the Medical Department of the University of Pennsylvania from Its Foundation in 1765.* Philadelphia, 1869.

15 CHEYNEY, Edwards P. *A History of the University of Pennsylvania, 1740-1940.* Philadelphia, 1940.

16 LIPPINCOTT, Horace M. *The University of Pennsylvania: Franklin's College.* Philadelphia, 1919.

17 DUNWAY, Wayland F. *History of the Pennsylvania State College.* State College, Pa., 1946.

18 STARRETT, Agnes L. *Through One Hundred and Fifty Years: The University of Pittsburgh.* Pittsburgh, 1937.

19 MAC LEAN, John. *History of the College of New Jersey from Its Origins in 1746 to the Commencement of 1854.* 2 vols. Philadelphia, 1877. (Refers to Princeton University.)

20 WERTENBAKER, Thomas J. *Princeton, 1746-1896.* Princeton, 1946.

21 HEPBURN, William M., and Louis M. SEARS. *Purdue University: Fifty Years of Progress.* Indianapolis, 1925.

22 CORNELIUS, Roberta D. *The History of Randolph-Macon Woman's College: From the Founding in 1891 Through the Year of 1949-1950.* Chapel Hill, 1951.

1 BAKER, Ray P. *A Chapter in American Education: Rensselaer Polytechnic Institute, 1824-1924*. New York, 1924.

2 RICKETTS, Palmer C. *History of Rensselaer Polytechnic Institute, 1824-1934*. 3d ed. New York, 1934.

3 ESCHENBACHER, Herman F. *The University of Rhode Island: A History of Land-Grant Education in Rhode Island*. New York, 1967.

4 ROSENBERGER, Jesse L. *Rochester: The Making of a University*. Rochester, 1927.

5 DEMAREST, William H. S. *A History of Rutgers College, 1766-1924*. New Brunswick, 1966.

6 MC CORMICK, Richard P. *Rutgers: A Bicentennial History*. New Brunswick, 1966.

7 FAHERTY, William B. *Better the Dream. Saint Louis: University and Community, 1818-1968*. St. Louis, 1968.

8 HOLLIS, Daniel W. *University of South Carolina*. 2 vols. Columbia, S.C., 1951, 1956.

9 ELLIOTT, Orrin L. *Stanford University: The First Twenty-Five Years*. Stanford, 1937.

10 MITCHELL, John P. *Stanford University, 1916-1941*. Stanford, 1958.

11 GALPIN, William F. *Syracuse University*. 2 vols. Syracuse, 1952, 1960.

12 BATTLE, W. J. "A Concise History of the University of Texas, 1883-1950." *SW Hist Q*, LIV (1951), 391-411.

13 PERRY, George S. *The Story of Texas A and M*. New York, 1951.

14 HICKERSON, Frank R. "The Founding of the Toledo University of Arts and Trades." *NW Ohio Q*, XX (1948), 68-86, 97-119, 168-191.

15 HICKERSON, Frank R. "The University of Toledo Comes of Age." *NW Ohio Q*, XXI (1949), 38-68.

16 MILLER, Russell E. *Light on the Hill: A History of Tufts College, 1852-1952*. Boston, 1966.

17 DYER, John P. *Tulane: The Biography of a University, 1834-1965*. New York, 1966.

18 FOX, Dixon R. *Union College: An Unfinished History*. Schenectady, N.Y., 1945.

19 RAYMOND, Andrew V. V., ed. *Union University: Its History, Influence, Characteristics and Equipment*. 3 vols. New York, 1907.

20 MIMS, Edwin. *History of Vanderbilt University*. Nashville, 1946.

21 TAYLOR, James M., and Elizabeth H. HAIGHT. *Vassar*. New York, 1915.

22 LINDSAY, Julian I. *Tradition Looks Forward: The University of Vermont, a History, 1791-1904*. Burlington, Vt., 1954.

23 BRUCE, Philip A. *The History of the University of Virginia, 1819-1919*. 5 vols. New York, 1920-1922.

1 COUPER, William. *One Hundred Years of VMI.* Charlottesville, Va., 1936.

2 SMITH, Francis H. *History of the Virginia Military Institute.* Lexington, Va., 1912.

3 HANAWALT, Leslie L. *A Place of Light: The History of Wayne State University.* Detroit, 1968.

4 HACKETT, Alice P. *Wellesley: Part of the American Story.* New York, 1949.

5 PRICE, Carl F. *Wesleyan's First Century.* Middletown, Conn., 1932.

6 AMBROSE, Stephen E. *Duty, Honor, Country: A History of West Point.* Baltimore, 1966.

7 FLEMING, Thomas J. *West Point: The Men and Times of the United States Military Academy.* New York, 1969.

8 FORMAN, Sidney. *West Point: A History of the United States Military Academy.* New York, 1950.

9 ADAMS, Herbert B. *The College of William and Mary.* U S Bur Ed, Circ Info 1887, no. 1. Washington, D.C., 1887.

10 TYLER, Lyon G. *The College of William and Mary in Virginia: Its Work and History, 1693-1907.* Richmond, Va., 1907.

11 SPRING, Leverett W. *A History of Williams College.* Boston, 1917.

12 CURTI, Merle, and Vernon CARSTENSEN. *The University of Wisconsin: A History, 1848-1925.* 2 vols. Madison, 1949.

13 GLOVER, Wilbur H. *Farm and College: The College of Agriculture of the University of Wisconsin, A History.* Madison, 1952.

14 WYMAN, Walker D. *History of the Wisconsin State Universities.* River Falls, Wis., 1968.

15 LENTZ, Harold. *A History of Wittenberg College.* Columbus, Ohio, 1946.

16 CLOUGH, Wilson O. *A History of the University of Wyoming, 1887-1937.* Laramie, Wyo., 1937.

17 CHITTENDEN, Russell H. *History of the Sheffield Scientific School of Yale University, 1846-1922.* 2 vols. New Haven, 1928.

18 DEXTER, Franklin B. *Sketch of the History of Yale University.* New York, 1887.

19 GABRIEL, Ralph H. *Religion and Learning at Yale: The Church of Christ in the College and University, 1757-1957.* New Haven, 1958.

20 KINGSLEY, William L., ed. *Yale College: A Sketch of Its History.* 2 vols. New York, 1879.

21 PIERSON, George W. *Yale: College and University, 1871-1937.* 2 vols. New Haven, 1952, 1955.

22 KLAPERMAN, Gilbert. *The Story of Yeshiva University: The First Jewish University in America.* New York, 1969.

See also 13.19, 14.9, 14.13, 25.20, 40.9, 41.3, 41.6, 42.10, 43.3, 43.11, 44.10, 44.11, 45.5, 45.17, 46.1, 47.4, 48.11, 49.1, 49.5, 49.8, 49.12, 49.16, 59.9, 59.18, 59.19, 60.5, 63.3, 63.11, 64.7, 64.10, 69.1, 69.5, 70.9, 78.4, 78.5, 78.11, 78.12, 78.14, 78.20, 79.1, 79.2, 79.5, 79.6, 79.7, 79.10, 79.20, 80.10, 80.12, 80.17, 80.22, 81.8, 81.9, 81.14, 82.15, 94.4, 94.14, 94.18, 95.17, 99.9, 113.16, 114.1, 114.3, 114.4, 114.5, 114.9, 114.19, 115.4, 115.6, 115.8, 115.10, 115.11, 115.13, 116.1, 116.5, 116.9, 116.13, 116.17, 117.1, 117.4, 118.13, 119.16, 119.20, 120.2, 120.3, 120.4, 120.22, 120.23, 121.4, 121.20, 121.21, 122.6, 122.7, 123.9, 126.9, 126.20, 127.11, 127.12, 127.15, 127.18, 128.2, 128.16.

D. UNIVERSITY EXTENSION

1   ADAMS, Herbert B. "American Pioneers of University Extension." *Ed Rev*, II (1891), 220-230.

2   ADAMS, Herbert B. "Educational Extension in the United States." *U S Bur Ed, Rep Comm 1899-1900*. Vol. I. Washington, D.C., 1901, pp. 175-379.

3   BITTNER, W. S. *The University Extension Movement*. U S Bur Ed Bull 1919, no. 84. Washington, D.C., 1920.

4   CARRIER, Lyman. "The United States Agricultural Society, 1852-1860: Its Relation to the Origin of the United States Department of Agriculture and the Land Grant Colleges." *Ag Hist*, XI (1937), 278-288.

5   GALPIN, Charles J. "The Development of the Science and Philosophy of American Rural Society." *Ag Hist*, XII (1938), 195-208.

6   LARSON, Vernon C. "The Development of Short Courses at the Land Grant Institutions." *Ag Hist*, XXXI (1957), 31-35.

7   "The Place of University Extension in American Education." *U S Bur Ed, Rep Comm 1891-1892*. Vol. II. Washington, D.C., 1894, pp. 743-752.

8   REBER, Louis E. *University Extension in the United States*. U S Bur Ed Bull 1914, no. 19. Washington, D.C., 1914.

9   ROSENTRETER, Frederick M. *The Boundaries of the Campus: A History of the University of Wisconsin Extension Division, 1885-1945*. Madison, 1957.

10   STEPHAN, A. Stephen. "Backgrounds and Beginnings of University Extension in America." *Har Ed Rev*, XVIII (1948), 99-108.

11   TRUE, Alfred C. *A History of Agricultural Extension Work in the United States, 1785-1923*. U S D A Misc Pub, no. 15. Washington, D.C., 1928.

12   WOODWARD, Carl R., and Ingrid N. WALLER. *New Jersey's Agricultural Experiment Station, 1880-1930*. New Brunswick, 1932.

See also 35.5, 39.13, 40.13, 41.3, 83.20, 115.8, 115.14.

E. COMMUNITY COLLEGES, MUNICIPAL UNIVERSITIES, AND ADULT EDUCATION

13   ADAMS, Herbert B. "The Promotion of Higher Political Education." *U S Bur Ed, Rep Comm 1885-1886*. Washington, D.C., 1887, pp. 743-747.

1 ADAMS, James T. *Frontiers of American Culture.* New York, 1944. (Concerns history of adult education.)

2 BOGUE, Jesse P. *The Community College.* New York, 1950.

3 BURRELL, John A. *A History of Adult Education at Columbia University; University Extension and the School of General Studies.* New York, 1954.

4 CARTWRIGHT, Morse A. "History of Adult Education in the United States." *J Neg Ed*, XIV (1945), 283-292.

5 CARTWRIGHT, Morse A. *Ten Years of Adult Education.* New York, 1935.

6 COULTON, Thomas E. *A City College in Action: Struggle and Achievement at Brooklyn College, 1930-1955.* New York, 1955.

7 DIEKHOFF, John S. *Democracy's College: Higher Education in the Local Community.* New York, 1950.

8 ECKELBERRY, R. H. *The History of the Municipal University in the United States.* U S Off Ed Bull 1932, no. 2. Washington, D.C., 1932.

9 EELLS, Walter C. *The Junior College.* Boston, 1931.

10 GRATTAN, C. Hartley, ed. *American Ideas About Adult Education, 1710-1951.* New York, 1959.†

11 HILLWAY, Tyrus. *The American Two Year College.* New York, 1958.

12 JOHNSON, B. Lamar, et al. *The Public Junior College.* 55th Yrbk Nat Soc Stud Ed. Pt. I. Chicago, 1956.

13 KLOTSCHE, J. Martin. *The Urban University and the Future of Our Cities.* New York, 1966.

14 KNOWLES, Malcolm S. *The Adult Education Movement in the United States.* New York, 1962.

15 KOOS, Leonard V. *The Junior College.* 2 vols. Minneapolis, 1924.

16 MC DOWELL, F. M. *The Junior College.* U S Bur Ed Bull 1919, no. 35. Washington, D.C., 1919.

17 MEDSKER, Leland L. *The Junior College: Progress and Prospect.* New York, 1960.

18 ROSS, Hugh. "University Influence in the Genesis and Growth of Junior Colleges in California." *Hist Ed Q*, III (1963), 145-152.

19 SEXSON, John A., and John W. HARBESON. *The New American College: The Four Year Junior College.* New York, 1946.

20 WILLOUGHBY, W. W. "The History of Summer Schools in the United States." *U S Bur Ed, Rep Comm 1891-1892.* Vol. II. Washington, D.C., 1894, pp. 893-959.

See also 1.11, 2.13, 20.8, 26.5, 32.13, 33.12, 36.15, 37.18, 38.4, 38.7, 38.11, 38.14, 38.15, 39.3, 67.3, 67.17, 68.9, 77.12, 102.23.

F. ACCREDITATION, ADMISSION, EXAMINATIONS, DEGREES

21 BECKER, Howard S., et al. *Making the Grade: The Academic Side of College Life.* New York, 1968.

1   BROOME, Edwin C. "A Historical and Critical Discussion of College Admission Requirements." *Contrib Philos Psy Ed* (Colum), XI (1903). (Repr. by College Entrance Examination Board, Princeton, 1963, 1968.)

2   EELLS, Walter C. "Honorary Ph.D.s in theTwentieth Century." *School Soc*, LXXXV (1957), 74-75.

3   FUESS, Claude M. *The College Board: Its First Fifty Years.* New York, 1950.

4   GERHARD, Dietrich. "The Emergence of the Credit System in American Education Considered as a Problem of Social and Intellectual History." *Bull Am Assn Univ Prof*, XLI (1955), 647-668.

5   HAYS, Edna. *College Entrance Requirements in English: Their Effects on the High Schools. An Historical Survey.* New York, 1936.

6   HILLS, E. C. "The Degree of Doctor of Philosophy." *Bull Am Assn Univ Prof*, XIII (1927), 163-185.

7   PAYTON, Phillip W. "Origins of the Terms 'Major' and 'Minor' in American Higher Education." *Hist Ed Q*, I (June 1961), 57-63.

8   SELDEN, William K. *Accreditation: A Struggle over Standards in Higher Education.* New York, 1960.

9   "The Selection, Retention, and Promotion of Undergraduates in American Universities." *Bull Am Assn Univ Prof*, XII (1926), 373-481.

10   SMALLWOOD, Mary L. *An Historical Study of Examinations and Grading Systems in Early American Universities: A Critical Study of the Original Records of Harvard, William and Mary, Yale, Mount Holyoke, and Michigan from Their Founding to 1900.* Cambridge, Mass., 1935.

G. CURRICULUM, BOOKS, TEACHING

11   BLENNER-HASSETT, Roland. "A Brief History of Celtic Studies in North America." *PMLA*, LXIX, 4, pt. 2 (1954), 3-21.

12   COWLEY, W. H. "College and University Teaching, 1858-1958." *Ed Rec*, XXXIX (1958), 311-326.

13   COWLEY, W. H. "Three Curricular Conflicts." *Lib Ed*, XLVI (1960), 467-483.

14   FORD, Charles E. "Botany Texts: A Survey of Their Development in American Higher Education, 1643-1906." *Hist Ed Q*, IV (1964), 59-71.

15   HADDOW, Anna. *Political Science in American Colleges and Universities, 1636-1900.* New York, 1939.

16   HALL, G. Stanley. "On the History of American College Text-Books and Teaching in Logic, Ethics, Psychology and Allied Subjects." *Proc Am Ant Soc*, IX, (1893-1894), 137-174.

17   "The History of the Preceptorial or Tutorial System." *Bull Am Assn Univ Prof*, X (1924), 534-562.

18   JACOB, Philip E. *Changing Values in College: An Exploratory Study of the Impact of College Teaching.* New York, 1957.

1   KNIGHT, Edgar W. "Some Early Discussions of the College Curriculum." *S Atl Q*, XXXIV (1935), 60-78.

2   POWELL, J. P. "Some Nineteenth Century Views on the University Curriculum." *Hist Ed Q*, V (1965), 97-109.

3   RAND, Benjamin. "Philosophical Instruction in Harvard University from 1636 to 1906." *Har Grad Mag*, XXXVII (1928-1929), 29-47, 188-200, 296-311.

4   SCHWAB, John C. "The Yale College Curriculum, 1701-1901." *Ed Rev*, XXII (1901), 1-17. (Also as book, New York, 1901.)

5   SHORES, Louis. *Origins of the American College Library, 1638-1800*. Nashville, 1934.

6   SIMONS, Lao G. *Introduction of Algebra into American Schools in the Eighteenth Century*. U S Bur Ed Bull 1924, no. 18. Washington, D.C., 1924.

7   SNOW, Louis F. *The College Curriculum in the United States*. New York, 1907.

8   WALLACE, Karl R., ed. *History of Speech Education in America*. New York, 1954.

See also 58.10, 58.19, 59.15, 60.4, 60.14, 61.14, 62.14, 64.1, 64.5, 65.6, 66.2, 79.13, 79.16, 79.19, 79.20, 81.19, 82.2, 82.4, 82.14, 113.17, 116.4, 120.11, 120.21, 128.9.

H. STUDENTS, ATHLETICS, AND COLLEGE LIFE

9   CORNER, George W. "Apprenticed to Aesculapius: The American Medical Student, 1765-1965." *Proc Am Philos Soc*, CIX (1965), 249-258.

10   COULTER, Ellis M. *College Life in the Old South*. 2d ed. Athens, Ga., 1951.

11   CUTTING, George R. *Student Life at Amherst College: Its Organization, Their Membership, and History*. Amherst, 1871.

12   FARNSWORTH, Dana L. *Mental Health in College and University*. Cambridge, Mass., 1957.

13   KOUWENHOVEN, John A. "The New York Undergraduate 1830-1850." *Colum U Q*, XXXI (1939), 75-103.

14   LEWIS, Guy. "The Beginning of Organized Collegiate Sport." *Am Q*, XXII (1970), 222-229.

15   OLIN, Stephen. *College Life: Its Theory and Practice*. New York, 1867.

16   PATTON, Cornelius H., and Walter T. FIELD. *Eight O'Clock Chapel: A Study of New England College Life in the Eighties*. Boston, 1927.

17   PHELPS, Reginald H. "150 Years of Phi Beta Kappa at Harvard." *Am Sch*, I (1932), 58-63.

18   POTTER, David. *Debating in the Colonial Chartered Colleges: An Historical Survey, 1642-1900*. New York, 1944.

19   RAPHAEL, Theophile, and Mary A. GORDON. "Psychoses Among College Students." *Am J Psy*, XCV (1938), 659-675.

1 RAUSHENBUSH, Esther. *The Student and His Studies.* Middletown, Conn., 1964.

2 ROACH, Helen. "The Early Speaking Societies at Columbia College." *Bull Am Assn Univ Prof*, XLI (1955), 639-644.

3 ROBERTS, Howard. *The Big Nine: The Story of Football in the Western Conference.* New York, 1948.

4 RUDOLPH, Frederick. "Neglect of Students as a Historical Tradition." *The College and the Student.* Ed. by Lawrence E. Dennis and Joseph F. Kauffman. Washington, D.C., 1966.

5 RYAN, W. Carson, Jr. *The Literature of American School and College Athletics.* Carnegie Foundation Bull no. 24. New York, 1929.

6 SACK, Saul. "Student Life in the Nineteenth Century." *Pa Mag Hist Bio*, LXXXV (1961), 255-288.

7 SAVAGE, Howard J., et al. *American College Athletics.* New York, 1929.

8 SHELDON, Henry D. *The History and Pedagogy of American Student Societies.* New York, 1901.

9 SHELDON, Henry D. *Student Life and Customs.* New York, 1901.

10 SOLBERG, Winton U. "The University of Illinois and the Reform of Discipline in the Modern University, 1868-1891." *Bull Am Assn Univ Prof*, LII (1966), 305-314.

11 STOKES, Anson P. *Memorials of Eminent Yale Men: A Biographical Study of Student Life and University Influences in the Eighteenth and Nineteenth Centuries.* 2 vols. New Haven, 1914.

12 WEDGE, Bryant M., ed. *The Psycho-Social Problems of College Men.* New Haven, 1958.

See also 1.1, 41.21, 46.16, 58.13, 59.17, 60.1, 62.10, 62.11, 63.7, 63.9, 63.15, 79.1, 79.8, 79.17, 79.20, 81.7, 114.1.

I. FACULTY, SCHOLARSHIP, SCIENCE

13 BATES, Ralph S. *The American Academy of Arts and Sciences, 1780-1940.* Boston, 1940.

14 BATES, Ralph S. *Scientific Societies in the United States.* 2d ed. New York, 1958.

15 BONNER, Thomas N. *Medicine in Chicago, 1850-1950: A Chapter in the Social and Scientific Development of a City.* Madison, 1957.

16 BORING, Edwin G. *A History of Experimental Psychology.* 2d ed. New York, 1950.

17 CALVERT, Monte A. *The Mechanical Engineer in America, 1830-1910.* Baltimore, 1967.

18 CARRELL, William D. "American College Professors; 1750-1800." *Hist Ed Q*, VIII (1968), 289-305.

1 CARRELL, William D. "Biographical List of American College Professors to 1800." *Hist Ed Q*, VIII (1968), 358-374.

2 COHEN, I. Bernard. "Science in America: The Nineteenth Century." *Paths of American Thought*. Ed. by A. M. Schlesinger, Jr., and Morton White. Boston, 1963, pp. 167-189.

3 CURTI, Merle. "The American Scholar in Three Wars." *J Hist Ideas*, III (1942), 241-264.

4 EELLS, Walter C., and Ernest V. HOLLIS. *Sabbatical Leave in American Higher Education: Origin, Early History, and Current Practices.* Washington, D.C., 1962.

5 FLEMING, Donald H. *Science and Technology in Providence: An Essay in the History of Brown University in the Metropolitan Community.* Providence, 1952.

6 FLEMING, Donald H. *William H. Welch and the Rise of Modern Medicine.* Boston, 1954.

7 FLEXNER, Simon and James T. *William Henry Welch and the Heroic Age in American Medicine.* New York, 1941.†

8 GOODE, George B., ed. *The Smithsonian Institution, 1846-1896: The History of Its First Half-Century.* Washington, D.C., 1897.

9 HALL, Courtney R. *History of America's Industrial Science.* New York, 1954.

10 HENDRICKSON, Walter. "Nineteenth Century State Geological Surveys." *Isis*, LII (1961), 357-371.

11 HUNT, Charles W. *Historical Sketch of the American Society of Civil Engineers.* New York, 1897.

12 HURST, J. Willard. *The Growth of American Law: The Law Makers.* Boston, 1950.

13 JAFFE, Bernard. *Men of Science in America: The Story of American Science Told Through the Lives and Achievements of Twenty Outstanding Men from Earliest Colonial Times to the Present Day.* Rev. ed. New York, 1958.

14 KENNEDY, Sister M. St. Mel. "The Changing Academic Characteristics of the Nineteenth Century American College Teacher." *Pae Hist*, V (1965), 351-401.

15 KIGER, Joseph C. *American Learned Societies.* Washington, D.C., 1963.

16 MOULTON, Forest R., ed. *Liebig and After Liebig: A Century of Progress in Agricultural Chemistry.* Washington, D.C., 1942.

17 MYERS, Burton D. "A Study of Faculty Appointments at Indiana University, 1824-1937." *Ind Mag Hist*, XL (1944), 129-155.

18 OEHSER, Paul H. *Sons of Science: The Story of the Smithsonian Institution and Its Leaders.* New York, 1949.

19 OLIVER, John W. *History of American Technology.* New York, 1956.

20 SHRYOCK, Richard H. "The Academic Profession in the United States." *Bull Am Assn U Prof*, XXXVIII (1952), 32-70.

21 SHRYOCK, Richard H. *Medicine and Society in America, 1660-1860.* New York, 1960.†

1 SHRYOCK, Richard H. *The University of Pennsylvania Faculty: A Study in American Higher Education.* Philadelphia, 1959.

2 SIGERIST, Henry E. *American Medicine.* New York, 1934.

3 STRUIK, Kirk J. *Yankee Science in the Making.* New rev. ed. New York, 1962.†

4 WILSON, Logan. *The Academic Man: A Study in the Sociology of a Profession.* New York, 1942.

See also 48.4, 51.5, 57.3, 57.11, 57.16, 111.20, 112.2.

J. GOVERNANCE AND ADMINISTRATION

5 BLACKWELL, Thomas E. *College and University Administration.* New York, 1966.

6 BRUBACHER, John S. "The Autonomy of the University." *J High Ed*, XXXVIII (1967), 237-249.

7 BURNS, Gerald P. *Administrators in Higher Education.* New York, 1962.

8 BURNS, Gerald P. *Trustees in Higher Education.* New York, 1966.

9 CLAPP, Gordon R. "The College Charter." *J High Ed*, V (1934), 79-87.

10 CORSON, John J. *Governance of Colleges and Universities.* New York, 1960.

11 COWLEY, W. H. "Some Myths About Professors, Presidents, and Trustees." *Tchr Col Rec*, LXIV (1962), 159-171.

12 DAVIS, Calvin O. *A History of the North Central Association of Colleges and Secondary Schools, 1895-1945.* Ann Arbor, 1945.

13 DEMERATH, Nicholas J., et al. *Power, Presidents, and Professors.* New York, 1967.

14 DIEKHOFF, John S. *The Domain of the Faculty in Our Expanding Colleges.* New York, 1956.

15 DODDS, Harold W. *The Academic President: Educator or Caretaker?* New York, 1962.

16 FALVEY, Frances E. *Student Participation in College Administration.* New York, 1952.

17 HARTNETT, Rodney T. *College and University Trustees: Their Backgrounds, Roles, and Educational Attitudes.* Princeton, 1969.

18 HOLMES, Lulu H. *A History of the Position of the Dean of Women in a Selected Group of Coeducational Colleges and Universities in the United States.* New York, 1939.

19 LUNN, Harry H., Jr. *The Student's Role in College Policy-Making.* Washington, D.C., 1957.

20 MC GRATH, Earl J. "The Control of Higher Education in America." *Ed Rec*, XVII (1936), 259-279.

21 MC GRATH, Earl J. *The Evolution of Administrative Offices in Institutions of Higher Education in the United States from 1860 to 1933.* Chicago, 1938.

1 MARTORANA, S. V. *College Boards of Trustees.* Washington, D.C., 1963.

2 MILLETT, John D. *The Academic Community: An Essay on Organization.* New York, 1962.

3 MILLETT, John D. *Decision Making and Administration in Higher Education.* Kent, Ohio, 1968.

4 MORISON, Samuel E. "The Harvard Presidency." *N Eng Q,* XXXI (1958), 435-446.

5 OTTEN, C. Michael. *University Authority and the Student: The Berkeley Experience.* Berkeley, 1970.

6 ROURKE, Francis E., and Glenn E. BROOKS. *The Managerial Revolution in Higher Education.* Baltimore, 1966.

7 RUML, Beardsley, and Donald MORRISON. *Memo to a College Trustee: A Report on Financial and Structural Problems of the Liberal College.* New York, 1959.

8 SELDEN, William K. "The Governance of Higher Education." *Ed Rec,* XLV (1964), 317-324.

9 STOKE, Harold W. *The American College President.* New York, 1959.

10 STROUP, Herbert H. *Bureaucracy in Higher Education.* Glencoe, Ill., 1966.

11 "Toryism in American College Government." *Bull Am Assn Univ Prof,* IX (1923), 349-356.

12 WILLIAMS, Robert L. *The Administration of Academic Affairs in Higher Education.* Ann Arbor, 1965.

See also 1.12, 36.18, 58.4, 59.16, 59.17, 61.1, 61.3-5, 62.13, 62.16, 78.7, 78.8, 80.1, 114.9, 114.10, 128.11.

K. RELATION WITH GOVERNMENT AND THE COURTS

13 ABBOTT, Frank C. *Government Policy and Higher Education: A Study of the Regents of the State of New York, 1784-1949.* Ithaca, N.Y., 1958.

14 AXT, Richard G. *The Federal Government and Financing Higher Education.* New York, 1952.

15 BABBIDGE, Homer D., Jr., and Robert M. ROSENZWEIG. *The Federal Interest in Higher Education.* New York, 1962.

16 BARTLETT, Lester W. *State Control of Private Incorporated Institutions of Higher Education as Defined in Decisions of the United States Supreme Court, Laws of the States Governing the Incorporation of Institutions of Higher Education, and Charters of Selected Private Colleges and Universities.* New York, 1926.

17 BLACKMAR, Frank W. *The History of Federal and State Aid to Higher Education in the United States.* U S Bur Ed, Circ Info 1890, no. 1. Washington, D.C., 1890.

18 BLACKWELL, Thomas E. *College Law: A Guide for Administrators.* Washington, D.C., 1961.

1 CHAMBERS, Merritt M. *The Colleges and the Courts, 1936-1941.* New York, 1942. (Subsequent volumes published under the same title for *1941-1945, 1946-1950, Since 1950*, and *1962-1966*, in 1945, 1952, 1964, and 1967 respectively, the last two volumes being published in Danville, Ill.)

2 CHAMBERS, Merritt M. "A Decade of Progress in Higher Education Law." *Ed Forum*, XXIX (1964), 79-84.

3 CHAMBERS, Merritt M. *Freedom and Repression in Higher Education.* Bloomington, 1965.

4 DUPREE, A. Hunter. *Science in the Federal Government: A History of Policies and Activities to 1940.* Cambridge, Mass., 1957.

5 ELLIOTT, Edward C., and Merritt M. CHAMBERS. *Charters and Basic Laws of Selected American Universities and Colleges.* New York, 1934.

6 ELLIOTT, Edward C., and Merritt M. CHAMBERS. *The Colleges and the Courts: Judicial Decisions Regarding Institutions of Higher Education in the United States.* New York, 1936.

7 KELLY, Fred J., and John H. MC NEELY. *The State and Higher Education; Phases of Their Relationship.* New York, 1933.

8 KELLY, Robert L. "The Colleges and the National Recovery Act." *Bull Am Assn Univ Prof*, XIX (1933), 478-482.

9 KNIGHT, Douglas M., ed. *The Federal Government and Higher Education.* Englewood Cliffs, N.J., 1960.

10 MOOS, Malcolm C., and Francis E. ROURKE. *The Campus and the State.* Baltimore, 1959.

11 PENNYPACKER, Samuel W. "The University of Pennsylvania in Its Relations to the State of Pennsylvania." *Pa Mag Hist Bio*, XV (1891), 88-100.

12 PRICE, Richard R. *The Financial Support of State Universities.* Cambridge, Mass., 1924.

13 RIVLIN, Alice M. *The Role of the Federal Government in Financing Higher Education.* Washington, D.C., 1961.†

See also 30.9, 32.3, 46.6, 46.9, 46.21, 60.11, 61.10, 61.11, 62.13, 78.8, 80.3, 80.8, 80.16, 81.11, 126.5, 126.6, 127.1, 127.12, 128.10.

L. ACADEMIC FREEDOM AND TENURE

14 BYSE, Clark, and Louis JOUGHIN. *Tenure in American Higher Education: Plans, Practices, and the Law.* Ithaca, N.Y., 1959.

15 COSER, Lewis. "Some Reflections on Academic Freedom Today." *Dissent*, XI (1964), 76-79.

16 DARLINGTON, C. D. "Freedom and Responsibility in Academic Life." *Bull Atomic Scientists*, XIII (1957), 131-134.

17 DONNAN, Elizabeth. "A Nineteenth Century Cause Célèbre." *Bull Am Assn Univ Prof*, XXXVIII (1952), 368-389.

1 ENGEL, Mary. "The Case of Alexander Winchell: A Chapter in the History of Academic Freedom." *Hist Ed J*, X (1959), 73-80; also in *Hist Ed J*, VII (1956). (At Vanderbilt University in 1878.)

2 FELLMAN, David. "Academic Freedom in American Public Law." *Tchr Col Rec*, LXII (1961), 368-386.

3 GIDEONSE, Harry D. "Changing Issues in Academic Freedom in the United States Today." *Proc Am Philos Soc*, XCIV (1950), 91-104.

4 HEPBURN, William M. "Academic Freedom and Tenure." *Bull Am Assn Univ Prof*, XXIII (1937), 642-653.

5 HERFURTH, Theodore. *Sifting and Winnowing: A Chapter in the History of Academic Freedom at the University of Wisconsin.* Madison, 1949.

6 JONES, Howard M. "The American Concept of Academic Freedom." *Bull Am Assn Univ Prof*, XLVI (1960), 66-72.

7 JOUGHIN, Louis, ed. *Academic Freedom and Tenure: A Handbook of the American Association of University Professors.* Madison, 1967.†

8 KINNEY, Stanley N. "The Speaker Ban Extended at the University of Michigan, 1920-1935." *Hist Ed J*, VIII (1956), 1-17.

9 MAC IVER, Robert M. *Academic Freedom in Our Time.* New York, 1955.

10 METZGER, Walter P. "The German Contribution to the American Theory of Academic Freedom." *Bull Am Assn Univ Prof*, XLI (1955), 214-230.

11 MEYER, Richard J. "Academic Freedom in the United States." *Brit J Ed Stud*, XV (1967), 28-39.

12 RADIN, Max. "The Loyalty Oath at the University of California." *Bull Am Assn Univ Prof*, XXXVI (1950), 237-248.

13 ROCKWELL, Leo L. "Academic Freedom—German Origin and American Development." *Bull Am Assn Univ Prof*, XXXVI (1950), 225-236.

14 ROSE, Arnold M. *Libel and Academic Freedom: A Lawsuit Against Political Extremists.* Minneapolis, 1968.

15 STARR, Joseph R. "The Hatch Act and Academic Freedom." *Bull Am Assn Univ Prof*, XXVII (1941), 61-69.

16 "The University of California Loyalty Oath Situation." *Bull Am Assn Univ Prof*, XXXVII (1951), 92-101.

See also 8.11, 14.13, 30.10, 30.12, 31.1, 69.3, 105.8.

II. The Colonial Period

1. European Background

17 BALDWIN, Thomas W. *William Shakespere's Petty School.* Urbana, Ill., 1943.

18 BALDWIN, Thomas W. *William Shakespere's Small Latine & Lesse Greeke.* 2 vols. Urbana, Ill., 1944.

1 BRIDENBAUGH, Carl. *Vexed and Troubled Englishmen: 1590-1642.* New York, 1968.

2 BRINSLEY, John. *A Consolation for Our Grammar Schools.* London, 1622; New York, 1943.

3 BROWN, John H. *Elizabethan Schooldays: An Account of the English Grammar Schools in the Second Half of the Sixteenth Century.* Oxford, 1933.

4 CAMPBELL, Mildred L. *The English Yeoman Under Elizabeth and the Early Stuarts.* New York, 1942.

5 CASPARI, Fritz. *Humanism and the Social Order in Tudor England.* New York, 1954.

6 CHARLTON, Kenneth. *Education in Renaissance England.* London, 1965.

7 COSTELLO, William T. *The Scholastic Curriculum at Early Seventeenth-Century Cambridge.* Cambridge, Mass., 1958.

8 CURTIS, Mark H. *Oxford and Cambridge in Transition, 1552-1642: An Essay on Changing Relations Between the English Universities and English Society.* Oxford, 1959.

9 CURTIS, Mark H. "The Alienated Intellectuals of Early Stuart England." *P and P,* XXIII (1962), 25-43.

10 DAVIES, Margaret. *The Enforcement of English Apprenticeship: A Study in Applied Mercantilism, 1563-1642.* Cambridge, Mass., 1956.

11 DUNLOP, Olive J. *English Apprenticeship and Child Labor.* London, 1912.

12 FISH, Carl R. "The English Parish and Education at the Beginning of American Colonization." *School Rev,* XXIII (1915), 433-449.

13 GREAVES, Richard L. *The Puritan Revolution and Educational Thought: Background for Reform.* New Brunswick, 1969.

14 HEXTER, Jack H. "The Education of the Aristocracy in the Renaissance." *J Mod Hist,* XXII (1950), 1-20.

15 JONES, Mary G. *The Charity School Movement: A Study of Eighteenth Century Puritanism in Action.* London, 1964.

16 JORDAN, Wilbur K. *Philanthropy in England: 1480-1660.* New York, 1964.

17 KELLETT, J. R. "The Breakdown of Gild and Corporation Control over the Handicraft and Retail Trade in London." *Econ Hist Rev,* 2d ser., X (1958), 381-394.

18 KRAMER, Stella. *The English Craft Gilds: Studies in Their Progress and Decline.* New York, 1927.

19 LASLETT, Peter. "The Gentry of Kent in 1640." *Cam Hist J,* IX (1948), 148-164.

20 LEACH, Arthur F. *English Schools at the Reformation: 1546-1548.* New York, 1968. (Repr. of 1896 ed.)

21 MC LACHLAN, Herbert. *English Education Under the Test Acts: Being the History of the Nonconformist Academies, 1662-1820.* Manchester, Eng., 1931.

22 MC MAHON, Clara P. *Education in Fifteenth-Century England.* Baltimore, 1947.

1 MERTON, Robert K. "Puritanism, Pietism, and Science." *Social Theory and Social Structure*. Rev. and enl. ed. Glencoe, Ill., 1959.

2 MERTON, Robert K. "Science, Technology and Society in Seventeenth Century England." *Osiris*, IV (1938), 360-632.

3 MULDER, John. *The Temple of the Mind: Education and Literary Taste in Seventeenth-Century England*. New York, 1969.†

4 NOTESTEIN, Wallace. *The English People on the Eve of Colonization*. New York, 1954.†

5 ORNSTEIN, Martha. *The Role of Scientific Societies in the Seventeenth Century*. Chicago, 1928.

6 PARKER, Irene. *Dissenting Academies in England: Their Rise and Progress and Their Place Among the Educational Systems of the Country*. Cambridge, 1914.

7 PINCHBECK, Ivy. "The State and the Child in Sixteenth Century England." *Brit J Socio*, VII (1956), 273-285.

8 PORTER, Harry C. *Reformation and Reaction in Tudor Cambridge*. Cambridge, 1958.

9 POWELL, Chilton L. *English Domestic Relations, 1487-1653: A Study of Matrimony and Family Life in Theory and Practice as Revealed by the Literature, Law, and History of the Period*. New York, 1917.

10 ROBBINS, Caroline. *The Eighteenth-Century Commonwealthman: Studies in the Transmission, Development, and Circumstance of English Liberal Thought from the Restoration of Charles II Until the War with the Thirteen Colonies*. Cambridge, Mass., 1961.

11 ROWSE, Alfred L. "Education and the Social Order." *The England of Elizabeth: The Structure of Society*. London, 1964.

12 SIMON, Joan. *Education and Society in Tudor England*. Cambridge, 1966.

13 SIMON, Joan. "The Social Origins of Cambridge Students, 1603-1640." *P and P*, XXVI (1963), 58-67.

14 STONE, Lawrence. *The Crisis of the Aristocracy: 1558-1641*. Oxford, 1965.†

15 STONE, Lawrence. "The Educational Revolution in England, 1560-1640." *P and P*, XXVIII (1964), 41-80.

16 STOWE, Ancel R. M. *English Grammar Schools in the Reign of Queen Elizabeth*. New York, 1908.

17 TREVOR-ROPER, Hugh R. *The Gentry, 1540-1640*. London, 1953.

18 WATSON, Foster. *The English Grammar Schools to 1660: Their Curriculum and Practise*. London, 1968. (New impression; 1st ed., 1908.)

19 WESTFALL, Richard S. *Science and Religion in Seventeenth-Century England*. New Haven, 1964.

20 WRIGHT, Louis B. *Middle Class Culture in Elizabethan England*. Ithaca, N.Y., 1965.

21 YOUNG, Robert F., ed. *Comenius in England*. London, 1932.

See also 52.1.

2. General Works

1 BELOK, Michael V. "The Courtesy Tradition and Early Schoolbooks." *Hist Ed Q*, VIII (1968), 306-318.

2 CHASE, Wayland J. " 'The Great Awakening' and Its Educational Consequences." *School Soc*, XXXV (1932), 443-449.

3 CLEWS, Elsie W. *Educational Legislation and Administration of the Colonial Governments.* New York, 1899. (Same as 52.16.)

4 CREMIN, Lawrence A. *American Education: The Colonial Experience, 1607-1783.* New York, 1970.

5 EARLE, Alice. *Child Life in Colonial Days.* New York, 1909.

6 EARLE, Alice. *Home Life in Colonial Days.* New York, 1899.

7 GREENE, Evarts B. "The Anglican Outlook on the American Colonies in the Early Eighteenth Century." *Am Hist Rev*, XX (1914), 64-85.

8 JERNEGAN, Marcus W. "Factors Influencing the Development of American Education Before the Revolution." *Proc Miss Val Hist Assn*, V (1911-1912), 190-206.

9 JERNEGAN, Marcus W. *Laboring and Dependent Classes in Colonial America, 1607-1783: Studies of the Economic, Educational, and Social Significance of Slaves, Servants, Apprentices, and Poor Folk.* Chicago, 1931.

10 KLASSEN, Frank. "Persistence and Change in Eighteenth Century Colonial Education." *Hist Ed Q*, II (1962), 83-99.

11 KNIGHT, Edgar W. "Early Opposition to the Teaching of American Children Abroad." *Ed Forum*, XI (1947), 193-204.

12 KNIGHT, Edgar W. "An Improved Plan of Education, 1775: An Eighteenth-Century Activity Curriculum." *School Soc*, LXIX (1949), 409-411.

13 LANDRUM, Grace W. "The First Colonial Grammar in English." *Wm Mar Col Q Hist Mag*, XIX (1939), 272-285.

14 MAYO, Amory D. "Public Schools During The Colonial and Revolutionary Period in the United States." *U S Bur Ed, Rep Comm 1893-1894.* Vol. I. Washington, D.C., 1896, pp. 639-738.

15 MERIWETHER, Colyer. *Our Colonial Curriculum, 1607-1776.* Washington, D.C., 1907.

16 PARSONS, Elsie W. *Educational Legislation and Administration of the Colonial Governments.* New York, 1899. (Same as 52.3.)

17 PASCOE, Charles F. *Two Hundred Years of the SPG: An Historical Account of the Society for the Propagation of the Gospel in Foreign Parts, 1701-1900.* London, 1901.

18 PENNINGTON, Edgar L. *The Reverend Thomas Bray.* Philadelphia, 1934.

19 PLIMPTON, George A. "The Hornbook and Its Use in America." *Proc Am Ant Soc*, XXV (1916), 264-272.

20 ROTHMAN, David. "A Note on the Study of the Colonial Family." *Wm Mar Q*, XXIII (1966), 627-634.

1 SALISBURY, Stephen. "Early Books and Libraries in America." *Proc Am Ant Soc*, V (1884), 171-215.

2 SEYBOLT, Robert F. *Apprenticeship and Apprenticeship Education in Colonial New England and New York.* New York, 1917.

3 SEYBOLT, Robert F. *The Evening School in Colonial America.* Bur Ed Res Col Ed (Ill.), Bull no. 24. Urbana, Ill., 1925.

4 SEYBOLT, Robert F. *Source Studies in American Colonial Education: The Private School.* Bur Ed Res Col Ed (Ill.), Bull no. 28. Urbana, Ill., 1925.

5 SHORES, Louis. *Origins of the American College Library, 1638-1800.* Hamden, Conn., 1966.

6 SIDWELL, Robert T. " 'Writers, Thinkers and Fox Hunters'—Educational Theory in the Almanacs of Eighteenth-Century Colonial America." *Hist Ed Q*, VIII (1968), 275-288.

7 STEINER, Bernard C. "Rev. Thomas Bray and His American Libraries." *Am Hist Rev*, II (1896-97), 59-75.

8 THOMPSON, Henry P. *Into All Lands: The History of the Society for the Propagation of the Gospel in Foreign Parts, 1701-1950.* London, 1951.

9 THOMPSON, Henry P. *Thomas Bray.* London, 1954.

10 WRIGHT, Louis B. *The Cultural Life of the American Colonies, 1607-1763.* New York, 1957.†

See also 3.1, 10.2, 12.7, 12.11, 12.19, 20.17.

3. The South

11 AMES, Susie M. *Reading, Writing and Arithmetic in Virginia, 1607-1699.* Williamsburg, 1957. (Jamestown 350th Anniversary Historical Booklets, no. 15.)

12 ANDERSON, Dice R. "The Teacher of Jefferson and Marshall." *S Atl Q*, XV (1916), 327-343. (Chancellor Thomas Wythe, 1726-1806.)

13 CAMPBELL, Helen J. "The Syms and Eaton Schools and Their Successor." *Wm Mar Col Q Hist Mag*, XX (1940), 1-61.

14 CORRY, John P. "Education in Colonial Georgia." *Ga Hist Q*, XVI (1932), 136-145.

15 CUTTS, A. B. "Educational Influence of Aberdeen in Seventeenth Century Virginia." *Wm Mar Col Q Hist Mag*, XV (1935), 229-249.

16 EASTERBY, J. H. "The South Carolina Education Bill of 1770." *S C Hist Mag*, XLVIII (1947), 95-111.

17 EAVES, Robert W. "A History of the Educational Developments of Alexandria, Virginia, Prior to 1800." *Wm Mar Col Q Hist Mag*, XVI (1936), 111-161.

18 GOODWIN, Mary F. "Christianizing and Educating the Negro in Colonial Virginia." *Hist Mag P E Ch*, I (1932), 143-152.

19 LAND, Robert H. "Henrico and Its College." *Wm Mar Col Q Hist Mag*, XVIII (1938), 453-498.

1 LAWRENCE, James B. "Religious Education of the Negro in the Colony of Georgia." *Ga Hist Q*, XIV (1930), 41-57.

2 MACLENNY, W. E. "Yeates Free Schools." *Wm Mar Col Q Hist Mag*, V (1925), 30-38.

3 MC CAUL, Robert L. "Education in Georgia During the Period of Royal Government, 1752-1776: Financial Support of Schools and Schoolmasters." *Ga Hist Q*, XL (1956), 103-112.

4 MC CAUL, Robert L. "Education in Georgia During the Period of Royal Government, 1752-1776: Public School Masters and Private Venture Teachers." *Ga Hist Q*, XL (1956), 248-259.

5 MC CRADY, Edward. *Education in South Carolina Prior to and During the Revolution.* Charleston, 1883.

6 MORGAN, Edmund S. *Virginians at Home: Family Life in the Eighteenth Century.* Williamsburg, 1952.†

7 NOBLE, Stuart G., and Arthur G. NUHRAH. "Education in Colonial Louisiana." *La Hist Q*, XXXII (1949), 759-776.

8 POWELL, William S. "Books in the Virginia Colony Before 1624." *Wm Mar Q*, V (1948), 177-184.

9 ROBINSON, W. Stitt. "Indian Education and Missions in Colonial Virginia." *J S Hist*, XVIII (1952), 152-168.

10 SEYBOLT, Robert F. "South Carolina's Schoolmasters of 1744." *S C Hist Mag*, XXXI (1930), 314-315; XXXVIII (1937), 64-65.

11 SMART, George K. "Private Libraries in Colonial Virginia." *Am Lit*, X (1938), 24-52.

12 TYLER, Lyon G. "Education in Colonial Virginia: Comparative Results." *Wm Mar Col Q Hist Mag*, VII (1898), 65-76.

13 TYLER, Lyon G. "Education in Colonial Virginia: Free Schools." *Wm Mar Col Q Hist Mag*, VI (1897), 71-85.

14 TYLER, Lyon G. "Education in Colonial Virginia: Poor Children and Orphans." *Wm Mar Col Q Hist Mag*, V (1897), 219-223.

15 TYLER, Lyon G. "Education in Colonial Virginia: Private Schools and Tutors." *Wm Mar Col Q Hist Mag*, VI (1897), 1-6.

16 TYLOR, Lyon G. "Grammar and Model School, Founded by Mrs. Mary Whaley in 1706." *Wm Mar Col Q Hist Mag*, IV (1895), 3-14.

17 WARING, Martha G. "Savannah's Earliest Private Schools, 1733-1800." *Ga Hist Q*, XIV (1930), 324-334.

18 WELLS, Guy F. *Parish Education in Colonial Virginia.* New York, 1923.

19 WRIGHT, Louis B. "Intellectual History and the Colonial South." *Wm Mar Q*, XVI (1959), 214-227.

See also 5.19, 15.3, 19.9, 20.13, 26.12, 28.18, 43.10, 61.16, 61.17.

4. The Middle Colonies

1 BELL, Whitfield J., Jr. "Benjamin Franklin and the German Charity Schools." *Proc Am Philos Soc*, XCIX (1955), 381-387.

2 BROOKES, George S. *Friend Anthony Benezet*. Philadelphia, 1937.

3 BRUMBAUGH, Martin G. *The Life and Works of Christopher Dock: America's Pioneer Writer on Education*. Philadelphia, 1908.

4 GEGENHEIMER, Albert F. *William Smith: Educator and Churchman, 1727-1803*. Philadelphia, 1943.

5 HALLER, Mabel. *Early Moravian Education in Pennsylvania*. Nazareth, Pa., 1953.

6 HAMLIN, Paul M. *Legal Education in Colonial New York*. New York, 1939.

7 JACKSON, Joseph. "A Philadelphia Schoolmaster of the Eighteenth Century." *Pa Mag Hist Bio*, XXXV (1911), 315-332. (David James Dove, 1696-1769.)

8 KEMP, William W. *The Support of Schools in Colonial New York by the Society for the Propagation of the Gospel in Foreign Parts*. New York, 1913.

9 KIEFER, Sister Monica. "Early American Childhood in the Middle Atlantic Area." *Pa Mag Hist Bio*, LXVIII (1944), 3-37.

10 KILPATRICK, William H. *The Dutch Schools of New Netherland and Colonial New York*. U S Bur Ed Bull 1912, no. 12. Washington, D.C., 1912.

11 KLEIN, Milton M. "Church, State, and Education: Testing the Issue in Colonial New York." *N Y Hist*, XLV (1964), 291-303.

12 KLINGBERG, Frank J. *Anglican Humanitarianism in Colonial New York*. Philadelphia, 1940.

13 LAMBERTON, E. V. "Colonial Libraries of Pennsylvania." *Pa Mag Hist Bio*, XLII (1918), 193-234.

14 LEARNED, Marion D. *Life of Francis Daniel Pastorius: The Founder of Germantown*. Philadelphia, 1908.

15 LIVINGWOOD, Frederick G. *Eighteenth Century Reformed Schools*. Morristown, Pa., 1930. (Schools of Pennsylvania Germans.)

16 MC ANEAR, Beverly. "The Charter of the Academy of Newark." *Del Hist*, IV (1950), 149-156.

17 MAURER, Charles L. *Early Lutheran Education in Pennsylvania*. Philadelphia, 1932.

18 PRATT, Daniel J. *Annals of Public Education in the State of New York, From 1626 to 1746*. Rev. and enl. ed. Albany, 1872.

19 SAVIN, Marion B., and Harold J. ABRAHAMS. "The Young Ladies' Academy of Philadelphia." *Hist Ed J*, VIII (1956), 58-67.

20 SEYBOLT, Robert F. *The Evening Schools of Colonial New York City*. Albany, 1921.

1 SEYBOLT, Robert F. "The S.P.G. Myth: A Note on Education in Colonial New York." *J Ed Res*, XIII (1926), 129-137.

2 SIDWELL, Robert T. " 'An Odd Fish'–Samuel Keimer and a Footnote to American Educational History." *Hist Ed Q*, VI (1966), 16-30.

3 STRAUB, Jean S. "Quaker School Life in Philadelphia Before 1800." *Pa Mag Hist Bio*, LXXXIX (1965), 447-458.

4 STUDER, Gerald C. *Christopher Dock; Colonial Schoolmaster: The Biography and Writings of Christopher Dock.* Scottdale, Pa., 1967.

5 TYACK, David. "Education as Artifact: Benjamin Franklin and Instruction of 'A Rising People.' " *Hist Ed Q*, VI (1966), 3-15.

6 VAN VECHTEN, Emma. *Early Schools and Schoolmasters of New Amsterdam.* New York, 1898.

7 WEAVER, Glenn. "Benjamin Franklin and the Pennsylvania Germans." *Wm Mar Q*, XIV (1957), 535-559.

8 WEBER, Samuel E. *Charity School Movement in Colonial Pennsylvania, 1754-1763.* Philadelphia, 1905.

9 WOODY, Thomas. *Early Quaker Education in Pennsylvania.* New York, 1920.

See also 58.18.

5. New England

10 BUSH, George G. "The First Common Schools of New England." *U S Bur Ed, Rep Comm 1896-1897.* Vol. II. Washington, D.C., 1898, pp. 1165-1186.

11 COLE, Norwood M. "The Licensing of Schoolmasters in Colonial Massachusetts." *Hist Ed J*, VIII (1956), 68-74.

12 DEMOS, John. *A Little Commonwealth: Family Life in Plymouth Colony.* New York, 1970.

13 GAMBRELL, Mary L. *Ministerial Training in Eighteenth-Century New England.* New York, 1937.

14 GOULD, Elizabeth P. *Ezekiel Cheever: Schoolmaster.* Boston, 1904.

15 HENDRICK, Irving G. "A Reappraisal of Colonial New Hampshire's Effort in Public Education." *Hist Ed Q*, VI (1966), 43-60.

16 JACKSON, George L. *The Development of School Support in Colonial Massachusetts.* New York, 1909.

17 LITTLEFIELD, George E. *Early Schools and School-Books of New England.* Boston, 1904.

18 MIDDLEKAUFF, Robert. *Ancients and Axioms: Secondary Education in Eighteenth Century New England.* New Haven, 1963.

19 MILLER, Perry. *The New England Mind.* 2 vols. Boston, 1939.†

20 MILLER, Perry, and Thomas H. JOHNSON. *The Puritans.* New York, 1938, pp. 1-63, 695-727.

21 MORGAN, Edmund S. *The Puritan Family: Religion and Domestic Relations in Seventeenth-Century New England.* Rev. and enl. ed. New York, 1966.†

1 MORISON, Samuel E. *The Puritan Pronaos: Studies in the Intellectual Life of New England in the Seventeenth Century.* New York, 1935. (Also published as *The Intellectual Life of Colonial New England.* 3d ed. New York, 1965.)†

2 MURDOCK, Kenneth B. "The Teaching of Latin and Greek at the Boston Latin School in 1712." *Pub Colonial Soc Mass*, XXVII (1927), 21-29.

3 MURDOCK, Kenneth B. *Literature and Theology in Colonial New England.* Cambridge, Mass., 1949.†

4 O'BRIEN, Michael J. "Early Irish Schoolmasters in New England." *Cath Hist Rev*, III (1917), 52-71.

5 SCHLESINGER, Elizabeth B. "Cotton Mather and His Children." *Wm Mar Q*, X (1953), 181-189.

6 SEYBOLT, Robert F. *The Private Schools of Colonial Boston.* Cambridge, Mass., 1935.

7 SEYBOLT, Robert F. "The Private Schools of Seventeenth-Century Boston." *N Eng Q*, VIII (1935), 418-424.

8 SEYBOLT, Robert F. *The Public Schools of Colonial Boston, 1635-1775.* Cambridge, Mass., 1935.

9 SEYBOLT, Robert F. "Schoolmasters of Colonial Boston." *Pub Colonial Soc Mass*, XXVII (1928), 130-156.

10 SHIPTON, Clifford K. "Secondary Education in the Puritan Colonies." *N Eng Q*, VII (1934), 646-661.

11 SHIPTON, Clifford K. "The New England Clergy of the 'Glacial Age.' " *Pub Colonial Soc Mass*, XXXII (1937), 24-54.

12 SHIPTON, Clifford K. "The Puritan Influence on Education." *Pa Hist*, XXV (1958), 223-233.

13 SMALL, Walter H. *Early New England Schools.* Boston, 1914.

14 SMITH, Wilson. "The Teacher in Puritan Culture." *Har Ed Rev*, XXXVI (1966), 394-411.

15 UPDEGRAFF, Harlan. *The Origin of the Moving School in Massachusetts.* New York, 1908.

16 WRIGHT, Thomas G. *Literary Culture in Early New England, 1620-1730.* New York, 1966.

See also 6.14, 9.7, 10.1, 26.9, 27.13, 28.2-4, 28.11, 29.6, 30.3.

6. Higher Education

A. GENERAL

17 BRINTON, Howard H. "Quaker Contributions to Higher Education in Colonial America." *Pa Hist*, XXV (1958), 234-250.

18 CASTANEDA, Carlos E. "The Beginnings of University Life in America." *Cath Hist Rev*, XXIV (1938), 153-174.

1 CONNOR, R. D. W. "The Genesis of Higher Education in North Carolina." *N C Hist Rev*, XXVIII (1951), 1-14. (Concerns years from 1763 to 1789.)

2 "Correspondence of Ezra Stiles, President of Yale College, and James Madison, President of William and Mary." *Wm Mar Col Hist Mag*, VII (1927), 292-296.

3 DEXTER, Franklin B. "On Some Social Distinctions at Harvard and Yale Before the Revolution." *Proc Am Ant Soc*, IX (1893), 34-59.

4 DURNIN, Richard G. "The Role of the Presidents in the American Colleges of the Colonial Period." *Hist Ed Q*, I (1961), 23-31.

5 EELLS, Walter C. *Baccalaureate Degrees Conferred by American Colleges in the Seventeenth and Eighteenth Centuries.* Washington, D.C., 1958.

6 EELLS, Walter C. "First Directory of American Colleges." *Hist Ed Q*, II (1962), 225-233.

7 FROST, S. E., Jr. "Higher Education Among the American Indians During the Colonial Period." *Hist Ed J*, IX (1958), 59-66.

8 HALBER, Mabel. "Moravian Influence on Higher Education in Colonial America." *Pa Hist*, XXV (1958), 205-222.

9 KIRKPATRICK, J. E. "The British College in the American Colonies." *School Soc*, XVII (1923), 449-454.

10 KRAUS, Joe W. "The Development of a Curriculum in the Early American Colleges." *Hist Ed Q*, I (1961), 64-76.

11 MC ANEAR, Beverly. "College Founding in the American Colonies, 1745-1775." *Miss Val Hist Rev*, XLII (1955), 24-44.

12 MC ANEAR, Beverly. "The Raising of Funds by the Colonial Colleges." *Miss Val Hist Rev*, XXXVIII (1952), 591-612.

13 MC ANEAR, Beverly. "The Selection of an Alma Mater by Pre-Revolutionary Students." *Pa Mag Hist Bio*, LXXIII (1949), 429-440.

14 MC CAUL, Robert L. "Whitefield's Bethesda College Projects and Other Major Attempts to Found Colonial Colleges." *Ga Hist Q*, XLIV (1960), 263-277, 381-398.

15 MIDDLETON, Arthur P. "Anglican Contributions to Higher Education in Colonial America." *Pa Hist*, XXV (1958), 251-268.

16 MORISON, Samuel E. "American Colonial Colleges." *Rice Institute Pamphlets*, XXIII (1936), 246-282.

17 SHIPTON, Clifford K. "Ye Mystery of Ye Ages Solved, or How Placing Worked at Colonial Harvard and Yale." *Har Al Bull*, LVII (1954-55), 258-59, 262-63, 417.

18 SMITH, William. *A General Idea of the College of Mirania.* New York, 1753. (Repr. 1969.)

19 WALSH, James J. *Education of the Founding Fathers of the Republic: Scholasticism in the Colonial Colleges, a Neglected Chapter in the History of American Education.* New York, 1935.

See also 43.18, 44.18, 45.1, 53.19.

B. HARVARD

1 CADBURY, Henry J. "John Harvard's Library." *Pub Colonial Soc Mass,* XXXIV (1940), 353-388.

2 CHAPLIN, Jeremiah. *Life of Henry Dunster, First President of Harvard College.* Boston, 1872.

3 DAVIS, Andrew M. "The First Scholarship at Harvard." *Proc Am Ant Soc,* V (1884), 129-140.

4 DAVIS, Andrew M. "John Harvard's Life in America, 1637-1638." *Pub Colonial Soc Mass,* XII (1908), 4-44.

5 DUDLEY, Thomas. "The Harvard College Charter of 1650." *Pub Colonial Soc Mass,* XXXI (1935), 1-6.

6 EDES, Henry H. "A College Commencement: Some Harvard Theses of 1663, and a Note on Their Significance." *Pub Colonial Soc Mass,* V (1898), 322-340.

7 EDES, Henry H. "A Letter of President Dunster of Harvard to a Committee of the General Court in 1653, Concerning the Affairs of Harvard College." *Pub Colonial Soc Mass,* III (1897), 415-425.

8 FOSTER, Francis A. "The Burning of Harvard Hall in 1764, and Its Consequences." *Pub Colonial Soc Mass,* XIV (1911), 2-43.

9 FOSTER, Margery S. *"Out of Smalle Beginnings . . . ": An Economic History of Harvard College in the Puritan Period, 1636-1712.* Cambridge, Mass., 1962.

10 HUDSON, Winthrop S. "The Morison Myth Concerning the Founding of Harvard College." *Church Hist,* VIII (1939), 148-159.

11 LAW, William C. "Early Harvard Broadsides." *Proc Am Ant Soc,* XXIV (1914), 264-304.

12 LITTLEFIELD, George E. "Elijah Corlet and the 'Faire Grammar Schoole' at Cambridge." *Pub Colonial Soc Mass,* XVII (1913), 131-142.

13 MATTHEWS, Albert. "The Harvard College Charter of 1672." *Pub Colonial Soc Mass,* XXI (1919), 363-409.

14 MATTHEWS, Albert. "Harvard Commencement Days, 1642-1916." *Pub Colonial Soc Mass,* XVIII (1916), 309-385.

15 MATTHEWS, Albert. "The Teaching of French at Harvard College Before 1750." *Pub Colonial Soc Mass,* XVII (1914), 216-231.

16 MATTHEWS, Albert, et al., eds. "Corporation Records of Harvard College, 1636-1774." *Pub Colonial Soc Mass,* XV, XVI (1925).

17 MORISON, Samuel E. "College Laws and Customs." *Pub Colonial Soc Mass,* XXXI (1935), 322-401.

18 MORISON, Samuel E. *The Founding of Harvard College.* Cambridge, Mass., 1935.

19 MORISON, Samuel E. *Harvard College in the Seventeenth Century.* 2 vols. Cambridge, Mass., 1936.

20 MORISON, Samuel E. "Henry Dunster, President of Harvard." *Builders of the Bay Colony.* Boston, 1930.†

1 MORISON, Samuel E. "Precedence at Harvard College in the Seventeenth Century." *Proc Am Ant Soc*, XLII (1932), 371-431.

2 MORISON, Samuel E. "Urian Oake's Salutary Oration: Commencement, 1677." *Pub Colonial Soc Mass*, XXXI (1935), 405-436.

3 NOBLE, John. "Comments on an Old Harvard Commencement Program of 1730." *Pub Colonial Soc Mass*, VI (1899), 265-278.

4 NORTON, Arthur O. "Harvard Textbooks and Reference Books of the Seventeenth Century." *Pub Colonial Soc Mass*, XXVIII (1933), 361-438.

5 PEIRCE, Benjamin. *A History of Harvard University from Its Foundation in the Year 1636 to the Period of the American Revolution.* Cambridge, Mass., 1833.

6 POTTER, Alfred C. "The Harvard College Library, 1723-1735." *Pub Colonial Soc Mass*, XXV (1922), 1-13.

7 RAND, Edward K. "Liberal Education in Seventeenth Century Harvard." *N Eng Q*, VI (1933), 525-551.

8 SEYBOLT, Robert F. "Student Libraries at Harvard, 1763-1764." *Pub Colonial Soc Mass*, XXVIII (1935), 449-461.

9 YOUNG, Edward J. *Subjects for Master's Degrees in Harvard College, 1655-1791.* Cambridge, Mass., 1880.

See also 34.20, 34.21, 42.10, 43.3, 43.17, 43.18, 44.18, 45.1, 47.4, 58.3, 58.17, 63.11, 66.6, 66.10, 78.6, 79.16, 79.20, 80.15, 82.1, 82.2.

C. WILLIAM AND MARY

10 "Accounts of the College." *Wm Mar Col Q Hist Mag*, VIII (1900), 166-171.

11 CULLETON, Leo. "William and Mary College vs. Frewen, Chancery Suit, 1702." *Va Mag Hist Bio*, XXIV (1916), 374-378.

12 "Documents of William and Mary College, Recently Discovered." *Wm Mar Col Q Hist Mag*, X (1930), 239-253.

13 "Finances of the College in 1755-1765." *Wm Mar Col Q Hist Mag*, XI (1903), 149-153.

14 "The First Chair of Law and Police at William and Mary College." *Wm Mar Col Q Hist Mag*, IV (1896), 264-265.

15 GANTER, Herbert L. "Documents Relating to the Early History of the College of William and Mary and to the History of the Church in Virginia." *Wm Mar Col Q Hist Mag*, XIX-XX (1939-1940), 348-375, 446-470; 114-137, 212-236, 391-396, 524-544.

16 HUGHES, Robert M. "William and Mary, the First American Law School." *Wm Mar Col Q Hist Mag*, II (1922), 40-48.

17 JONES, E. Alfred. "Two Professors of William and Mary College." *Wm Mar Col Q Hist Mag*, XXVI (1918), 221-231. (Revs. Thomas Gwatkin and Dr. Samuel Henley.)

1   "Journal of the Meetings of the President and Masters of William and Mary College." *Wm Mar Col Q Hist Mag*, I (1893), 130-137, 214-220; II (1893), 50-57, 122-127; II (1894), 208-210, 256-258; III (1894), 60-64, 128-132; III (1895), 195-197, 262-265; IV (1895), 43-46, 130-132; IV (1896), 187-192; V (1896), 15-17, 83-89; V (1897), 187-189, 224-229; XIII (1904), 15-22, 133-137; XIII (1905), 148-156, 230-235; XIV (1905), 25-31; XIV (1906), 242-246; XV (1906), 1-14, 134-142; XV (1907), 164-174, 264-269.

2   KIRKPATRICK, John E. "Constitutional Development of the College of William and Mary." *Wm Mar Col Q Hist Mag*, VI (1926), 95-108. (1693-1779)

3   Ludwell Papers, Virginia Historical Society Collection. "Proceedings of the Visitors of William and Mary College, 1716." *Va Mag Hist Bio*, IV (1896), 161-175.

4   "Minutes of the College Faculty, 1758." *Wm Mar Col Q Hist Mag*, I (1921), 24-26.

5   NICHOLSON, Francis, and James BLAIR. "Papers Relating to the Administration of Governor Nicholson and to the Founding of William and Mary College." *Va Mag Hist Bio*, VII (1899-1900), 153-172, 275-286, 386-401; VIII (1900-1901), 46-64, 126-146, 366-385; IX (1901-1902), 18-29, 152-162, 251-262.

6   "Notes Relative to Some of the Students Who Attended the College of William and Mary, 1753-1778." *Wm Mar Col Q Hist Mag*, I (1921), 27-41, 116-130.

7   "Papers Concerning the College of William and Mary." *Wm Mar Col Q Hist Mag*, II, (1893), 36-37.

8   "Papers Relating to the College." *Wm Mar Col Q Hist Mag*, XVI (1908), 162-180.

9   "Papers Relating to the Founding of William and Mary College." *Wm Mar Col Q Hist Mag*, VII (1899), 158-174.

10   "The Statutes of the College of William and Mary in Virginia." *Wm Mar Col Q Hist Mag*, XVI (1908), 239-256.

11   "The Statutes of the College of William and Mary, Codified in 1736." *Wm Mar Col Q Hist Mag*, XXII (1914), 281-296.

12   SWEM, Earl G. "The Lee Free School and the College of William and Mary." *Wm Mar Q*, XVI (1959), 207-213.

13   TYLER, Lyon G. "A Few Facts from the Records of William and Mary College." *Pap Am Hist Assn*, IV (1890), 129-141.

14   TYLER, Lyon G. "Early Courses and Professors at William and Mary College." *Wm Mary Col Q Hist Mag*, XIV (1905), 71-83.

15   TYLER, Lyon G. "Early Presidents of William and Mary." *Wm Mar Col Q Hist Mag*, I (1892), 63-75.

16   TYLER, Lyon G. "Education in Colonial Virginia: The Higher Education." *Wm Mar Col Q Hist Mag*, VI (1898), 171-187.

17   TYLER, Lyon G. "Education in Colonial Virginia: The Influence of William and Mary College." *Wm Mar Col Q Hist Mag*, VII (1898), 1-9.

18   TYLER, Lyon G. "William and Mary College and Its Influence on the Founding of the Republic." *Wm Mar Col Q Hist Mag*, XV (1935), 324-333.

1 TYLER, Lyon G. "William and Mary College as Expressing the American Principle of Democracy." *Wm Mar Col Q Hist Mag*, XV (1935), 282-293.

2 VASSAR, Rena. "The College Battle: Political Factionalism in the Founding of the College of William and Mary." *Pae Hist*, IV (1964), 444-456.

3 "William and Mary College in 1774." *Wm Mar Col Q Hist Mag*, II (1922), 101-113.

4 "William and Mary College, 1771." *Wm Mar Col Q Hist Mag*, IV (1924), 277-279.

See also 39.9, 39.10, 42.10, 43.18, 44.18, 45.1, 58.2, 79.5, 81.19, 82.6, 82.7, 82.12-14.

D. YALE

5 BALDWIN, Ebenezer. *Annals of Yale College.* 2d ed. New Haven, 1838.

6 BALDWIN, Simeon E. "The Ecclesiastical Constitution of Yale College." *Pap New Haven Colony Hist Soc*, III (1882), 406-442.

7 CLAP, Thomas. *The Annals or History of Yale College.* New Haven, 1766. (Evans Bibliography No. 10262.)

8 CLAP, Thomas. *The Answer of the Friend in the West.* New Haven, 1755. (Evans Bibliography No. 7385.)

9 CLAP, Thomas. *The Religious Constitution of Colleges, Especially of Yale College.* New London, Conn., 1754. (Evans Bibliography No. 7171.)

10 COHEN, Sheldon S. "Tradition and Change in the Ivy League: Benjamin Trumbull, the Years at Yale 1755-1759." *Hist Ed Q*, VI (1966), 33-48.

11 COWIE, Alexander. *Educational Problems at Yale College in the Eighteenth Century.* New Haven, 1936. (Published for the Tercentenary Commission of Connecticut, Committee on Historical Publications.)

12 CUNINGHAM, Charles E. *Timothy Dwight, 1752-1817.* New York, 1942.

13 DANA, Samuel W. *Yale College Subject to the General Assembly.* New Haven, 1784.

14 DEXTER, Franklin B. *Biographical Sketches of Graduates of Yale: Yale College with Annals of the College History.* 6 vols. New York, 1885-1912.

15 DEXTER, Franklin B. "The Founding of Yale College." *Pap New Haven Colony Hist Soc*, III (1882), 1-31.

16 DEXTER, Franklin B. "An Historical Sketch of the Powers and Duties of the Presidency in Yale College." *Proc Am Ant Soc*, XII (1896), 27-42.

17 DEXTER, Franklin B., ed. *Extracts from the Itineraries and Other Miscellanies of Ezra Stiles.* New Haven, 1916.

18 DEXTER, Franklin B. "The Removal of Yale College to New Haven in October, 1716." *Pap New Haven Hist Soc*, IX (1918), 70-89.

19 DEXTER, Franklin B. "Student Life at Yale in the Early Days of Connecticut Hall." *Pap New Haven Colony Hist Soc*, VII (1908), 288-297.

1 DEXTER, Franklin B. "Thomas Clap and His Writings." *Pap New Haven Colony Hist Soc*, V (1894), 247-274.

2 DEXTER, Franklin B. "Yale College in Saybrook." *Pap New Haven Colony Hist Soc*, VII (1908), 129-140.

3 DEXTER, Franklin B., ed. *Documentary History of Yale University, Under the Original Charter of the Collegiate School of Connecticut, 1701-1745.* New Haven, 1916.

4 DEXTER, Franklin B., ed. *Literary Diary of Ezra Stiles.* 3 vols. New York, 1901.

5 FULLER, Henry M. "Bishop Berkeley as a Benefactor of Yale." *Yale Univ Lib Gaz*, XXVIII (1953), 1-18.

6 KINGSLEY, William L. "History of Yale College." *Am J Ed*, V (1858), 541-566.

7 LARNED, Ellen D. "Yale Boys of the Last Century: The Journal of Elijah Backus, Jr., at Yale College, from January 1 to December 31, 1777." *Conn Q*, I (1895), 355-361.

8 MC KEEHAN, Louis W. *Yale Science: The First Hundred Years, 1701-1801.* New York, 1947.

9 MORGAN, Edmund S. "Ezra Stiles: The Education of a Yale Man, 1742-1746." *Hunt Lib Q*, XVII (1954), 251-268.

10 MORGAN, Edmund S. *The Gentle Puritan: A Life of Ezra Stiles, 1727-1795.* New Haven, 1962.

11 MURDOCK, Kenneth B. "Cotton Mather and the Rectorship of Yale College." *Pub Colonial Soc Mass*, XXVI (1926), 388-401.

12 OVIATT, Edwin. *The Beginnings of Yale, 1701-1726.* New Haven, 1916.

13 PARSONS, Francis. "Elisha Williams, Minister, Soldier, President of Yale." *Pap New Haven Colony Hist Soc*, VII (1908), 188-214.

14 PARSONS, Francis. "Ezra Stiles of Yale." *N Eng Q*, IX (1936), 286-316.

15 SCOTT, Kenneth. "A 'Dust' at Yale and a 'Blessing' for President Clap." *Bull Conn Hist Soc*, XXIII (1958), 46-49.

16 SHIPTON, Clifford K. "Thomas Clap (1703-1767)." *Sibley's Harvard Graduates.* Vol. VII. Boston, 1945.

17 SMITH, Charles H. "The Founding of Yale College." *Pap New Haven Colony Hist Soc*, VII (1908), 34-64.

18 TUCKER, Louis L. "President Thomas Clap and the Rise of Yale College, 1740-1766." *Historian*, XIX (1956-1957), 66-81.

19 TUCKER, Louis L. "The Church of England and Religious Liberty at Pre-Revolutionary Yale." *Wm Mar Q*, XVII (1960), 314-328.

20 TUCKER, Louis L. *Puritan Protagonist: President Thomas Clap of Yale College.* Chapel Hill, 1962.

See also 13.19, 39.18-20, 42.10, 43.4, 43.18, 44.11, 44.18, 45.1, 58.2, 58.3, 58.17, 66.17, 79.1, 79.13, 80.19, 82.4.

E. OTHER COLLEGES

1 BRODERICK, Francis L. "Pulpit, Physics, and Politics: The Curriculum of the College of New Jersey, 1746-1794." *Wm Mar Q*, VI (1949), 42-67.

2 COLLINS, Varnum L. *President Witherspoon.* 2 vols. Princeton, 1925.

3 FOX, Bertha S. "Provost Smith and the Quest for Funds." *Pa Hist*, II (1935), 225-238.

4 HASKETT, Richard C. "Princeton Before the Revolution." *Wm Mar Q*, V (1949), 90-93.

5 HORNBERGER, Theodore. "A Note on the Probable Source of Provost Smith's Famous Curriculum for the College of Philadelphia." *Pa Mag Hist Bio*, LVIII (1934), 370-377.

6 INGRAM, George H. "The Story of the Log College." *J Presb Hist Soc*, XII (1927), 487-511.

7 KEEN, William W. *The Early Years of Brown University, 1764-1770.* Boston, n.d.

8 LIVELY, Bruce R. "William Smith, the College and Academy of Philadelphia, and Pennsylvania Politics, 1753-1758." *Hist Mag P E Church*, XXXVIII (1969), 237-258.

9 MC CALLUM, James D. *Eleazar Wheelock: Founder of Dartmouth College.* Hanover, N.H., 1939.

10 MONTGOMERY, Thomas H. *A History of the University of Pennsylvania from Its Foundation to A.D. 1770.* Philadelphia, 1900.

11 OLSON, Alison B. "The Founding of Princeton University: Religion and Politics in Eighteenth Century New Jersey." *N J Hist*, LXXXVII (1969), 133-150.

12 PATERSON, William. *Glimpses of Colonial Society and the Life at Princeton College, 1766-1773.* Ed. by W. Jay Mills. Philadelphia, 1903.

13 SCHMIDT, George P. *Princeton and Rutgers: The Two Colonial Colleges of New Jersey.* Princeton, 1964.

14 *The Reverend Samuel Davies Abroad: The Diary of a Journey to England and Scotland, 1753-55.* Ed. by George William Pilcher. Urbana, Ill., 1967. (Concerns the College of New Jersey.)

15 SCHNEIDER, Herbert W., and Carol, eds. *Samuel Johnson, President of King's College; His Career and Writings.* 4 vols. New York, 1929.

16 SMITH, Perry W. " 'Exercises' Presented During the Commencements of the College of Philadelphia and Other Colonial Colleges." *Pae Hist*, VII (1967), 182-222.

17 THORPE, Francis N., ed. *Benjamin Franklin and the University of Pennsylvania.* U S Bur Ed, Circ Info 1892, no. 2. Washington, D.C., 1893.

See also 12.6, 33.1, 33.17, 33.19, 34.2, 34.3, 37.14-16, 37.19, 37.20, 38.5, 38.6, 43.18, 44.2, 44.18, 45.1, 55.4, 58.18, 82.15.

7. The Professions, Science, and Learning

1 ALDRIDGE, Alfred O. *Benjamin Franklin: Philosopher and Man.* Philadelphia, 1965.

2 BECKER, Carl. *Benjamin Franklin.* Ithaca, N.Y., 1946. Also in *Dictionary of American Biography*, VI, 585-598.

3 BELL, Whitfield J. *Early American Science: Needs and Opportunities for Study.* Williamsburg, 1955.

4 BEST, John H., ed. *Benjamin Franklin on Education.* New York, 1962.†

5 BRASCH, Frederick E. "The Newtonian Epoch in the American Colonies." *Proc Am Ant Soc*, XLIX (1939), 314-332.

6 BURANELLI, Vincent. "Colonial Philosophy." *Wm Mar Q*, XVI (1959), 343-362.

7 BUTTERFIELD, Lyman H. "A Sketch of the Revolution and Improvement in Science, Arts, and Literature in America." *Wm Mar Q*, X (1953), 579-627. (Repr. from Samuel Miller, "A Brief Retrospect of the Eighteenth Century [1803].")

8 COHEN, I. Bernard. *Franklin and Newton.* Philadelphia, 1956.

9 COHEN, I. Bernard. *Some Early Tools of American Science: An Account of the Early Scientific Instruments and Mineralogical and Biological Collections in Harvard University.* Cambridge, Mass., 1950.

10 CONROY, Graham P. "Berkeley and Education in America." *J Hist Ideas*, XXI (1960), 211-220.

11 GAY, Peter. *A Loss of Mastery: Puritan Historians in Colonial America.* Berkeley and Los Angeles, 1966.†

12 GOODE, G. Brown. "The Beginning of Natural History in America." *Smith Inst, Ann Rep 1897.* Washington, D.C., 1901, pp. 355-408.

13 GRABO, Norman S. "The Veiled Vision: The Role of Aesthetics in Early American Intellectual History." *Wm Mar Q*, XIX (1962), 493-510.

14 GRANGER, Bruce I. *Benjamin Franklin, an American Man of Letters.* Ithaca, N.Y., 1964.

15 HINDLE, Brooke. *David Rittenhouse.* Princeton, 1964.

16 HINDLE, Brooke. *The Pursuit of Science in Revolutionary America, 1735-1789.* Chapel Hill, 1956.†

17 HINDLE, Brooke. "The Quaker Background and Science in Colonial Philadelphia." *Isis*, XLVI (1955), 243-250.

18 HINDLE, Brooke. *Technology in Early America.* Chapel Hill, 1966. (With a directory of artifact collections by Lucius F. Ellsworth.)

19 HORNBERGER, Theodore. "Samuel Johnson of Yale and King's College: A Note on the Relation of Science and Religion in Provincial America." *N Eng Q*, VIII (1935), 378-397.

1 HORNBERGER, Theodore. *Scientific Thought in the American Colleges, 1638-1800*. Austin, Tex., 1945.

2 KIMMEL, Herbert. "The Status of Mathematics and Mathematical Instruction During the Colonial Period." *School Soc*, IX (1919), 195-202.

3 KOCH, Adrienne. "Pragmatic Wisdom and the American Enlightenment." *Wm Mar Q*, XVIII (1961), 313-329.

4 LABAREE, Leonard W., ed. *The Autobiography of Benjamin Franklin*. New Haven, 1964.†

5 LABAREE, Leonard W., et al., eds. *The Papers of Benjamin Franklin*. Several vols. New Haven, 1959-

6 LANE, William C. "Benjamin Franklin's Relations with Harvard College." *Pub Colonial Soc Mass*, X (1906), 229-239.

7 LOVELL, Robert W. "William Crosswell: Eccentric Scholar." *N Eng Q*, XXXVIII (1965), 35-53.

8 MESSERLI, Jonathan. "Benjamin Franklin: Colonial and Cosmopolitan Educator." *Brit J Ed Stud*, XVI (1968), 43-59.

9 MILES, Richard D. "The American Image of Benjamin Franklin." *Am Q*, IX (1957), 117-143.

10 MORGAN, Morris H. "The First Harvard Doctors of Medicine." *Pub Colonial Soc Mass*, XII (1909), 312-321.

11 POOL, Rev. David de Sola. "Hebrew Learning Among the Puritans of New England Prior to 1700." *Pub Am Jew Hist Soc*, XX (1911), 31-83.

12 SACK, Saul. "The Birth of American Medical Education." *Pae Hist*, III (1963), 97-132.

13 SMALLWOOD, William M. *Natural History and the American Mind*. New York, 1941.

14 SMITH, Edgar F. "Early Scientists of Philadelphia." *Pa Mag Hist Bio*, XLVII (1923), 1-27.

15 STEARNS, Raymond P. "James Petiver, Seventeenth Century Promoter of Natural Science." *Proc Am Ant Soc*, LXII (1952), 243-365.

16 TOLLES, Frederick B. "Philadelphia's First Scientist, James Logan." *Isis*, XLVII (1956), 20-30.

17 TUCKER, Leonard. "President Thomas Clap of Yale College: Another 'Founding Father' of American Science." *Isis*, LII (1961), 55-77.

18 VAN DOREN, Carl. *Benjamin Franklin*. New York, 1964.†

19 WOODY, Thomas, ed. *Educational Views of Benjamin Franklin*. New York, 1931.

See also 7.18, 11.12, 12.5, 37.14, 43.9, 45.21, 46.3, 56.5, 56.13, 58.19, 62.17, 63.1, 63.4, 63.8, 63.10, 63.14, 63.20, 64.17.

III.   From Revolution to Reconstruction

1.   General Works

1   ANDERSON, Lewis F. "The Manual Labor School Movement." *Ed Rev*, XLVI (1913), 369-386.

2   BIDWELL, Charles E. "The Moral Significance of the Common School." *Hist Ed Q*, VI (1966), 50-91.

3   BODE, Carl. *The American Lyceum: Town Meeting of the Mind.* New York, 1956.†

4   BROWN, Marianna C. *Sunday School Movements in America.* New York, 1901.

5   BURGESS, Charles O. "Two Tendencies of Educational Thought in the New Nation: America as a Presbyterian's City on a Hill or as a Deist's Island in the Sea." *Pae Hist*, IV (1964), 326-342.

6   BURGESS, Charles O. "William Maclure and Education for a Good Society." *Hist Ed Q*, III (1963), 58-76.

7   BURTON, Warren. *The District School as It Was by One Who Went to It.* Boston, 1833.

8   CARLTON, Frank T. *Economic Influences upon Educational Progress in the United States, 1820-1850.* New York, 1965, c. 1908.†

9   COPE, Henry F. *The Evolution of the Sunday School.* Boston, 1911.

10   CRANDALL, John C. "Patriotism and Humanitarian Reform in Children's Literature, 1825-1860." *Am Q*, XXI (1969), 3-22.

11   CREMIN, Lawrence A. *The American Common School: An Historic Conception.* New York, 1951.

12   DRAPER, Andrew S. "Public School Pioneering in New York and Massachusetts." *Ed Rev*, III (1892), 313-336. (See also replies and counter-replies to this article. *Ibid.*, IV (1892-1893), 241-252, 345-362.)

13   ESCHENBACHER, Herman. "Education and Social Unity in the Ante-Bellum Period." *Har Ed Rev*, XXX (1960), 154-163.

14   FOSTER, Ashley. "An 1803 Proposal to Improve the American Teaching Profession." *School Soc*, LXXX (1954), 69-73.

15   GOOD, Harry G. "Emerson, An Educational Liberal." *Hist Ed J*, I (1949), 7-20.

16   HARDING, Walter. "Henry D. Thoreau, Instructor." *Ed Forum*, XXIX (1964), 89-97.

17   HAYES, Cecil B. *The American Lyceum, Its History and Contribution to Education.* U S Off Ed Bull 1932, no. 12. Washington, D.C., 1932.

18   HOYL, William D., Jr. "Richard Henry Dana and the Lecture System, 1841." *N Eng Q*, XVIII (1945), 93-96.

1 JACKSON, Sidney L. *America's Struggle for Free Schools: Social Tensions and Education in New England and New York, 1827-1842.* Washington, D.C., 1941.

2 JACKSON, Sidney L. "Labor, Education and Politics in the 1830s." *Pa Mag Hist Bio*, LXVI (1942), 279-293.

3 JEWETT, James P. "Moral Education in American Secondary Schools Before the Civil War." *Hist Ed J*, III (1951), 18-26.

4 JONES, Howard M., ed. *Emerson on Education: Selections.* New York, 1966.†

5 LEWIS, Albert. "Emerson and Educational Reconstruction." *Ed Forum*, VIII (1944), 449-457.

6 MANLY, John M. "Educational Ideals of 1850." *School Rev*, XXIV (1916), 746-751.

7 MANSFIELD, Edward A. *American Education: Its Principles and Elements.* New York, 1854.

8 MEAD, Arthur R. *The Development of Free Schools in the United States as Illustrated by Connecticut and Michigan.* New York, 1918.

9 NOFFSINGER, John S. *Correspondence Schools, Lyceums, Chautaquas.* New York, 1926.

10 REISNER, Edward H. *The Evolution of the Common School.* New York, 1930.

11 RICHEY, Herman G. "Reappraisal of the State School Systems of the Pre-Civil War Period." *El School J*, XLI (1940), 118-129.

12 RICHEY, Herman G. "The Persistence of Educational Progress During the Decade of the Civil War." *El School J*, XLII (1942), 358-366, 456-463.

13 ROORBACH, Agnew O. *The Development of the Social Studies in American Secondary Education Before 1861.* Philadelphia, 1937. (A study of academies from 1820 to 1860.)

14 SARGENT, Walter. "The Evolution of the Little Red School House." *School Rev*, XI (1903), 435-455.

15 SALOMON, Louis B. "The Straight-Cut Ditch: Thoreau on Education." *Am Q*, XIV (Spring, 1962), 52-61.

16 SHEPARD, Grace F. "Emerson as an Educator." *Har Ed Rev*, III (1933), 188-197.

17 SMITH, Timothy L. "Protestant Schooling and American Nationality." *J Am Hist*, LIII (1966-1967), 679-696.

18 TRAVERS, Paul D. "John Orville Taylor: A Forgotten Educator." *Hist Ed Q*, IX (1969), 57-63.

19 WILSON, John B. "Bronson Alcott: Platonist or Pestalozzian?" *School Soc*, LXXXI (1955), 49-54.

20 WILSON, Lawrence. "Thoreau on Education." *Hist Ed Q*, II (1962), 19-29.

21 WRIGHT, Louis B. *Culture on the Moving Frontier.* Bloomington, 1955.†

See also 6.11-13, 6.15, 7.2, 7.5-10, 10.3, 10.7, 10.8, 12.17-21, 15.17, 19.1, 21.15, 26.8, 28.19, 29.2, 29.17.

2. The Founding Fathers and National Leaders

1 ADAMS, Herbert B. *Thomas Jefferson and the University of Virginia.* U S Bur Ed, Circ Info 1888, no. 1. Washington, D.C., 1888.

2 ARROWOOD, Charles F. *Thomas Jefferson and Education in a Republic.* New York, 1930.

3 BAKER, Gordon E. "Thomas Jefferson and Academic Freedom." *Bull Am Assn Univ Prof,* XXXIX (1953), 377-387.

4 BUTTS, R. Freeman. "James Madison, the Bill of Rights, and Education." *Tchr Col Rec,* LX (1958), 121-128.

5 CABELL, Nathaniel F., ed. *Early History of the University of Virginia as Contained in the Letters of Thomas Jefferson and Joseph C. Cabell.* Richmond, Va., 1856.

6 CASTEL, Albert. "The Founding Fathers and the Vision of a National University." *Hist Ed Q,* IV (1964), 280-302.

7 CHINARD, Gilbert. "Thomas Jefferson as a Classical Scholar." *Am Sch,* I (1932), 133-143.

8 CHINARD, Gilbert, ed. *The Correspondence of Jefferson and DuPont de Nemours.* Baltimore, 1931.

9 COLBOURN, H. Trevor. "Thomas Jefferson's Use of the Past." *Wm Mar Q,* XV (1958), 56-70.

10 CONANT, James B. *Thomas Jefferson and the Development of American Public Education.* Berkeley, 1962.

11 DU PONT DE NEMOURS, Pierre S. *National Education in the United States of America.* Newark, Del., 1923.

12 GOOD, Harry G. "Who First Proposed a National University?" *School Soc,* III (1916), 387-391. (Benjamin Rush)

13 GREENE, Evarts B. "Some Educational Values of the American Revolution." *Proc Am Philos Soc,* LXVIII (1929), 85-194.

14 HANSEN, Allen O. *Liberalism and American Education in the Eighteenth Century.* New York, 1926.

15 HEALEY, Robert M. *Jefferson on Religion in Public Education.* New Haven, 1962.

16 HENDERSON, John C. *Thomas Jefferson's Views on Public Education.* New York, 1890.

17 HESLEP, Robert D. *Jefferson and Education.* New York, 1969.†

18 HESLEP, Robert D. "Thomas Jefferson's View of Equal Social Opportunity." *Ed Theory,* XIII (1963), 142-148.

19 HIMES, Charles F. *Life and Times of Judge Thomas Cooper: Jurist, Scientist, Educator, Author, Publicist.* Carlisle, Pa., 1918.

20 HONEYWELL, Roy J. *The Educational Work of Thomas Jefferson.* Cambridge, Mass., 1931.

21 KELLEY, Maurice. *Additional Chapters on Thomas Cooper.* Orono, Me., 1930.

22 KURITZ, Hyman. "Benjamin Rush: His Theory of Republican Education." *Hist Ed Q,* VII (1967), 432-451.

1 LEE, Gordon C., ed. *Crusade Against Ignorance: Thomas Jefferson on Education.* New York, 1961.†

2 LEHMANN, Karl. *Thomas Jefferson, American Humanist.* New York, 1947.†

3 LONG, Orie W. *Thomas Jefferson and George Ticknor: A Chapter in American Scholarship.* Williamstown, Mass., 1933.

4 MALONE, Dumas. *The Public Life of Thomas Cooper, 1783-1839.* New Haven, 1926.

5 MARTIN, Edwin T. *Thomas Jefferson: Scientist.* New York, 1952.†

6 MESSERLI, Jonathan. "The Columbian Complex: The Impulse to National Consolidation." *Hist Ed Q*, VII (1967), 417-431.

7 MINTZ, Max M. "Robert Morris and John Jay on Education: Two Letters." *Pa Mag Hist Bio*, LXXIV (1950), 340-347.

8 ODGERS, Merle M. *Alexander Dallas Bache: Scientist and Educator, 1806-1867.* Philadelphia, 1947.

9 PATTON, John S. *Jefferson, Cabell, and the University of Virginia.* New York, 1906.

10 PLEASANTS, Samuel A. "Thomas Jefferson: Educational Philosopher." *Proc Am Philos Soc*, CXI (1967), 1-4.

11 RUDOLPH, Frederick, ed. *Essays on Education in the Early Republic: Benjamin Rush, Noah Webster, Robert Coram, Simeon Doggett, Samuel Harrison Smith, Amable-Louis-Rose de Lafitte du Courteil, Samuel Knox.* Cambridge, Mass., 1965.

12 SHOEMAKER, Ervin C. *Noah Webster: Pioneer of Learning.* New York, 1936.

13 SHRYOCK, Richard H. "The Psychiatry of Benjamin Rush." *Am J Psy*, CI (1945), 429-432.

14 SWAN, William O. "The Northwest Ordinances, So-Called, and Confusion." *Hist Ed Q*, V (1965), 235-240.

15 TYACK, David. "Forming the National Character: Paradox in the Educational Thought of the Revolutionary Generation." *Har Ed Rev*, XXXVI (1966), 29-41.

16 WARFEL, Harry R. *Noah Webster: Schoolmaster to America.* New York, 1936, 1966.

17 WARFEL, Harry R., ed. *Letters of Noah Webster.* New York, 1953.

18 YOUNG, Homer H. "The 'National University' of the Early National Period." *Ed Forum*, XV (1951), 343-352.

See also 6.7, 30.15, 31.12, 53.12, 58.19, 61.18.

3. New England

19 BIXLER, Paul. "Horace Mann: Mustard Seed." *Am Sch*, VII (1938), 24-38.

20 BLAIR, Anna L. *Henry Barnard: School Administrator.* Minneapolis, 1938.

21 BRUBACHER, John S., ed. *Henry Barnard on Education.* New York, 1931.

1   BUTLER, Vera M. *Education as Revealed by New England Newspapers Prior to 1850.* Philadelphia, 1935.

2   CARTER, James G. *Letters to the Hon. William Prescott, L.L.D., on the Free Schools of New England: With Remarks upon the Principles of Instruction.* Boston, 1824.

3   COMPAYRE, Gabriel. *Horace Mann and the Public Schools in the United States.* New York, 1907.

4   *Connecticut Common School Journal and Annals of Education.* Ed. by Henry Barnard. New Britain, Conn., 1838-1855.

5   CREMIN, Lawrence A. *The Republic and The School: Horace Mann on the Education of Free Men.* New York, 1957.†

6   CULVER, Raymond B. *Horace Mann and Religion in the Massachusetts Public Schools.* New Haven, 1929.

7   FOSTER, Frank C. "Horace Mann as Philosopher." *Ed Theory*, X (1960), 9-25.

8   HARRIS, William T. "On Horace Mann." *U S Bur Ed, Rep Comm 1895-1896.* Vol. I. Washington, D.C., 1897, pp. 887-897. (Also in *Ed Rev*, XII (1896), 105-119.)

9   "Henry Barnard." *U S Bur Ed, Rep Comm 1902.* Vol. I. Washington, D.C., 1903, pp. 887-928.

10   HINSDALE, Burke A. *Horace Mann and the Common School Revival in the United States.* New York, 1898.

11   HUTCHISON, Keith R. "James Gordon Carter, Educational Reformer." *N Eng Q*, XVI (1943), 376-396.

12   JENKINS, Ralph C., and Gertrude C. WARNER. *Henry Barnard: An Introduction.* Hartford, Conn., 1937.

13   JONES, Howard M. "Horace Mann's Crusade." *America in Crisis.* Ed. by Daniel Aaron. New York, 1952.

14   *Journal of the Rhode Island Institute of Instruction.* Ed. by Henry Barnard. Providence, 1845-1849.

15   KATZ, Michael B. *The Irony of Early School Reform: Educational Innovation in Mid-Nineteenth Century Massachusetts.* Cambridge, Mass., 1968; Boston, 1970.†

16   MANN, Horace. *Horace Mann on the Crisis in Education.* Ed. by Louis Filler. Antioch, Ohio, 1965.

17   MANN, Horace. *Lectures on Education.* Boston, 1845.

18   MANN, Mary T. P. *The Life and Works of Horace Mann.* 5 vols. Boston, 1891.

19   MANN, Mary T. P. *Life of Horace Mann: By His Wife.* New York, 1865.

20   MARTIN, George H. "Horace Mann and the Revival of Education in Massachusetts." *Ed Rev*, V (1893), 434-450.

21   MAYO, Amory D. "The American Common School in New England from 1790 to 1840." *U S Bur Ed, Rep Comm 1894-1895.* Vol. II. Washington, D.C., 1896, pp. 1551-1615.

22   MAYO, Amory D. "Henry Barnard." *U S Bur Ed, Rep Comm 1896-1897.* Vol. I. Washington, D.C., 1898, pp. 769-810.

1 MAYO, Amory D. "Horace Mann and the Great Revival of the American Common School, 1830-1850." *U S Bur Ed, Rep Comm 1896-1897.* Vol. I. Washington, D.C., 1898, pp. 715-767.

2 MESSERLI, Jonathan C. "Horace Mann's Childhood: Myth and Reality." *Ed Forum,* XXX (1966), 159-168.

3 MESSERLI, Jonathan C. "James G. Carter's Liabilities as a Common School Reformer." *Hist Ed Q,* V (1965), 14-25.

4 MESSERLI, Jonathan C. "Localism and State Control in Horace Mann's Reform of the Common Schools." *Am Q,* XVII (1965), 104-118.

5 MONROE, Will S. *The Educational Labors of Henry Barnard: A Study in the History of American Pedagogy.* Syracuse, 1893.

6 NIETZ, John A. "Horace Mann's Ideas on General Methods in Education." *El School J,* XXXVII (1937), 742-751.

7 PARKER, Francis W. "Horace Mann." *Ed Rev,* XII (1896), 65-74.

8 ROBERTS, Josephine. "Elizabeth Peabody and the Temple School." *N Eng Q,* XV (1942), 497-508.

9 SIMPSON, Lewis P. "The Intercommunity of the Learned: Boston and Cambridge in 1800." *N Eng Q,* XXIII (1950), 491-503.

10 STEINER, Bernard C. *Life of Henry Barnard.* U S Bur Ed Bull 1919, no. 8. Washington, D.C., 1919.

11 THARP, Louise H. *Until Victory: Horace Mann and Mary Peabody.* Boston, 1953.

12 WIGHTMAN, Joseph M. *Annals of the Boston Primary School Committee: From Its First Establishment in 1818 to Its Dissolution in 1855.* Boston, 1860.

13 WILLIAMS, E. I. F. *Horace Mann: Educational Statesman.* New York, 1937.

See also 2.3, 2.15, 9.7, 9.8, 10.1, 10.4, 10.17, 11.13, 12.3, 12.4, 12.15, 13.1, 13.15, 17.1, 20.15, 20.18, 21.1, 21.2, 21.4, 21.6, 26.9, 27.20, 28.2-4, 28.10, 28.11, 28.14, 29.6, 30.3, 67.12, 68.1, 68.8, 74.16, 74.20, 74.21, 80.1, 80.2, 80.6, 80.13, 81.17, 89.14, 93.17, 94.7, 94.16, 94.20, 95.7, 95.11, 95.18, 95.20.

4. New York and the Middle States

14 BOURNE, William O. *History of the Public School Society of the City of New York.* New York, 1870.

15 BROWNE, Henry J. "Public Support of Catholic Education in New York, 1825-1842: Some New Aspects." *Cath Hist Rev,* XXXIX (1953), 1-27.

16 FITZPATRICK, Edward A. *The Educational Views and Influence of DeWitt Clinton.* New York, 1911.

17 HOBSON, Elsie G. *Educational Legislation and Administration in the State of New York from 1777 to 1850.* Chicago, 1918.

18 JACKSON, Sidney L. "An Unknown Ben Franklin." *Har Ed Rev,* XI (1941), 102-111. (Concerns Joseph Curtis, New York educational pioneer, 1782-1856.)

19 LANNIE, Vincent P. *Public Money and Parochial Education: Bishop Hughes, Governor Seward, and the New York School Controversy.* Cleveland, 1968.

1   LANNIE, Vincent P. "William Seward and Common School Education." *Hist Ed Q*, IV (1964), 181-192.

2   LANNIE, Vincent P. "William Seward and the New York School Controversy, 1840-1842: A Problem in Historical Motivation." *Hist Ed Q*, VI (1966), 52-71.

3   LANNIE, Vincent P., and Bernard C. DIETHORN. "For the Honor and Glory of God: The Philadelphia Bible Riots of 1840." *Hist Ed Q*, VIII (1968), 44-106.

4   MC CADDEN, Joseph J. "Bishop Hughes Versus the Public School Society of New York." *Cath Hist Rev*, L (1964), 188-207.

5   MC CADDEN, Joseph J. *Education in Pennsylvania, 1801-1835, and Its Debt to Robert Vaux.* Philadelphia, 1937.

6   MARTIN, William J. "The Old Log School, a Chronicle of Rural Education." *W Pa Hist Mag*, XVI (1933), 163-173.

7   MAYO, Amory D. "The American Common School in New York, New Jersey, and Pennsylvania During the First Half Century of the Republic." *U S Bur Ed, Rep Comm 1895-1896.* Vol. I. Washington, D.C., 1897, pp. 219-266.

8   MEYERS, Mary A. "The Children's Crusade: Philadelphia Catholics and the Public Schools, 1840-1844." *Rec Am Cath Hist Soc Phil*, LXXV (1964), 103-127.

9   MOHL, Raymond A. "Education as Social Control in New York City, 1784-1825." *N Y Hist*, LI (1970), 219-237.

10 MOHR, James C. "New York State's Free School Law of 1867: A Chapter in the Reconstruction of the North." *N Y Hist Soc Q*, LIII (1969), 230-249.

11 PRATT, John W. "Governor Seward and the New York City School Controversy, 1840-1842: A Milestone in the Advance of Nonsectarian Public Education." *N Y Hist*, XLII (1961), 351-364.

12 PRATT, John W. "Religious Conflict in the Development of the New York City Public School System." *Hist Ed Q*, V (1965), 110-120.

13 VAN DEUSEN, Glyndon G. "Seward and the School Question Reconsidered." *J Am Hist*, LII (1965), 313-319.

See also 13.3, 13.10, 13.11, 16.3, 16.19, 21.6, 21.10, 23.14, 29.11, 43.13, 67.12, 68.1.

5.   The South

14 AMBROSE, Stephen E. "Public Education in the Post-War South." *Ed Forum*, XXVI (1962), 353-362. (Concerns Reconstruction.)

15 BADGER, Henry G. "Colleges That Did Not Survive." *J Neg Ed*, XXXV (1966), 306-312.

16 BLAUNCH, L. E. "The First Uniform School System of Maryland, 1865-1868." *Md Hist Mag*, XXVI (1931), 205-227.

1   BRUCE, Philip A. "Recollections of My Plantation Teachers." *S Atl Q*, XVI (1917), 1-13.

2   COON, Charles L., ed. *The Beginnings of Public Education in North Carolina: A Documentary History, 1790-1840.* 2 vols. Raleigh, 1908.

3   COON, Charles L., ed. *North Carolina Schools and Academies, 1790-1840: A Documentary History.* Raleigh, 1915.

4   COULTER, E. Merton. "The Ante-Bellum Academy Movement in Georgia." *Ga Hist Q*, V (1921), 11-42.

5   COULTER, E. Merton. "A Georgia Educational Movement During the Eighteen Hundred Fifties." *Ga Hist Q*, IX (1925), 1-33.

6   DAVIS, Richard B. *Intellectual Life in Jefferson's Virginia, 1790-1830.* Chapel Hill, 1964.

7   EATON, Clement. *Freedom of Thought in the Old South.* Durham, N.C., 1940.†

8   FORD, Paul M. "Calvin Wiley's View of the Negro." *N C Hist Rev*, XLI (1964), 1-20.

9   HALL, D. D. "A Yankee Tutor in the Old South." *N Eng Q*, XXXIII (1960), 82-91.

10 HARRISON, Lowell H. "William Duane on Education: A Letter to the Kentucky Assembly, 1822." *Pa Mag Hist Bio*, LXXIII (1949), 316-325.

11 JOHNSTON, Richard M. "Early Educational Life in Middle Georgia." *U S Bur Ed, Rep Comm 1894-1895.* Vol. II; *U S Bur Ed, Rep Comm 1895-1896.* Vol. I. Washington, D.C., 1896, 1897, pp. 1699-1733, 839-886.

12 KILPATRICK, William H. "The Beginnings of the Public School System in Georgia." *Ga Hist Q*, V (1921), 3-19.

13 KNAUSS, J. O. "Education in Florida: 1821-1829." *Fla Hist Q*, III (1925), 22-35.

14 KNIGHT, Edgar W. *The Influence of Reconstruction on Education in the South.* New York, 1913.

15 KNIGHT, Edgar W. "Manual Labor Schools in the South." *S Atl Q*, XVI (1917), 209-221. (Concerns 1861-1862.)

16 KNIGHT, Edgar W. "More Evidence of Horace Mann's Influence in the South." *Ed Forum*, XII (1948), 167-184.

17 KNIGHT, Edgar W. "The Peabody Fund and Its Early Operation in North Carolina." *S Atl Q*, XIV (1915), 168-180.

18 KNIGHT, Edgar W. "Reconstruction and Education in South Carolina." *S Atl Q*, XVIII (1919), 350-364; XIX (1920), 55-66.

19 KNIGHT, Edgar W. "Reconstruction and Education in Virginia." *S Atl Q*, XV (1916), 25-40, 157-174.

20 KNIGHT, Edgar W. "Some Evidence of Horace Mann's Influence in the South." *School Soc*, LXV (1947), 33-37.

21 KNIGHT, Edgar W. "Some Evidence of Henry Barnard's Influence in the South." *Ed Forum*, XIII (1949), 301-312.

22 KNIGHT, Edgar W. "Some Fallacies Concerning the History of Public Education in the South." *S Atl Q*, XIII (1914), 371-381.

1   KNIGHT, Edgar W. "Southern Opposition to Northern Education." *Ed Forum*, XIV (1949), 47-58.

2   LEWIS, Miriam E. "The Minutes of the Wilmington Academy, 1777-1802." *Del Hist*, III (1949), 181-226.

3   MADDOX, William A. *The Free School Idea in Virginia Before the Civil War: A Phase of Political and Social Evolution.* New York, 1918.

4   MAYO, Amory D. "The American Common School in the Southern States During the First Half Century of the Republic, 1790-1840." *U S Bur Ed, Rep Comm 1895-1896.* Vol. I. Washington, D.C., 1897, pp. 267-338.

5   MAYO, Amory D. "Common School Education in the South from the Beginning of the Civil War to 1870-1876." *U S Bur Ed, Rep Comm 1900-1901.* Vol. I. Washington, D.C., 1902, pp. 429-541.

6   MAYO, Amory D. "The Organization and Development of the American Common School in the Atlantic and Central States of the South, 1830 to 1860." *U S Bur Ed, Rep Comm 1899-1900.* Vol. I. Washington, D.C., 1901, pp. 65-69.

7   MAYO, Amory D. "The Common School in the Southern States Beyond the Mississippi River from 1830 to 1860." *U S Bur Ed, Rep Comm 1900-1901.* Vol. I. Washington, D.C., 1902, pp. 285-314.

8   MOFFAT, Walter. "Arkansas Schools, 1819-1840." *Ark Hist Q*, XII (1953), 91-105.

9   PYBURN, Nita K. *Documentary History of Education in Florida, 1822-1860.* Tallahassee, 1951.

10 PYBURN, Nita K. "Public Schools in Mississippi Before 1860." *J Miss Hist*, XXI (1959), 113-130.

11 RILEY, Martin L. "The Development of Education in Louisiana Prior to Statehood." *La Hist Q*, XIX (1936), 595-634.

12 SHEPHARD, William. "Buckingham Female Collegiate Institute." *Wm Mar Col Q Hist Mag*, XX (1940), 167-193.

13 SLAPPYE, George H. "Early Foundations of Georgia's System of Common School Education." *Ga Hist Q*, XIV (1930), 139-149.

14 "Some Historical Documents Bearing upon Common School Education in Virginia and South Carolina Previous to the Civil War." *U S Bur Ed, Rep Comm 1899-1900.* Vol. I. Washington, D.C., 1901, pp. 431-441.

15 SWINT, Henry L. *The Northern Teacher in the South, 1862-1870.* Nashville, 1941; New York, 1967.

16 TAYLOR, William R. "Toward a Definition of Orthodoxy: The Patrician South and the Common Schools." *Har Ed Rev*, XXXVI (1966), 412-426.

17 TURNBULL, L. Minerva. "Early Public Schools in Norfolk and its Vicinity." *Wm Mar Col Q Hist Mag*, XII (1932), 4-9.

18 TURNBULL, L. Minerva. "Private Schools in Norfolk, 1800-1860." *Wm Mar Col Q Hist Mag*, XI (1931), 277-303.

19 TURNBULL, L. Minerva. "The Southern Educational Revolt." *Wm Mar Col Q Hist Mag*, XIV (1934), 60-76.

20 WEATHERSBY, William H. *History of Educational Legislation in Mississippi from 1798 to 1860.* Chicago, 1921.

1 WEEKS, Stephen B. "The Beginnings of the Common School System in the South; or Calvin Henderson Wiley and the Organization of Common Schools in North Carolina." *U S Bur Ed, Rep Comm 1896-1897.* Vol. II. Washington, D.C., 1898, pp. 1379-1474.

2 WHITAKER, A. P. "The Public School System of Tennessee, 1834-1860." *Tenn Hist Q*, II (1916), 1-30.

3 WOLCOTT, John D. "The Southern Educational Convention of 1863." *S Atl Q*, VIII (1909), 354-360.

See also 4.8, 4.18, 5.19, 6.6, 13.4, 15.3, 16.1, 17.13, 19.9, 20.13, 21.3, 21.8, 26.12, 28.8, 28.18, 29.14, 31.7, 43.10, 69.1, 69.19, 69.21, 70.4, 89.9.

6. The West

4 AURNER, Clarence R. "Some Early Educational Leaders in Iowa." *Iowa J Hist*, XXII (1924), 532-568.

5 BEECHER, Lyman. *A Plea for the West.* Cincinnati, 1835.

6 BELTING, Paul E. "The Development of the Free Public High School in Illinois to 1860." *J Ill State Hist Soc*, XI (1918), 269-370. (Also published as book, Springfield, Ill., 1919.)

7 BESTOR, Arthur E., Jr., ed. *Education and Reform at New Harmony: Correspondence of William Maclure and Marie Duclos Fretageot, 1820-1833.* Indianapolis, 1948.

8 BIBB, Thomas W. *History of Early Common School Education in Washington.* Seattle, 1929.

9 BONE, Robert G. "Education in Illinois Before 1857." *J Ill St Hist Soc*, L (1957), 119-140.

10 BROOKS, Harold C. "Founding of the Michigan Public School System." *Mich Hist*, XXXIII (1949), 291-306.

11 FERRIS, David F. *Judge Marvin and the Founding of the California Public School System.* Berkeley, 1962.

12 FULTON, C. J. "The Beginnings of Education in Iowa." *Iowa J Hist*, XXIII (1925), 171-191.

13 HANSEN, Allen O. *Early Educational Leadership in the Ohio Valley: A Study of Educational Reconstruction Through the Western Library Institute and College of Professional Teachers, 1829-1841.* Bloomington, 1923.

14 HINSDALE, Burke A. "The History of Popular Education on the Western Reserve." *Ohio Hist Q*, VI (1898), 35-59.

15 HOWISON, G. H. "Contributions to the History of American Teaching: Academy and College in Early Ohio." *Ed Rev*, XL (1910), 455-472.

16 HOYT, Charles O., and R. Clyde FORD. *John D. Pierce, Founder of the Michigan School System: A Study of Education in the Northwest.* Ypsilanti, Mich., 1905.

1 JOHNSON, T. Walter. "Peter Akers: Methodist Circuit Rider and Educator (1790-1886)." *J Ill St Hist Soc*, XXXII (1939), 417-441.

2 JONES, Edgar D. "Educational Pathfinders of Illinois." *J Ill St Hist Soc*, XXIV (1931), 1-11.

3 JORGENSON, Lloyd P. *The Founding of Public Education in Wisconsin.* Madison, 1956.

4 KLATT, Albert G. "A Brief Survey of the Events Pertaining to Education Previous to the Organization of Minnesota as a Territory." *School Rev*, XXIV (1916), 603-609.

5 LITTELL, Harold. "Development of the City School System of Indiana." *Ind Mag Hist*, XII (1916), 193-213, 299-325.

6 LOTTICH, Kenneth V. "Democracy and Education in the Early American Northwest." *Pae Hist*, II (1962), 234-254.

7 LOTTICH, Kenneth V. "Educational Leadership in Early Ohio." *Hist Ed Q*, II (1962), 52-61.

8 LOTTICH, Kenneth V. *New England Transplanted: A Study of the Development of Educational and Other Cultural Agencies in the Connecticut Western Reserve in Their National and Philosophical Setting.* Dallas, 1964.

9 MC ALPINA, William. "The Origin of Public Education in Ohio." *NW Ohio Q*, XXXVIII (1929), 409-447.

10 MAYO, Amory D. "The Development of the Common School in the Western States from 1830 to 1865." *U S Bur Ed, Rep Comm 1899*. Vol. I. Washington, D.C., 1900, pp. 1367-1371.

11 MAYO, Amory D. "Education in the Northwest During the First Half Century of the Republic, 1790-1840." *U S Bur Ed, Rep Comm 1894-1895*. Vol. II. Washington, D.C., 1896, pp. 1513-1550.

12 MEAD, David. *Yankee Eloquence in the Middle West: The Ohio Lyceum, 1850-1870.* East Lansing, Mich., 1951.

13 MILLER, Edward A. "High Schools in Ohio Prior to 1850." *School Rev*, XXVIII (1920), 454-469.

14 MILLER, Edward A. *The History of Educational Legislation in Ohio from 1803 to 1850.* Chicago, 1920. (Also in *NW Ohio Q*, XXVII (1918), 1-271.)

15 NEWMAN, Otto L. "Development of the Common Schools of Indiana." *Ind Mag Hist*, XXII (1926), 216-229.

16 NOLAN, Val, Jr. "Caleb Mills and the Indiana Free School Law." *Ind Mag Hist*, XLIX (1953), 81-90.

17 POLOS, Nicholas C. "A Yankee Patriot: John Swett, the Horace Mann of the Pacific." *Hist Ed Q*, IV (1964), 17-32.

18 PULLIAM, John. "Changing Attitudes Toward Free Public Schools in Illinois—1825-1860." *Hist Ed Q*, VII (1967), 191-208.

19 SCHAFER, Joseph. "Origins of Wisconsin's Free School System." *Wis Mag Hist*, IX (1925), 27-46.

20 SHOEMAKER, F. L. "Samuel Galloway: An Educational Statesman of First Rank." *Hist Ed J*, V (1954), 105-117.

1 THOMAS, J. H. "The Academies of Indiana." *Ind Mag Hist*, X (1914), 331-358; XI (1915), 8-39.

2 VENABLE, William H. *Beginnings of Literary Culture in the Ohio Valley: Historical and Biographical Sketches.* Louisville, Ky., 1956.

3 WHITTENBURG, Clarice. "The Frontier Schoolma'am on Ranch and Homestead." *Ed Forum*, XIII (1948), 79-89.

   See also 9.4, 12.12, 18.20, 21.5, 21.11, 21.16, 23.17, 26.11, 26.13, 29.8, 29.15, 30.2, 35.3, 68.8, 68.21, 75.7, 75.8, 90.1, 93.20, 94.21.

7. Higher Education: The Age of the College

4 ASHER, Helen D. "A Frontier College of the Middle West: Hamline University, 1854-1869." *Minn Hist*, IX (1928), 363-78.

5 AURNER, Clarence R. "The Founding of Iowa College." *Palimpsest*, XXV (1944), 65-77.

6 BAIL, Hamilton V. "Harvard's Commemoration Day, July Twenty First, 1865." *N Eng Q*, XV (1942), 256-279.

7 BARNARD, Frederick A. P. *Letters on College Government and the Evils Inseparable from the American College System in Its Present Form.* New York, 1855.

8 BAXTER, Maurice. "Should the Dartmouth College Case Have Been Reargued?" *N Eng Q*, XXXIII (1960), 19-36.

9 BORROWMAN, Merle. "The False Dawn of the State University." *Hist Ed Q*, I (1961), 6-22.

10 BROWN, Jerry W. *The Rise of Biblical Criticism in America, 1800-1870: The New England Scholars.* Middletown, Conn., 1969.

11 BURNETT, Howard R. "Early History of Vincennes University." *Ind Mag Hist*, XXIX (1933), 114-121.

12 CHURCHILL, Alfred V. "The Founding of Oberlin." *NW Ohio Q*, XXIII (1951), 107-132, 158-178.

13 COME, Donald R. "The Influence of Princeton on Higher Education in the South Before 1825." *Wm Mar Q*, II (1945), 359-396.

14 CONSTANTINE, Robert. "Minutes of the Board of Trustees for Vincennes University, 1801-1824." *Ind Mag Hist*, LIV (1958), 313-364; LV (1959), 247-294; LVII (1961), 311-368.

15 COULTER, E. Merton. "Why John and Joseph LeConte Left the University of Georgia, 1855-1856." *Ga Hist Q*, LIII (1969), 18-40.

16 CRANE, Theodore R. "Francis Wayland and the Residential College." *R I Hist*, XIX (1960), 65-78, 118-129.

17 CRANE, Theodore R. "Francis Wayland: Political Economist as Educator." *R I Hist*, XXI (1962), 65-90, 105-124. (Also in *Brown University Papers*, XXXIX. Providence, 1962.)

18 CRANE, Theodore R., ed. *The Colleges and the Public, 1787-1862.* New York, 1963.†

19 DAWES, Rufus C. "Marietta College and Early Education in the West." *Am Sch*, IV (1935), 373-376.

20 DE BLOIS, Austen K. *The Pioneer School: A History of Shurtleff College, The Oldest Institution in the West.* Chicago, 1900.

1   DEXTER, Franklin B. "Student Life at Yale College, 1795-1817." *Proc Am Ant Soc*, XXVII (1917), 318-335.

2   DODD, William G. "Early Education in Tallahassee and the West Florida Seminary, Now Florida State University." *Fla Hist Q*, XXVII (1948), 1-27, 157-180.

3   DRAKE, William E. *Higher Education in North Carolina Before 1860.* New York, 1964.

4   DUNBAR, Willis F. "Early Denominational Academies and Colleges in Michigan." *Mich Hist*, XXIV (1940), 451-466.

5   EWELL, B. S. "William and Mary College in the Years 1861-1865." *Wm Mar Col Q Hist Mag*, III (1923), 221-230.

6   FAHERTY, William B., S.J. "Nativism and Midwestern Education: The Experience of Saint Louis University, 1832-1856." *Hist Ed Q*, VIII (1968), 447-458.

7   FARGUHAR, Catherine G. B. "Tabor and Tabor College." *Iowa J Hist*, XLI (1943), 337-393.

8   FITSGERALD, Virginia. "A Southern College Boy Eighty Years Ago." *S Atl Q*, XX (1921), 236-246.

9   FLEMING, Walter L. "William Tecumseh Sherman as College President." *S Atl Q*, XI (1912), 33-54.

10 FLETCHER, Robert S. *A History of Oberlin College from Its Foundation Through the Civil War.* 2 vols. Oberlin, Ohio, 1943.

11 FLETCHER, Robert S. "Oberlin and Co-Education." *NW Ohio Q*, XLVII (1938), 1-19.

12 FOX, Dixon R. *Dr. Eliphalet Nott (1773-1866)–and the American Spirit.* Princeton, 1944. (President of Union College.)

13 FREIMARCK, Vincent. "Rhetoric at Yale in 1807." *Proc Am Philos Soc*, CX (1966), 235-255.

14 GARRETT, Jane N. "The Delaware College Lotteries, 1818-1845." *Del Hist*, VII (1957), 299-318.

15 GODBOLD, Albea. *The Church College of the Old South.* Durham, N.C., 1944.

16 GOODFELLOW, Donald M. "The First Boylston Professor of Rhetoric and History." *N Eng Q*, XIX (1946), 372-389. (J. Q. Adams, appointed in 1805.)

17 HARGRELL, Lester. "Student Life at the University of Georgia in the 1840s." *Ga Hist Q*, VIII (1924), 49-59.

18 HAUNTON, Richard H. "Education and Democracy: The Views of Philip Lindsley." *Tenn Hist Q*, XXI (1962), 131-139.

19 HEWITT, John H. "Contributions to the History of American Teaching: College Education Fifty Years Ago." *Ed Rev*, XXXIX (1910), 227-237.

20 HILL, Benjamin T. "Life at Harvard a Century Ago as Illustrated by the Papers of Stephen Salibury, Class of 1817." *Proc Am Ant Soc*, XX (1910), 197-248.

21 HOOVER, Thomas N. "The Beginning of Higher Education in the Northwest Territory." *NW Ohio Q*, L (1941), 244-260.

1 HUBBELL, George A. *Horace Mann in Ohio: A Study of the Application of His Public School Ideals to College Administration.* New York, 1900.

2 HUBBELL, George A. "Horace Mann and Antioch College." *Ohio Hist Q,* XIV (1905), 12-28.

3 HUTCHESON, James M. "Virginia's 'Dartmouth College Case.' " *Va Mag Hist Bio,* LI (1943), 134-140.

4 ISBELL, Egbert R. "The Universities of Virginia and Michigania." *Mich Hist,* XXVI (1942), 39-52.

5 JUDD, Romie D. *The Educational Contributions of Horace Holley.* Nashville, 1936.

6 KAPLAN, Sidney. "The Reduction of Teachers' Salaries in Post-Revolutionary Boston." *N Eng Q,* XXI (1948), 373-379.

7 KERR, Robert Y. "The Wittenberg Manual Labor College." *Iowa J Hist,* XXIV (1926), 290-304.

8 KNIGHT, Edward W. "North Carolina's Dartmouth College Case." *J High Ed,* XIX (1948), 116-122.

9 KNIGHT, George W. "Higher Education in the North West Territory." *U S Bur Ed, Rep Comm 1887-1888.* Washington, D.C., 1889, pp. 1039-1047.

10 LAZERSON, Marvin. "F. A. P. Barnard and Columbia College: Prologue to a University." *Hist Ed Q,* VI (1966), 49-64.

11 LOCKARD, E. Kidd. "The Influence of New England in Denominational Colleges in the Northwest (1830-1860)." *NW Ohio Q,* LIII (1944), 1-14.

12 LOTTICH, Kenneth V. "The Oldest University in the West." *School Soc,* LXXIII (1951), 193-196. (Williamette University, Ore.)

13 MESSERLI, Jonathan C. "Horace Mann at Brown." *Har Ed Rev,* XXXIII (1963), 285-311.

14 MILLER, James L., Jr. "Transylvania University as the Nation Saw It, 1818-1828." *Fil Club,* XXXIV (1960), 305-318.

15 MORISON, Samuel E. "The Great Rebellion in Harvard College and the Resignation of President Kirkland." *Pub Colonial Soc Mass,* XXVII (1927-1930), 54-112.

16 NORTH, William G. "The Political Background of the Dartmouth College Case." *N Eng Q,* XVIII (1945), 181-203.

17 PEDRICK, Samuel M. "Early History of Ripon College, 1850-1864." *Wis Mag Hist,* VIII (1924), 22-37.

18 PERRY, Charles M. *Henry Philip Tappan, Philosopher and University President.* Ann Arbor, 1933.

19 RAVITZ, Abe C. "Timothy Dwight: Professor of Rhetoric." *N Eng Q,* XXIX (1956), 63-72.

20 ROELKER, William G. "Francis Wayland: A Neglected Pioneer of Higher Education." *Proc Am Ant Soc,* LIII (1944), 27-98.

21 ROELKER, William G. "Francis Wayland, 1796-1865, President of Brown University and Citizen of Providence." *Coll R I Hist Soc,* XXXII (1939), 33-55.

22 RUDOLPH, Frederick. *Mark Hopkins and the Log: Williams College, 1836-1872.* New Haven, 1956.

1 RUDOLPH, Frederick. "Who Paid the Bills: An Inquiry into the Nature of Nineteenth-Century College Finance." *Har Ed Rev*, XXXI (1961), 144-157.

2 SACK, Saul. "A Nineteenth-Century Scheme for Financing Higher Education in Pennsylvania." *Hist Ed Q*, I (1961), 50-54.

3 SCHMIDT, George P. "Colleges in Ferment." *Am Hist Rev*, LIX (1953), 19-42.

4 SCHMIDT, George P. "Intellectual Crosscurrents in American Colleges, 1825-1855." *Am Hist Rev*, XLII (1936), 46-67.

5 SCHMIDT, George P. *The Liberal Arts College: A Chapter in American Cultural History.* New Brunswick, 1957.

6 SCHMIDT, George P. *The Old Time College President.* New York, 1930.

7 SELLERS, James B. "Student Life at the University of Alabama Before 1860." *Ala Rev*, II (1949), 269-293.

8 SHAW, Henry K. "The Founding of Butler University, 1847-1855." *Ind Mag Hist*, LVIII (1962), 233-264.

9 SHAW, Wilfred. "The Early Days of the University of Michigan." *Mich Hist*, XVI (1932), 439-463; XVII (1933), 52-107.

10 SHEPARD, Grace F. "Education at Wheaton College." *N Eng Q*, VI (1933), 803-824.

11 SHIRLEY, John M. *The Dartmouth College Causes and the Supreme Court of the United States.* St. Louis, 1879.

12 SILVERMAN, Robert and Mark BEACH. "A National University for Up-state New York." *Am Q*, XXII (1970), 701-713.

13 "Sketch of a Plan for Endowment and Establishment of a State University in Virginia." *Wm Mar Col Q Hist Mag*, IV (1924), 266-276.

14 SMITH, Joseph B. "A Frontier Experiment with Higher Education: Dickinson College (1783-1800)." *Pa Hist*, XVI (1949), 1-19.

15 SMITH, Wilson. *Professors and Public Ethics: Studies of Northern Moral Philosophers Before the Civil War.* Ithaca, N.Y., 1956.

16 SPILL, William A. "University of Michigan: Beginnings." *Mich Hist*, XII (1928), 635-661; XIII (1929), 41-54; 227-244.

17 STRAKER, Robert L. *The Unseen Harvest: Horace Mann and Antioch College.* Yellow Springs, Ohio, 1955.

18 TAPPAN, Henry P. *University Education.* New York, 1851.

19 "Teaching of Natural History at William and Mary College." *Wm Mar Col Q Hist Mag*, III (1923), 239-240.

20 TEWKSBURY, Donald G. *The Founding of American Colleges and Universities Before the Civil War: With Particular Reference to the Religious Influences Bearing upon the College Movement.* New York, 1932. (Repr. 1965.)

21 THORNTON, Harrison J. "Locating the State University of Iowa." *Iowa J Hist*, XLVII (1949), 50-62.

22 "The University of Virginia, a reprint from the *Richmond Enquirer* of the Nineteenth Century." *Wm Mar Col Q Hist Mag*, III (1923), 58-64.

1 TICKNOR, George. *Remarks on Changes Lately Proposed or Adopted in Harvard University.* Boston, 1825.

2 TODD, Edgeley W. "Philosophical Ideas at Harvard College, 1817-1837." *N Eng Q*, XVI (1943), 63-90.

3 TOWNSEND, John W. "Horace Holley, L.L.D. Third President of Old Transylvania." *Proc Miss Val Hist Assn*, VIII (1914-1915), 123-134.

4 UROFSKY, Melvin I. "Reforms and Response: The Yale Report of 1828." *Hist Ed Q*, V (1965), 53-67.

5 WAITE, Frederick C. "Manual Labor: An Experiment in American Colleges of the Early Nineteenth Century." *Bull Assn Am Col*, XXXVI (1950), 391-400.

6 WATSON, Joseph Shelton to David WATSON. "Letters from William and Mary College, 1798-1801." *Va Mag Hist Bio*, XXIX (1921), 129-179.

7 WATSON, Thomas S. "William and Mary Letters from 1795 to 1799." *Va Mag Hist Bio*, XXX (1922), 223-249.

8 WAYLAND, Francis. *Thoughts on the Present Collegiate System in the United States.* Boston, 1842.

9 WELLS, Herman G. "The Early History of Indiana University as Reflected in the Administration of Andrew Wylie, 1829-1851." *Fil Club*, XXXVI (1962), 113-127.

10 WHITE, Ruth W. "James Marsh, Educational Pioneer." *Ed Forum*, XXIX (1965), 217-224. (Univ. of Vt., President in 1820s.)

11 "William and Mary College, 1802-1804." *Wm Mar Col Q Hist Mag*, V (1925), 120-124.

12 "William and Mary College, 1806." *Wm Mar Col Q Hist Mag*, III (1923), 201-208.

13 "William and Mary College in 1858." *Wm Mar Col Q Hist Mag*, X (1902), 251-257.

14 WILLS, Elbert V. "Political Economy in the Early American College." *S Atl Q*, XXIV (1925), 131-153.

15 WOOD, George B. *Early History of the University of Pennsylvania from Its Origin to the Year 1827.* 3d ed. Philadelphia, 1896.

16 WOOLVERTON, John F. "Philip Lindsley and the Cause of Education in the Old Southwest." *Tenn Hist Q*, XIX (1960), 3-22.

See also 11.12, 12.15, 13.1, 13.8, 13.15, 14.2, 20.13, 20.18, 21.1, 21.2, 21.4, 21.8, 21.11, 21.16, 30.10, 30.15, 31.3, 31.7, 31.12, 34.3, 34.4, 34.5, 34.7, 34.9-11, 34.13, 34.18, 34.20, 34.21, 35.10, 35.11, 35.14, 35.18, 36.3-6, 36.9-12, 36.15, 36.17, 36.21, 37.4, 37.14-20, 38.7, 38.8, 38.16-23, 39.5, 39.11, 39.18-20, 42.10, 43.3, 43.10, 43.13, 43.15, 44.11, 44.18, 45.1, 45.14, 45.17, 45.20, 46.3, 59.14, 69.1, 69.5, 70.3, 73.15, 83.14, 123.6-8.

8. *Scientific, Technical, and Professional Education*

1 ASHE, Samuel A. "Memories of Annapolis." *S Atl Q*, XVIII (1919), 197-210.

2 ATHERTON, Lewis E. "Mercantile Education in the Ante-Bellum South." *Miss Val Hist Rev*, XXXIX (1952-1953), 623-641.

3 BROWN, R. M. "Agricultural Science and Education in Virginia Before 1860." *Wm Mar Col Q Hist Mag*, XIX (1939), 197-213.

4 BROWNE, C. A. "History of Chemical Education in America, 1820-1870." *J Chem Ed*, IX (1932), 718-720.

5 CALHOUN, F. Phinizy. "The Founding and the Early History of the Atlanta Medical College." *Ga Hist Q*, IX (1925), 34-54.

6 COULSON, Thomas. *Joseph Henry: His Life and Work*. Princeton, 1950.

7 DANIELS, George H. *American Science in the Age of Jackson*. New York, 1968.

8 DANIELS, George H. "The Process of Professionalization in American Science: The Emergent Period, 1820-1860." *Isis*, LVIII (1967), 151-166.

9 DITTRICK, William C. "An Ancestry of Ohio Medicine: Fairfield Medical School." *Ohio Hist Q*, LXI (1952), 365-371.

10 ENGLISH, William F. *The Pioneer Lawyer and Jurist in Missouri*. University of Missouri Studies, vol. 21, no. 2. Columbia, Mo., 1947.

11 FARMER, Fannie M. "Legal Education in North Carolina, 1820-1860." *N C Hist Rev*, XXVIII (1951), 271-297.

12 FISHER, Berenice M. "Public Education and 'Special Interest': An Example from the History of Mechanical Engineering." *Hist Ed Q*, VI (1966), 31-40.

13 FISHER, Samuel H. *The Litchfield Law School, 1775-1833*. New Haven, 1933.

14 FREIDEL, Frank. "A Plan for Modern Education in Early Philadelphia." *Pa Hist*, XIV (1947), 175-184. (Concerns Girard College.)

15 FULTON, John F., and Elizabeth H. THOMSON. *Benjamin Silliman, 1779-1864: Pathfinder in American Science*. New York, 1947.

16 GOOD, Harry G. "New Data on Early Engineering Education." *J Ed Res*, XXIX (1935-1936), 37-46.

17 GOODE, G. Brown. "The Origin of the National Scientific and Educational Institutions of the United States." *Ann Rep Am Hist Assn 1889*. Washington, D.C., 1890, pp. 53-161.

18 HAAR, Charles M. "E. L. Youmans: A Chapter in the Diffusion of Science in America." *J Hist Ideas*, IX (1948), 193-213.

19 HITCHCOCK, Edward. *The Religion of Geology*. Boston, 1859.

20 JACKSON, Sidney L. "Some Ancestors of the 'Extension Course.' " *N Eng Q*, XIV (1941), 505-518.

21 JUETTNER, Otto. "Rise of Medical Colleges in the Ohio Valley." *Ohio Hist Q*, XXII (1913), 481-491.

1 KETT, Joseph F. *The Formation of the American Medical Profession: The Role of Institutions, 1780-1860.* New Haven, 1968.

2 MERRITT, Raymond H. *Engineering in American Society, 1850-1875.* Lexington, Ky., 1969.

3 MILLS, Edward C. "Dental Education in Ohio (1838-1858)." *NW Ohio Q*, LI (1942), 332-340; LII (1943), 356-372.

4 NORWOOD, William F. *Medical Education in the United States Before the Civil War.* Philadelphia, 1944.

5 PEARE, C. O. *A Scientist of Two Worlds: Louis Agassiz.* Philadelphia, 1958.

6 REINGOLD, Nathan, ed. *Science in Nineteenth Century America: A Documentary History.* New York, 1964.†

7 REZNECK, Samuel. "The Emergence of a Scientific Community in New York State a Century Ago." *N Y Hist*, XLIII (1962), 209-225.

8 ROWLAND, Major T. "Letters of a Virginia Cadet at West Point, 1859-1861." *S Atl Q*, XIV (1915), 201-219, 330-347; XV (1916), 1-17, 142-156, 201-215.

9 SCOTT, Roy V. "Early Agricultural Education in Minnesota: The Institute Phase." *Ag Hist*, XXXVIII (1963), 21-34.

10 SHRYOCK, Richard H. "American Indifference to Basic Science During the Nineteenth Century." *Archives Internationales d'Histoire des Sciences*, V (1948), 50-65. Also in *The Sociology of Science.* Ed. by B. Barber and W. Hirsch. Glencoe, Ill., 1962.

11 STEPHENS, Roswell P. "Science in Georgia, 1800-1830." *Ga Hist Q*, IX (1925), 55-66.

12 STUART, Charles B. *Lives and Works of Civil and Military Engineers of America.* New York, 1871.

13 WAITE, Frederick C. "The Professional Education of Pioneer Ohio Physicians." *NW Ohio Q*, XLVIII (1939), 189-97.

14 WEBB, Lester A. *Captain Alden Partridge and the United States Military Academy, 1806-1833.* Northport, Ala., 1965.

See also 25.4, 34.19, 34.22, 34.23, 38.1, 38.2, 39.6, 39.8, 39.17, 44.13-15, 44.17, 45.2, 45.5, 45.8, 45.10, 45.16, 45.18, 45.21, 46.3, 70.5, 70.8, 70.13, 78.10, 78.17, 117.9, 123.1, 123.3, 123.4, 123.12, 123.20, 124.9, 124.19, 125.9.

9. Black Americans

15 ABBOTT, Martin. "The Freedmen's Bureau and Negro Schooling in South Carolina." *S C Hist Mag*, LVII (1956), 65-81.

16 ANDERSON, William T., Jr. "The Freedmen's Bureau and Negro Education in Virginia." *N C Hist Rev*, XXIX (1952), 64-90.

17 BIRNIE, C. W. "The Education of the Negro in Charleston, South Carolina, Before the Civil War." *J Neg Hist*, XII (1927), 13-21.

1   BLASSINGAME, John W. "The Union Army as an Educational Institution for Negroes, 1862-1865." *J Neg Ed*, XXXIV (1965), 152-159.

2   BOND, Horace M. *Negro Education in Alabama: A Study in Cotton and Steel.* Washington, D.C., 1939.

3   BOSKIN, Joseph. "The Origin of American Slavery: Education as an Index of Early Differentiation." *J Neg Ed*, XXXV (1966), 125-133.

4   BRIGHAM, R. I. "Negro Education in Ante-Bellum Missouri." *J Neg Hist*, XXX (1945), 405-420.

5   CARROLL, J. C. "The Beginnings of Public Education for Negroes in Indiana." *J Neg Ed*, VIII (1939), 649-658.

6   FEN, Sing-Nan. "Notes on the Education of Negroes in North Carolina During the Civil War." *J Neg Ed*, XXXVI (1967), 24-31.

7   GRESHAM, Luveta W. "Colonization Proposals for Free Negroes and Contrabands During the Civil War." *J Neg Ed*, XVI (1947), 28-33.

8   HAMILTON, J. G. de Roulhac. "The Freedmen's Bureau in North Carolina." *S Atl Q*, VIII (1909), 53-67, 154-163.

9   HARLAN, Louis R. "Desegregation in New Orleans Public Schools During Reconstruction." *Am Hist Rev*, LXVII (1962), 663-675.

10 HOLLINGSWORTH, R. R. "Education and Reconstruction in Georgia." *Ga Hist Q*, XIX (1935), 112-133, 229-250.

11 JACKSON, L. P. "The Educational Efforts of the Freedmen's Bureau and Freedmen's Aid Societies in South Carolina, 1862-1872." *J Neg Hist*, VIII (1923), 1-40.

12 JONES, Lewis W. "The Agent as a Factor in the Education of Negroes in the South." *J Neg Ed*, XIX (1950), 28-37.

13 KELLY, Alfred H. "The Congressional Controversy over School Segregation, 1867-1875." *Am Hist Rev*, LXIV (1959), 537-563.

14 KING, Emma. "Some Aspects of the Work of the Society of Friends for Negro Education in North Carolina." *N C Hist Rev*, I (1924), 403-411.

15 LEVY, Leonard W., and Harlan B. PHILLIPS. "The Roberts Case: Source of the 'Separate but Equal' Doctrine." *Am Hist Rev*, LVI (1951), 510-518.

16 LOW, W. A. "The Freedmen's Bureau and Education in Maryland." *Md Hist Mag*, XLVII (1952), 29-39.

17 MABEE, Carleton. "A Negro Boycott to Integrate Boston Schools." *N Eng Q*, XLI (1968), 341-361. (1844-1849.)

18 PARKER, Marjorie H. "Some Educational Activities of the Freedmen's Bureau." *J Neg Ed*, XXIII (1954), 9-21.

19 PORTER, Dorothy B. "The Organized Educational Activities of Negro Literary Societies, 1828-1846." *J Neg Ed*, V (1936), 555-576.

20 PRESTON, Emmett D., Jr. "The Development of Negro Education in the District of Columbia, 1800-1860." *J Neg Ed*, XII (1943), 189-198.

21 RICHARDSON, Joe M. "The Freedmen's Bureau and Negro Education in Florida." *J Neg Ed*, XXXI (1962), 460-467.

1 RILEY, Herman M. "A History of Negro Elementary Education in Indiana." *Ind Mag Hist*, XXVI (1930), 288-305.

2 ROBBINS, Gerald. "William F. Allen, Classical Scholar Among the Slaves." *Hist Ed Q*, V (1965), 211-223.

3 SAVAGE, W. Sherman. "Early Negro Education in the Pacific Coast States." *J Neg Ed*, XV (1946), 134-139.

4 SEIFMAN, Eli. "Education or Emigration: The Schism Within The African Colonization Movement, 1865-1875." *Hist Ed Q*, VII (1967), 36-57.

5 SMITH, James M. "The 'Separate but Equal' Doctrine: An Abolitionist Discusses Racial Segregation and Educational Policy During the Civil War, a Document." *J Neg Hist*, XLI (1956), 138-147. (Concerns Andrew D. White.)

6 VANCE, Joseph C. "Freedmen's Schools in Albemarle County During Reconstruction." *Va Mag Hist Bio*, LXI (1953), 430-438.

7 WESLEY, Edgar B. "Forty Acres and a Mule and a Speller." *Hist Ed J*, X (1959), 56-70. [Also in *Hist Ed J*, VIII (1957).]

8 WEST, Earle H. "The Peabody Education Fund and Negro Education, 1867-1880." *Hist Ed Q*, VI (1966), 3-21.

9 WILLIAMS, Henry S. "The Development of the Negro Public School System in Missouri." *J Neg Hist*, V (1920), 137-165.

See also 19.5, 20.11, 35.1, 73.15, 74.14, 103.8.

IV.   America in the Urban Age

1.   General Works and Essays

10 BETTS, John R. "P. T. Barnum and the Popularization of Natural History." *J Hist Ideas*, XX (1959), 353-368.

11 BOWERS, C. A. "The Ideologies of Progressive Education." *Hist Ed Q*, VII (1967), 452-473.

12 BUTLER, Nicholas M., ed. *Education in the United States.* 2 vols. Albany, 1900. (Repr. 1969.)

13 COHEN, Sol. "English Writers on the American Common Schools, 1884-1904." *School Rev*, LXXVI (1968), 127-146.

14 COHEN, Sol. *Progressives and Urban School Reform: The Public Education Association of New York City, 1895-1954.* New York, 1964.

15 COUNTS, George S. *The American Road to Culture.* New York, 1930.

16 COVELLO, Leonard, and Guido D'Agostino. *The Teacher in the Urban Community: A Half Century in City Schools.* Totowa, N.J., 1970. (Originally published as *The Heart Is the Teacher.* New York, 1958.)

17 CREMIN, Lawrence A. "The Progressive Movement in American Education: A Perspective." *Har Ed Rev*, XXVII (1957), 251-70.

1 CREMIN, Lawrence A. *The Transformation of the School: Progressivism in American Education, 1876-1957.* New York, 1961.†

2 CREMIN, Lawrence A. "What Happened to Progressive Education?" *Tchr Col Rec,* LXI (1959), 23-29.

3 CURRY, Jabez L. M. *Brief Sketch of George Peabody and a History of the George Peabody Fund Through Thirty Years.* Cambridge, Mass., 1898.

4 DOWNES, Randolph C. "The People's Schools: Popular Foundations of Toledo's Public School System." *N W Ohio Q,* XXIX (1956-1957), 9-26, and XXIX (1957), 108-116.

5 EMBREE, Edwin R., and Julia WAXMAN. *Investment in People: The Story of the Julius Rosenwald Fund.* New York, 1949.

6 FERGUSON, James S. "An Era of Educational Change." *N C Hist Rev,* XLVI (1969), 130-141. (Concerns 1895-1899 fusion of Populists and Republicans.)

7 FILLER, Louis. "Main Currents in Progressivist American Education." *Hist Ed J,* VIII (1956), 33-57.

8 FINDLEY, James. "Education and the Church Controversy. The Later Career of Dwight L. Moody." *N Eng Q,* XXXIX (1966), 210-232.

9 FOSDICK, Raymond B., et al. *Adventure in Giving: The Story of the General Education Board.* New York, 1962.

10 *The General Education Board: An Account of Its Activities, 1902-1914.* New York, 1915.

11 GRAHAM, Patricia A. *Progressive Education: From Arcady to Academe–A History of the Progressive Education Association, 1919-1955.* New York, 1967.

12 ISSEL, William H. "Teachers and Educational Reform During the Progressive Era: A Case Study of the Pittsburgh Teachers Association." *Hist Ed Q,* VII (1967), 220-233.

13 KANDEL, Isaac L. *American Education in the Twentieth Century.* Cambridge, Mass., 1957.

14 KANDEL, Isaac L., ed. *Twenty-Five Years of American Education.* New York, 1924.

15 KEPPEL, Ann M. "The Myth of Agrarianism in Rural Educational Reform, 1890-1914." *Hist Ed Q,* II (1962), 100-112.

16 KERSCHENSTEINER, Georg. *A Comparison of Public Education in Germany and in the United States.* U S Bur Ed Bull 1913, no. 24. Washington, D.C., 1913.

17 KNIGHT, Edgar W. *Fifty Years of American Education: A Historical Review and Critical Appraisal.* New York, 1952.

18 KNIGHT, Edgar W. "Public Education in the South: Some Inherited Ills and Some Needed Reforms." *School Soc,* XI (1920), 31-38.

19 MC COLLUM, M. G., Jr. "Robert L. Tidwell and Public Education in Alabama." *Pae Hist,* VIII (1968), 81-107.

1 MAYO, Amory D. "The Final Establishment of the American Common School System in North Carolina, South Carolina, and Georgia, 1863-1900." *U S Bur Ed, Rep Comm 1904.* Vol. I. Washington, D.C., 1906, pp. 999-1090.

2 MAYO, Amory D. "The Final Establishment of the American Common School System in West Virginia, Maryland, Virginia, and Delaware, 1863-1900." *U S Bur Ed, Rep Comm 1903.* Vol. I. Washington, D.C., 1905, pp. 391-462.

3 PERKINSON, Henry J. *The Imperfect Panacea: American Faith in Education, 1865-1965.* New York, 1968.†

4 RUDY, Willis. *Schools in an Age of Mass Culture: An Exploration of Selected Themes in the History of Twentieth-Century American Education.* Englewood Cliffs, N.J., 1965.

5 SMITH, Timothy L. "Progressivism in American Education, 1880-1900." *Har Ed Rev,* XXXI (1961), 168-193.

See also 3.15, 5.1, 5.3, 5.7, 10.6, 10.10, 10.13, 10.15, 14.17, 15.18, 16.21, 17.13, 21.13, 27.2, 27.10, 28.9, 29.1, 29.2, 29.10, 29.16, 29.21, 96.16, 97.15.

2. *The Response to Immigration*

6 *Americanization as a War Measure: Report of a Conference Called by the Secretary of the Interior, and Held in Washington, April 3, 1918.* U S Bur Ed Bull 1918, no. 18. Washington, D.C., 1918.

7 ATZMON, Ezri. "The Educational Programs for Immigrants in the United States." *Hist Ed J,* IX (1958), 75-80.

8 BORRIE, W. D. et al. *The Cultural Integration of Immigrants.* Washington, D.C., 1939.

9 BRUNNER, Edmund DeS. et al. "Migration and Education." *Tchr Col Rec,* XLIX (1947), 98-107.

10 BUTLER, Fred C. *Community Americanization.* U S Bur Ed Bull 1919, no. 76. Washington, D.C., 1920.

11 BUTLER, Fred C. *State Americanization: The Part of the State in the Education and Assimilation of the Immigrant.* U S Bur Ed Bull 1919, no. 77. Washington, D.C., 1920.

12 COHEN, Helen L. "Americanization By Classroom Practice." *Tchr Col Rec,* XX (1919), 238-249.

13 DILLINGHAM, William P., ed. *The Children of the Immigrants in Schools.* Reports of the Immigration Commission, United States Congress. Vols. 29-33. Washington, D.C., 1911. (With introductory essay by Francesco Cordasco. Metuchen, N.J., 1970.)

14 MAHONEY, John J. *Americanization in the United States.* U S Bur Ed Bull 1923, no. 31. Washington, D.C., 1923.

15 MILLER, Herbert A. *The School and the Immigrant.* Cleveland, 1916.

16 ROSENSTEIN, David. "Contributions of Education to Ethnic Fusion in America." *School Soc,* XIII (1921), 673-682.

1 SMITH, Timothy L. "Immigrant Social Aspirations and American Education, 1880-1930." *Am Q*, XXI (1969), 523-543.

2 THOMAS, Alan M., Jr. "American Education and the Immigrant." *Tchr Col Rec*, LV (1954), 253-267.

3 THOMPSON, Frank V. *Schooling of the Immigrant.* New York, 1920.

4 TYACK, David B. "Education and Social Unrest, 1873-1878." *Har Ed Rev*, XXXI (1961), 194-212.

See also 16.4, 16.6, 16.9, 17.3.

3.   The Response to Industrial Civilization

5 ADDAMS, Jane. *The Spirit of Youth and the City Streets.* New York, 1909.

6 BECK, John M. "The Public Schools and the Chicago Newspapers: 1890-1920." *School Rev*, LXII (1954), 288-295.

7 BERROL, Selma C. "William Henry Maxwell and a New Educational New York." *Hist Ed Q*, VIII (1968), 215-228.

8 COHEN, Sol. "The Industrial Education Movement, 1906-17." *Am Q*, XX (1968), 95-110.

9 COON, Charles L. "The Beginnings of North Carolina City Schools, 1867-1887." *S Atl Q*, XII (1913), 235-247.

10 CUBBERLY, Ellwood P. *The Portland Survey.* Yonkers-on-Hudson, N.Y., 1916.

11 ELIOT, Charles W. "The Unity of Educational Reform." *U S Bur Ed, Rep Comm 1892-1893.* Vol. II. Washington, D.C., 1895, pp. 1465-1473.

12 GERSMAN, Elinor M. "Progressive Reform of the St. Louis School Board, 1897." *Hist Ed Q*, X (1970), 3-21.

13 ISSEL, William H. "Modernization in Philadelphia School Reform, 1882-1905." *Pa Mag Hist Bio*, XCIV (1970), 358-383.

14 KATZ, Michael B. "The Emergence of Bureaucracy in Urban Education: The Boston Case, 1850-1884." *Hist Ed Q*, VIII (1968), 155-188, 319-357.

15 MERK, Lois B. "Boston's Historic Public School Crisis." *N Eng Q*, XXXI (1958), 172-200.

16 MEZVINSKY, Norton. "Scientific Temperance Instruction in the Schools." *Hist Ed Q*, I (March 1961), 48-56. (Concerns activities of the Women's Christian Temperance Union, 1869-1920.)

17 RICE, Joseph M. *The Public School System of the United States.* New York, 1893.

18 RICKARD, Garrett E. "Establishment of Graded Schools in American Cities." *El School J*, XLVII (1947), 575-585; XLVIII (1948), 326-335.

19 SPRING, Joel. "Education and Progressivism." *Hist Ed Q*, X (1970), 53-71.

20 STAMBLER, Moses. "The Effect of Compulsory Education and Child Labor Laws on High School Attendance in New York City 1898-1917." *Hist Ed Q*, VIII (1968), 189-214.

1 TYACK, David. "Bureaucracy and the Common School: The Example of Portland, Oregon, 1851-1913." *Am Q*, XIX (1967), 475-498.

2 VALENTINE, Marian G. "William H. Maxwell and Progressive Education." *School Soc*, LXXV (1952), 353-356.

3 WEISS, Robert M. "He Wanted to Abolish Public Schools." *Tchr Col Rec*, LVII (1956), 222-231. (Richard Grant White, journalist, 1821-1885.)

4 WORMELEY, G. Smith. "Educators of the First Half-Century of the Public Schools of the District of Columbia." *J Neg Hist*, XVII (1932), 124-140.

See also 6.9, 25.1, 25.5, 25.7-11, 25.19, 26.7, 27.4, 27.5, 27.7-10, 27.19, 28.7, 28.13, 29.18, 86.14, 108.4.

4. Progressive Education, Youth, the Arts, and Psychoanalysis

5 BECK, Robert H. "Progressive Education and American Progressivism." *Tchr Col Rec*, LX (1958-59), 77-89, 129-37, 198-208.

6 BOURNE, Randolph S. *The Gary Schools.* Boston, 1916.

7 BURRIS, William P. *The Public School System of Gary, Indiana.* U S Bur Ed Bull 1914, no. 18. Washington, D.C., 1914.

8 CASE, Roscoe D. *The Platoon School in America.* Stanford, 1931.

9 COBB, Stanwood. *The New Leaven.* New York, 1928.

10 CORIAT, Isador H. "The Psycho-Analytic Approach to Education." *Prog Ed*, III (1926), 19-25.

11 DE LIMA, Agnes. *Our Enemy the Child.* New York, 1926.

12 DEWEY, Evelyn. *New Schools for Old: The Regeneration of the Porter School.* New York, 1919.

13 FLEXNER, Abraham. *A Modern School.* New York, 1916.

14 FREUD, Anna. *Psychoanalysis for Teachers and Parents: Introductory Lectures.* New York, 1935.†

15 GEORGE, Anne E. "The Montessori Movement in America." *U S Bur Ed, Rep Comm 1914.* Vol. I. Washington, D.C., 1915, pp. 355-362.

16 HAMILTON, A. E. *The Real Boy and the New School.* New York, 1925.

17 JOHNSON, Marietta L. *Youth in a World of Men: The Child, the Parent and the Teacher.* New York, 1930.

18 KARIER, Clarence J. "The Rebel and the Revolutionary: Sigmund Freud and John Dewey." *Tchr Col Rec*, LXIV (1963), 605-613.

19 LEWIS, Mary H. *An Adventure with Children.* New York, 1928.

20 LINDSEY, Ben B., and Wainwright EVANS. *The Revolt of Modern Youth.* New York, 1925.

21 MEARNS, Hughes. *Creative Youth: How a School Environment Set Free the Creative Spirit.* Garden City, N.Y., 1926.

1 Members of the Faculty of the South Philadelphia High School for Girls. *Educating for Responsibility: The Dalton Laboratory Plan in a Secondary School.* New York, 1926.

2 NAUMBURG, Margaret. *The Child and the World: Dialogues in Modern Education.* New York, 1928.

3 OBERNDORF, Clarence P. *A History of Psychoanalysis in America.* New York, 1953.

4 PARKHURST, Helen. *Education on the Dalton Plan.* New York, 1922.

5 PARKHURST, Helen. *An Explanation of the Dalton Laboratory Plan.* London, 1926.

6 PFISTER, Oskar R. *Psycho-Analysis in the Service of Education: Being an Introduction to Psycho-Analysis.* London, 1922.

7 PRATT, Caroline. *I Learn from Children: An Adventure in Progressive Education.* New York, 1948.

8 PRATT, Caroline, ed. *Experimental Practice in the City and Country School.* New York, 1924.

9 PRATT, Caroline, and Jessie STANTON. *Before Books.* New York, 1926.

10 RUGG, Harold, and Ann SHUMAKER. *The Child-Centered School: An Appraisal of the New Education.* Yonkers-on-Hudson, N.Y., 1928.

11 SMITH, Eugene R. *Education Moves Ahead: A Survey of Progressive Methods.* Boston, 1926.

12 SPAIN, Charles L. *The Platoon School: A Study of the Adaptation of the Elementary School Organization to the Curriculum.* New York, 1924.

13 STEERE, Geoffrey H. "Freudianism in Child-Rearing in the Twenties." *Am Q*, XX (1968), 759-767.

14 TYLER, Louise L. "Psychoanalysis and Curriculum Theory." *School Rev*, LXVI (1958), 446-460.

15 VAN WATERS, Miriam. *Youth in Conflict.* New York, 1932.

16 VOORHEES, Margaretta R. "Social Studies in the Beaver Country Day School." *Prog Ed*, II (1925), 241-246.

17 WASHBURNE, Carleton W., and Sidney P. MARLAND. *Winnetka: The History and Significance of an Educational Experiment.* Englewood Cliffs, N.J., 1968.

18 WASHBURNE, Carleton W., and Myron M. STEARNS. *Better Schools: A Survey of Progressive Education in American Public Schools.* New York, 1928.

19 WHITE, William A. *The Mental Hygiene of Childhood.* Boston, 1929.

20 WILLCOTT, Paul. "The Initial American Reception of the Montessori Method." *School Rev*, LXXVI (1968), 147-165.

21 YEOMANS, Edward. *Shackled Youth: Comments on Schools, School People, and Other People.* Boston, 1921.

See also 2.5, 86.11, 86.14, 86.17, 87.1, 87.2, 87.7, 87.11, 87.12, 88.5, 89.5, 89.19, 90.2, 99.4-6, 99.19, 100.7, 105.4, 105.11, 106.3, 106.13, 108.4, 118.3.

5. Education as a Discipline

A. NINTEENTH CENTURY PEDAGOGY

1 BENNE, Kenneth D. "The Educational Outlook of Herbert Spencer." *Har Ed Rev*, X (1940), 436-453.

2 BUTTON, Henry W. "Committee of Fifteen." *Hist Ed Q*, V (1965), 253-263.

3 CAMPBELL, Jack K. *Colonel Francis W. Parker: The Children's Crusader.* New York, 1968.

4 CHAMBLISS, J. J. "William Torrey Harris' Philosophy of Education." *Pae Hist*, V (1965), 319-339.

5 COMPAYRE, Gabriel. *Herbart and Education By Instruction.* New York, 1907.

6 COOKE, Flora J. "Colonel Francis W Parker as Interpreted Through the Work of the Francis W. Parker School." *El School Tchr*, XII (1912), 397-544.

7 DALE, Edward E. "Teaching on the Prairie Plains, 1890-1900." *Miss Val Hist Rev*, XXXIII (1946-1947), 293-307.

8 DARROCH, Alexander. *Herbart and the Herbartian Theory of Education: A Criticism.* London, 1903.

9 DAVIS, Sheldon E. *Educational Periodicals During the Nineteenth Century.* U S Bur Ed Bull 1919, no. 28. Washington, D.C., 1919.

10 DEARBORN, Ned H. *The Oswego Movement in American Education.* New York, 1925.

11 DE GARMO, Charles. *Herbart and the Herbartians.* New York, 1896.

12 ELIOT, Charles W. "Contributions to the History of American Teaching." *Ed Rev*, XLII (1911), 346-366.

13 FISHER, Sara C. "The Psychological and Educational Work of Granville Stanley Hall." *Am J Psy*, XXXVI (1925), 1-52.

14 "Francis Wayland Parker and His Work for Education." *U S Bur Ed, Rep Comm 1902.* Vol. I. Washington, D.C., 1903, pp. 231-284.

15 GRINDER, Robert E., and Charles E. STRICKLAND. "G. Stanley Hall and the Social Significance of Adolescence." *Tchr Col Rec*, LXIV (1963), 390-399.

16 HALL, G. Stanley. *Adolescence: Its Psychology and Its Relations to Physiology, Anthropology, Sociology, Sex, Crime, Religion, and Education.* 2 vols. New York, 1904.

17 HARRIS, William T. "Educational Values." *U S Bur Ed, Rep Comm 1893-1894.* Vol. I. Washington, D.C., 1896, pp. 617-637.

18 HARRIS, William T. "The Old Psychology v. the New." *U S Bur Ed, Rep Comm 1893-1894.* Vol. I. Washington, D.C., 1896, pp. 433-436.

19 HERBST, Jurgen. "Herbert Spencer and the Genteel Tradition in American Education." *Ed Theory*, XI (1961), 99-111.

20 HOLMES, Brian. "Some Writings of William Torrey Harris." *Brit J Ed Stud*, V (1956-57), 47-66.

1 KATZ, Michael B. "The New Departure in Quincy, 1873-1881: The Nature of Nineteenth Century Educational Reform." *N Eng Q*, XL (1967), 3-30.

2 KOHLBRENNER, Richard J. "William Torrey Harris: Superintendent of Schools, St. Louis." *Hist Ed J*, II (1950-1951), 18-24, 54-61.

3 LEIDECKER, Kurt F. *Yankee Teacher: The Life of William Torrey Harris.* New York, 1946.

4 MC MURRY, Charles A. *The Elements of General Method Based on the Principles of Herbart.* Rev. and enl. ed. New York, 1903.

5 MC RAE, Donald G. "Education and Sociology in America: 1865-1900, A Paradox of Creativity." *Ed Forum*, XXXIII (1969), 143-151.

6 MICHAEL, Richard B. "The American Institute of Instruction." *Hist Ed J*, III (1951), 27-32.

7 MOSIER, Richard D. "The Educational Philosophy of William T. Harris." *Peabody J Ed*, XXIX (1951), 24-33.

8 MOULTON, Gerald L. "The American Herbartian: A Portrait from His Yearbooks." *Hist Ed Q*, III (1963), 134-142, 187-197.

9 PARKER, Francis W. *Talks on Pedagogics: An Outline of the Theory of Concentration.* New York, 1894.

10 PARKER, Franklin. "Francis Wayland Parker, 1837-1902." *Pae Hist*, I (1961), 120-133.

11 RADOSAVLJEVICH, Paul R. "The Oswego Movement and the New Education." *Ed Forum*, II (1937), 90-100.

12 ROBARTS, Jason R. "The Quest for a Science of Education in the Nineteenth Century." *Hist Ed Q*, VIII (1968), 431-446.

13 ROBERTS, John S. *William Torrey Harris: A Critical Study of His Educational and Related Philosophical Views.* Washington, D.C., 1924.

14 RUDY, Willis. "Josiah Royce and the Art of Teaching." *Ed Theory*, II (1952), 158-169.

15 STAFFORD, Douglas K. "Roots of the Decline of Herbartianism in Nineteenth Century America." *Har Ed Rev*, XXV (1955), 231-241.

16 STRICKLAND, Charles E. "The Child, The Community, and Clio: The Uses of Cultural History in Elementary School Experiments of the Eighteen-Nineties." *Hist Ed Q*, VII (1967), 474-492.

17 THURSFIELD, Richard E. *Henry Barnard's American Journal of Education.* Baltimore, 1945.

18 TOSTBERG, Robert E. "Colonel Parker's Quest for 'A School in Which All Good Things Come Together.' " *Hist Ed Q*, VI (1966), 22-42.

19 WESLEY, Edgar B. *NEA: The First Hundred Years.* New York, 1957.

20 WEST, H. F. "Common School Advocate—The Earliest Indiana School Journal." *Ind Mag Hist*, VI (1910), 118-126.

See also 10.17, 11.14, 12.3, 12.9, 12.10, 12.13, 13.2, 13.5, 13.6, 13.9 13.12, 13.13, 13.16, 71.4, 71.14, 71.17, 72.5, 72.6, 76.13.

B. TEACHER TRAINING

1 ALMACK, John C. "History of Oregon Normal Schools." *Ore Hist Soc Q*, XXI (1920), 95-169.

2 ARMSTRONG, W. Earle. *The College and Teacher Education.* Washington, D.C., 1944.

3 BIGELOW, Karl W. "The Passing of the Teachers College." *Tchr Col Rec*, LVIII (1957), 409-417.

4 BIGELOW, Maurice A. "Thirty Years of Practical Arts in Teachers College Under the Administration of Dean James E. Russell, 1897-1927." *Tchr Col Rec*, XXVIII (1927), 765-775.

5 BORROWMAN, Merle L. *The Liberal and Technical in Teacher Education.* New York, 1956.

6 BORROWMAN, Merle L., ed. *Teacher Education in America: A Documentary History.* New York, 1965.†

7 CARTER, James G. *Essays upon Popular Education Containing a Particular Examination of the Schools of Massachusetts and an Outline of an Institution for the Education of Teachers.* Boston, 1826.

8 COLEMAN, Charles H. "The Normal School Comes to Charleston." *J Ill St Hist Soc*, XLI (1948), 117-133.

9 CONANT, James B. *The Education of American Teachers.* New York, 1963.†

10 DEWEY, John, et al. *The Relation of Theory to Practice in the Education of Teachers.* 3d *Yrbk Nat Soc Stud Ed.* Pt. I. Bloomington, Ill., 1904.

11 DEYOE, George P. *Certain Trends in Curriculum Practices and Policies in State Normal Schools and Teachers Colleges.* New York, 1934.

12 DUNN, Joan. *Retreat from Learning: Why Teachers Can't Teach, a Case History.* New York, 1955.

13 EDELFELT, Roy A., ed. "A Symposium on James Bryant Conant's *The Education of American Teachers.*" *J Tchr Ed*, XV (1964), 5-49.

14 GOOD, Harry G. *The Rise of the College of Education of the Ohio State University.* Columbus, Ohio, 1960.

15 GORDY, J. P. *Rise and Growth of the Normal School Idea in the United States.* U S Bur Ed, Circ Info 1891, no. 8. Washington, D.C., 1891.

16 HALL, Samuel R. *Lectures on School-Keeping.* 4th ed. Boston, 1832.

17 HARPER, Charles A. *A Century of Public Teacher Education: The Story of the State Teachers Colleges as They Evolved from the Normal Schools.* Washington, D.C., 1939.

18 HERVERY, Walter L. "Historical Sketch of Teachers College from Its Foundation to 1897." *Tchr Col Rec*, I (1900), 12-35.

19 HOLLIS, Andrew P. *The Contribution of the Oswego Normal School to Educational Progress in the United States.* Boston, 1898.

20 JENKINS, Ralph C. "Henry Barnard: Educator of Teachers." *Ed Forum*, IV (1939), 25-34.

21 KERSEY, Harry A. "Michigan Teachers' Institutes in the Mid-Nineteenth Century: A Representative Document." *Hist Ed Q*, V (1965), 40-52.

1 KNIGHT, Edgar W. "A Century of Teacher Education." *Ed Forum*, IX (1945), 149-161.

2 KOERNER, James D. *The Miseducation of American Teachers*. Boston, 1963.†

3 LA BUE, Anthony C. "Teacher Certification in the United States: A Brief History." *J Tchr Ed*, XI (1960), 147-172.

4 LINTON, Clarence, and Joseph J. KATSURANIS. "Study of Alumni of Teachers College Receiving Degrees from 1928 to 1935." *Tchr Col Rec*, XXXIX (1938), 407-422, 734-746; XL (1938), 150-159.

5 LUCKEY, George W. A. *The Professional Training of Secondary Teachers in the United States*. New York, 1903.

6 LYTE, Eliphalet O. "The State Normal Schools of the United States." *U S Bur Ed, Rep Comm 1903*. Vol. I. Washington, D.C., 1905, pp. 1103-1136.

7 MANGUN, Vernon L. *The American Normal School: Its Rise and Development in Massachusetts*. Baltimore, 1928.

8 MEYER, Karl W. "Post-World War II Conversion of the Teachers College." *J Tchr Ed*, XI (1960), 335-339.

9 MONROE, Walter S. *Teacher-Learning Theory and Teacher Education, 1890 to 1950*. Urbana, Ill., 1952.

10 NEWELL, M. A. "Contributions to the History of Normal Schools in the United States." *U S Bur Ed, Rep Comm 1898-1899*. Vol. II. Washington, D.C., 1900, pp. 2263-2290.

11 NORTON, Arthur O., ed. *The First State Normal School in America: The Journals of Cyrus Peirce and Mary Swift*. Cambridge, Mass., 1926.

12 O'DONNELL, W. F. "Five Decades of Teacher Education in Kentucky." *Fil Club*, XXX (1956), 115-124.

13 PANGBURN, Jesse M. *The Evolution of the American Teachers College*. New York, 1932.

14 PANNELL, Henry C. *The Preparation and Work of Alabama High School Teachers*. New York, 1933. (Concerns in-service training of teachers from 1901 to 1928.)

15 PARKER, Francis W. "An Account of the Work of the Cook County and Chicago Normal School from 1883 to 1899." *El School Tchr*, II (1901-1902), 752-780.

16 REAVIS, G. H. "The Development of Teacher Training as a Profession." *Tchr Col Rec*, XXIV (1923), 208-212.

17 ROGERS, Dorothy. *Oswego: Fountainhead of Teacher Education: A Century in the Sheldon Tradition*. New York, 1961.

18 RUDY, Willis. "America's First Normal School: The Formative Years." *J Tchr Ed*, V (1954), 263-270. (Lexington, Mass., 1839.)

19 RUSSELL, James E. *Founding Teachers College: Reminiscences of the Dean Emeritus*. New York, 1937.

20 STONE, Mason S. "The First Normal School in America." *Tchr Col Rec*, XXIV (1923), 263-271.

21 WEISS, Robert M. *The Conant Controversy in Teacher Education*. New York, 1969.†

1 WILLIAMSON, Obed J. *Provisions for General Theory Courses in the Professional Education of Teachers.* New York, 1936.

2 WOFFORD, Kate V. *A History of the Status and Training of Elementary Rural Teachers of the United States, 1860-1930.* New York, 1903.

3 WRIGHT, Frank W. "The Evolution of the Normal Schools." *El School J,* XXX (1930), 363-371.

   See also 3.2, 3.8, 3.11, 3.19-21, 33.15, 35.4, 36.16, 99.9.

C. THE SCIENCE AND PROFESSION OF EDUCATION

4 AUERBACH, Eugene. "Aspects of the History and Present Status of Liberal Arts Opposition to Professors of Education." *Ed Forum,* XXII (1957), 83-94.

5 AYRES, Leonard P., et al. *The Measurement of Educational Products.* 17th *Yrbk Nat Soc Stud Ed.* Pt. II. Bloomington, Ill., 1918.

6 BAKER, James H. *Report of the Committee of the National Council of Education on Economy of Time in Education.* U S Bur Ed Bull 1913, no. 38. Washington, D.C., 1913.

7 BROWN, Elmer E. "The Development of Education as a University Subject." *Tchr Col Rec,* XXIV (1923), 190-196.

8 BURKS, Jesse D. "History of the Speyer School." *Tchr Col Rec,* III (1902), 6-12. (Teachers College Laboratory School.)

9 BUSHNELL, Don D., and Dwight W. ALLEN, eds. *The Computer in American Education.* New York, 1967.

10 BUTLER, Leslie A. *The Michigan Schoolmasters' Club: A Story of the First Seven Decades, 1886-1957.* Ann Arbor, 1958.

11 CALLAHAN, Raymond E. "Leonard Ayres and the Educational Balance Sheet." *Hist Ed Q,* I (1961), 5-13.

12 CALLAHAN, Raymond E. *Education and the Cult of Efficiency.* Chicago, 1962.†

13 COURTIS, Stuart A. *The Gary Public Schools: Measurement of Classroom Products.* New York, 1919.

14 COXE, Warren W., et al. *The Grouping of Pupils.* 35th *Yrbk Nat Soc Stud Ed.* Pt. I. Bloomington, Ill., 1936.

15 DE PENCIER, Ida B. *History of the Laboratory Schools, The University of Chicago, 1896-1965.* Chicago, 1967.

16 DIENER, Thomas J. "The United States Office of Education: One Hundred Years of Service to Higher Education." *Ed Forum,* XXXIII (1969), 453-466.

17 DROST, Walter H. "Clarence Kingsley—'The New York Years.'" *Hist Ed Q,* VI (1966), 18-34.

18 DROST, Walter H. *David Snedden and Education for Social Efficiency.* Madison, 1967.

19 EDWARDS, Newton D. "General Methods: Historical, Comparative, and Documentary." *The Scientific Movement in Education.* Ed. by Frank N. Freeman et al. 37th *Yrbk Nat Soc Stud Ed.* Pt. II. Chicago, 1938, pp. 273-281.

1 FREEMAN, Frank N. *Mental Tests: Their History, Principles, and Applications.* Rev. ed., Boston, 1939.

2 FREEMAN, Frank N., et al. *The Scientific Movement in Education.* 37th *Yrbk Nat Soc Stud Ed.* Pt. II. Chicago, 1938.

3 GOODENOUGH, Florence L. *Mental Testing: Its History, Principles, and Applications.* New York, 1949.

4 GORE, Joseph. "The Economy of Time Movement in Elementary Education: The Impact of Social Forces upon Curriculum Organization in the United States." *Pae Hist,* VII (1967), 489-518.

5 HARMS, Ernest. "Child Guidance Yesterday, Today, and Tomorrow." *School Soc,* LXXII (1950), 129-132.

6 HOLLINGWORTH, Leta S. "The Founding of Public School 500: Speyer School." *Tchr Col Rec,* XXXVIII (1936), 119-128. (Teachers College Laboratory School.)

7 JERSILD, Arthur T. "Child Psychology in the United States." *Tchr Col Rec,* L (1948), 114-127.

8 JOHANNINGMEIER, Erwin V. "William Chandler Bagley's Changing Views on the Relationship Between Psychology and Education." *Hist Ed Q,* IX (1969), 3-27.

9 JONCICH, Geraldine. *The Sane Positivist: A Biography of Edward L. Thorndike.* Middletown, Conn., 1968.

10 JONCICH, Geraldine M., ed. *Psychology and the Science of Education: Selected Writings of Edward L. Thorndike.* New York, 1962.†

11 JONES, Howard M., et al. "On the Conflict Between the 'Liberal Arts' and the 'Schools of Education.'" *ACLS Newsletter,* V (1954), 17-38.

12 JUDD, Charles H. "A Century of Applications of Psychology to Education." *Tchr Col Rec,* XXVII (1926), 771-781.

13 KIRSCHNER, Joseph. "Programmed Learning: An Historical Antecedent." *Ed Forum,* XXXII (1967), 97-103.

14 KOOS, Leonard V., et al. *Extracurricular Activities.* 25th *Yrbk Nat Soc Stud Ed.* Pt. II. Bloomington, Ill., 1926.

15 KURSH, Harry. *The United States Office of Education: A Century of Service.* Philadelphia, 1965.

16 LIEBERMAN, Myron. *Education as a Profession.* Englewood Cliffs, N.J., 1956.

17 LORGE, Irving. "Thorndike's Contribution to the Psychology of Learning of Adults." *Tchr Col Rec,* XLI (1940), 778-788.

18 MC GAUGHY, J. R. "The Extension of the Frontier in Elementary Education Since 1900." *Tchr Col Rec,* XXIV (1933), 580-586.

19 MAYHEW, Katherine C., and Anna C. EDWARDS. *The Dewey School: The Laboratory School of the University of Chicago, 1896-1903.* New York, 1936.†

20 MOSSMAN, Lois C., et al. *The Activity Movement.* 33rd *Yrbk Nat Soc Stud Ed.* Pt. II. Bloomington, Ill., 1934.†

1 MOWRER, O. Hobart. "Learning Theory: Historical Review and Re-interpretation." *Har Ed Rev*, XXIV (1954), 37-58.

2 OETTINGER, Anthony, and Sema MARKS. *Run, Computer, Run: The Mythology of Educational Innovation.* Cambridge, Mass., 1969.

3 PARKER, Franklin. "The Case of Harold Rugg." *Pae Hist*, II (1962), 95-122.

4 PATERSON, Donald G. "The Genesis of Modern Guidance." *Ed Rec*, XIX (1938), 36-46.

5 PAX, Rev. Walter T. *A Critical Study of Thorndike's Theory and Laws of Learning.* Washington, D.C., 1938.

6 PELTIER, Gary L. "Teacher Participation in Curriculum Revision: An Historical Case Study." *Hist Ed Q*, VII (1967), 209-219.

7 PETERSON, Joseph. *Early Conceptions and Tests of Intelligence.* Yonkers-on-Hudson, N.Y., 1925.

8 PHILLIPS, Richard C. "The Historical Development of the Term, Experience Curriculum." *Hist Ed Q*, V (1965), 121-130.

9 RIVLIN, Harry N., et al. *Mental Health in Modern Education.* 54th *Yrbk Nat Soc Stud Ed.* Pt. II. Chicago, 1955.

10 ROCK, Robert T., Jr. "Thorndike's Contribution to the Psychology of Learning." *Tchr Col Rec*, XLI (1940), 751-761.

11 RUGG, Harold. "After Three Decades of Scientific Method in Education." *Tchr Col Rec*, XXXVI (1934), 111-122.

12 RUGG, Harold, et al. *The Foundations and Technique of Curriculum-Making: Curriculum-Making, Past and Present.* 26th *Yrbk Nat Soc Stud Ed.* Pt. I. Bloomington, Ill., 1926.

13 SEARS, Jesse B., and Adin D. HENDERSON. *Cubberley of Stanford and His Contribution to American Education.* Stanford, 1957.

14 SEAY, Maurice F., et al. *The Community School.* 52nd *Yrbk Nat Soc Stud Ed.* Pt. II. Chicago, 1953.†

15 STRANG, Ruth, et al. *Juvenile Delinquency and the Schools.* 47th *Yrbk Nat Soc Stud Ed.* Pt. I. Chicago, 1948.

16 STRAYER, George D., et al. *Report of the Committee of the National Council of Education on Standards and Tests for Measuring the Efficiency of Schools or Systems of Schools.* U S Bur Ed Bull 1913, no. 13. Washington, D.C., 1913.

17 STRAYER, George D., et al. *Standards and Tests for the Measurement of the Efficiency of Schools and School Systems.* 15th *Yrbk Nat Soc Stud Ed.* Pt. I. Chicago, 1916.

18 TERMAN, Lewis M., et al. *Genetic Studies of Genius.* Stanford, 1925.

19 TERMAN, Lewis M., et al. *Nature and Nurture.* 27th *Yrbk Nat Soc Stud Ed.* Pts. I and II. Bloomington, Ill., 1928.

20 THORNDIKE, Edward L. "The Measurement of Educational Products." *School Rev*, XX (1912), 289-299.

21 THORNDIKE, Edward L. *The Teaching Staff of Secondary Schools in the United States: Amount of Education, Length of Experience, Salaries.* U S Bur Ed Bull 1909, no. 4. Washington, D.C., 1909.

1   THORNDIKE, Edward L., et al. *Intelligence Tests and Their Use.* 21st *Yrbk Nat Soc Stud Ed.* Pts. I and II. Bloomington, Ill., 1922.

2   THURSFIELD, Richard E. "Ellwood Patterson Cubberley." *Har Ed Rev*, IX (1939), 43-62.

3   TYLER, Ralph W., et al. *Graduate Study in Education.* 50th *Yrbk Nat Soc Stud Ed.* Pt. I. Chicago, 1951.

4   WASHBURNE, Carleton W. *Adjusting the School to the Child: Practical First Steps.* Yonkers-on-Hudson, N.Y., 1932.

5   WASHBURNE, Carleton W., ed. *Adapting the School to Individual Differences.* 24th *Yrbk Nat Soc Stud Ed.* Pt. II. Bloomington, Ill., 1925.

6   WASHBURNE, Carleton W., et al. *Results of Practical Experiments in Fitting Schools to Individuals.* Bloomington, Ill., 1926.

7   WESTERBERG, Virginia. "A History of the University Elementary School, State University of Iowa, 1915-1958." *Pae Hist*, IV (1964), 457-496.

8   WHITTEMORE, Richard. "Nicholas Murray Butler and the Teaching Profession." *Hist Ed Q*, I (1961), 22-37.

9   WHITTEMORE, Richard. "Sovereignty in the University: Teachers College and Columbia." *Tchr Col Rec*, LXVI (1965), 509-518.

10 WINTERS, Elmer A. "Man and His Changing Society: The Textbooks of Harold Rugg." *Hist Ed Q*, VII (1967), 493-514.

11 WYLIE, Andrew T. "A Brief History of Mental Tests." *Tchr Col Rec*, XXIII (1922), 19-33.

See also 1.5, 1.14, 2.16, 3.7, 6.5, 8.15, 9.5, 29.3, 46.12, 87.12, 89.10, 89.11, 93.19, 95.3, 95.4, 105.18, 108.14, 108.16, 109.1, 110.6.

D. PHILOSOPHY AND JOHN DEWEY

12 ARCHAMBAULT, Reginald D., ed. *Dewey on Education: Appraisals.* New York, 1966.†

13 ARCHAMBAULT, Reginald D., ed. *John Dewey on Education: Selected Writings.* New York, 1964.

14 ARCHAMBAULT, Reginald D., ed. *Lectures in the Philosophy of Education, by John Dewey.* New York, 1966.

15 BAKER, Melvin C. *Foundations of John Dewey's Educational Theory.* New York, 1955.†

16 BERKSON, Issac B. "Science, Ethics, and Education in the Deweyan Experimentalist Philosophy." *School Soc*, LXXXVIII (1959), 387-391.

17 BLAU, Joseph L. "John Dewey and American Social Thought." *Tchr Col Rec*, LXI (1959), 121-127.

18 BODE, Boyd H. *Modern Educational Theories.* New York, 1927.†

19 BODE, Boyd H. *Progressive Education at the Crossroads.* New York, 1938.

20 BRICKMAN, William W. "Essentialism Ten Years After." *School Soc*, LXVII (1948), 361-365.

21 BRICKMAN, William W., and Stanley LEHRER, eds. *John Dewey: Master Educator.* New York, 1946.

1 CHAMBERS, Gurney. "Michael John Demiashkevich and the Essentialist Committee for the Advancement of American Education." *Hist Ed Q*, IX (1969), 46-56.

2 CHAMBLISS, Joseph J. *Boyd H. Bode's Philosophy of Education.* Columbus, Ohio, 1963.

3 CHILDS, John L. *American Pragmatism and Education: An Interpretation and Criticism.* New York, 1956.

4 CHILDS, John L. "Boyd H. Bode and the Experimentalists." *Tchr Col Rec*, LV (1953), 1-9.

5 CHILDS, John L. "Experimentalism and American Education." *Tchr Col Rec*, XLIV (1943), 539-543.

6 CHILDS, John L. "John Dewey and American Education." *Tchr Col Rec*, LXI (1959), 128-133.

7 CREMIN, Lawrence A. "John Dewey and the Progressive-Education Movement, 1915-1952." *School Rev*, LXVII (1959), 160-173.

8 DEWEY, John and Evelyn. *Schools of To-Morrow.* New York, 1915.†

9 DEWEY, John. *Democracy and Education.* New York, 1916.†

10 DEWEY, John. *Experience and Education.* New York, 1938.†

11 DWORKIN, Martin S., ed. *Dewey on Education.* New York, 1959.†

12 DYKHUIZEN, George. "John Dewey, the Vermont Years, 1859-1882." *J Hist Ideas*, XX (1959), 515-544.

13 DYKHUIZEN, George. "John Dewey and the University of Michigan, 1889-1904." *J Hist Ideas*, XXIII (1962), 513-544.

14 DYKHUIZEN, George. "John Dewey at Johns Hopkins, 1882-1884." *J Hist Ideas*, XXII (1961), 103-116.

15 FEUER, Lewis S. "John Dewey and the Back to the People Movement in American Thought." *J Hist Ideas*, XX (1959), 545-568.

16 FEUER, Lewis S. "John Dewey's Reading at College." *J Hist Ideas*, XIX (1958), 415-421.

17 FRANKEL, Charles. "John Dewey's Legacy." *Am Sch*, XXIX (1960), 313-331.

18 FRANKEL, Charles. "Appearance and Reality in Kilpatrick's Philosophy." *Tchr Col Rec*, LXVI (1965), 352-364.

19 GEIGER, George R. *John Dewey in Perspective.* New York, 1958.

20 GREENE, Maxine. "Dewey and American Education, 1894-1920." *School Soc*, LXXXVII (1959), 381-386.

21 GUTEK, Gerald L. *The Educational Theory of George S. Counts.* Columbus, Ohio, 1970.

22 HANDLIN, Oscar. *John Dewey's Challenge to Education: Historical Perspectives on the Cultural Context.* New York, 1959.

23 KILPATRICK, William H. "Dewey's Philosophy of Education." *Ed Forum*, XVII (1953), 143-154.

24 KILPATRICK, William H. *Foundations of Method: Informal Talks on Teaching.* New York, 1925.

1 KILPATRICK, William H. "The Philosophy of American Education." *Tchr Col Rec*, XXX (1928), 13-22.

2 "Letters of John Dewey to Robert V. Daniels, 1946-1950." *J Hist Ideas*, XX (1959), 569-576.

3 LILGE, Frederic. "John Dewey in Retrospect; An American Reconsideration." *Brit J Ed Stud*, VIII (1960), 99-111.

4 MC CAUL, Robert L. "Dewey and the University of Chicago." *School Soc*, LXXXIX (1961), 152-157, 179-183, 202-206.

5 MC CAUL, Robert L. "Dewey in College, 1875-1879." *School Rev*, LXX (1962), 437-456.

6 MC CAUL, Robert L. "Dewey's School Days, 1867-75." *El School J*, LXIII (1962), 15-21.

7 MILLER, Henry. "John Dewey on Urban Education: An Extrapolation." *Tchr Col Rec*, LXIX (1968), 771-783.

8 NEWLON, Jesse H. "John Dewey's Influence in the Schools." *Tchr Col Rec*, XXXI (1929), 224-238.

9 RATNER, Joseph, ed. *Intelligence in the Modern World: John Dewey's Philosophy*. New York, 1939.

10 RUSSELL, William F. "Philosophical Bases of Organization and Operation of American Schools: The Influence of American Ideals." *Tchr Col Rec*, L (1949), 221-231.

11 RUSSELL, William F. "Philosophical Bases of Organization and Operation of American Schools: The Influence of the New Psychology." *Tchr Col Rec*, L (1949), 386-395.

12 SOMJEE, A. H. *The Political Theory of John Dewey*. New York, 1968.

13 STEINBERG, Ira S. *Ralph Barton Perry on Education for Democracy*. Columbus, Ohio, 1970.

14 TENNEBAUM, Samuel. *William Heard Kilpatrick: Trail Blazer in Education*. New York, 1951.

15 WATSON, Goodwin. "John Dewey as a Pioneer in Social Psychology." *Tchr Col Rec*, LI (1949), 139-143.

16 WHITE, Morton G. *The Origin of Dewey's Instrumentalism*. New York, 1943.

17 WIRTH, Arthur G. *John Dewey as Educator: His Work in Education, 1894-1904*. New York, 1966.†

18 YENGO, Carmine A. "John Dewey and the Cult of Efficiency." *Har Ed Rev*, XXXIV (1964), 33-53.

See also 2.14, 10.15, 10.17, 94.10, 97.19, 110.14, 119.6.

6. *The Schools*

A. MINORITIES IN THE CLASSROOM – BOOKER T. WASHINGTON AND W. E. B. DU BOIS. SEGREGATION AND INTEGRATION

19 BENDER, William A. "Desegregation in the Public Schools of Mississippi." *J Neg Ed*, XXIV (1955), 287-292.

1   BILLINGTON, Monroe. "Public School Integration in Missouri, 1954-65." *J Neg Ed*, XXXV (1966), 252-262.

2   BLAUSTEIN, Albert P., and Clarence C. FERGUSON, Jr. *Desegregation and the Law: The Meaning and Effect of the School Segregation Cases*. 2d rev. ed. New Brunswick, 1962.†

3   BOND, Horace M. "Negro Education: A Debate in the Alabama Constitutional Convention of 1901." *J Neg Ed*, I (1932), 49-59.

4   BRODERICK, Francis L. "The Academic Training of W. E. B. Du Bois." *J Neg Ed*, XXVII (1958), 10-16.

5   CALISTA, Donald J. "Booker T. Washington: Another Look." *J Neg Hist*, XLIX (1964), 240-255.

6   CALVER, Ambrose. "Certain Significant Developments in the Education of Negroes During the Past Generation." *J Neg Hist*, XXXV (1950), 18-27.

7   CARMICHAEL, Omer, and Weldon JAMES. *The Louisville Story*. New York, 1957.

8   COX, Oliver C. "The Leadership of Booker T. Washington." *Social Forces*, XXX (1951), 91-97.

9   CURRY, J. L. M. *Education of Negroes Since 1860*. Baltimore, 1894.

10 DAVIS, Allison, and John DOLLARD. *Children of Bondage: The Personality Development of Negro Youth in the Urban South*. Washington, D.C., 1940.†

11 DAVIS, William R. *The Development and Present Status of Negro Education in East Texas*. New York, 1934. (Concerns years from the 1850s to 1932.)

12 DU BOIS, W. E. B. *The Autobiography of W. E. B. Du Bois*. New York, 1968.†

13 DU BOIS, W. E. B. *Black Reconstruction in America*. New York, 1935.†

14 DU BOIS, W. E. B. *Dusk of Dawn: An Essay Toward an Autobiography of a Race Concept*. New York, 1940.†

15 DU BOIS, W. E. B. *Mansart Builds a School*. New York, 1959.

16 DU BOIS, W. E. B. *The Ordeal of Mansart*. New York, 1957.

17 DU BOIS, W. E. B. *The Souls of Black Folk: Essays and Sketches*. Chicago, 1903.†

18 FARRISON, W. Edward. "Booker T. Washington: A Study in Educational Leadership." *S Atl Q*, XLI (1942), 313-319.

19 GATES, Robbins L. *The Making of Massive Resistance*. Chapel Hill, 1964.

20 HARLAN, Louis R. *Separate and Unequal: Public School Campaigns in the Southern Seaboard States, 1901-1915*. Chapel Hill, 1958.†

21 HARLAN, Louis R. "Booker T. Washington and the White Man's Burden." *Am Hist Rev*, LXXI (1966), 441-467.

22 HARLAN, Louis R. "Booker T. Washington in Biographical Perspective." *Am Hist Rev*, LXXV (1970), 1581-1599.

23 HORTON, Aimee. "The Highlander Folk School: Pioneer of Integration in the South." *Tchr Col Rec*, LXVIII (1966), 242-250.

24 JONES, Lewis W. "Desegregation of Public Education in Alabama." *J Neg Ed*, XXIV (1955), 165-171.

1 JONES, Lewis W. "Two Years of Desegregation in Alabama." *J Neg Ed*, XXV (1956), 205-211.

2 JONES, Thomas J. *Recent Progress in Negro Education.* U S Bur Ed Bull 1919, no. 27. Washington, D.C., 1919.

3 KEPPEL, Ann M., and James I. CLARK. "James H. Stout and the Menomonie Schools." *Wis Mag Hist*, XLII (1959), 200-210.

4 LANE, Russell A. "Legal Trends Toward Increased Provisions for Negro Education in the United States Between 1920 and 1940." *J Neg Ed*, I (1932), 396-399.

5 LOGAN, Frenise A. "Legal Status of Public School Education for Negroes in North Carolina, 1877-1894." *N C Hist Rev*, XXXII (1955), 346-357.

6 MC PHERSON, James M. "White Liberals and Black Power in Negro Education, 1865-1915." *Am Hist Rev*, LXXV (1970), 1357-1386.

7 MATHEWS, Basil J. *Booker T. Washington: Educator and Interracial Interpreter.* Cambridge, Mass., 1948; College Park, Md., 1969.

8 MAYO, Amory D. "The Work of Certain Northern Churches in the Education of the Freedmen, 1861-1900." *U S Bur Ed, Rep Comm 1902.* Vol. I. Washington, D.C., 1903, pp. 285-314.

9 MEIER, August, and Elliott M. RUDWICK. "Early Boycotts of Segregated Schools: The Alton, Illinois Case, 1897-1908." *J Neg Ed*, XXXVI (1967), 394-402.

10 MEIER, August, and Elliott M. RUDWICK. "Early Boycotts of Segregated Schools: The East Orange, New Jersey, Experience, 1899-1906." *Hist Ed Q*, VII (1967), 22-35.

11 MILLER, Arthur S. *Racial Discrimination and Private Education: A Legal Analysis.* Chapel Hill, 1957.

12 MILLER, Carroll L. "Trends in Negro Education from 1930 to 1939 and Prospects for the 1940s." *J Neg Ed*, X (1941), 280-293.

13 MILLER, Kelly. "Forty Years of Negro Education." *Ed Rev*, XXXVI (1908), 484-498.

14 NOBLE, Stuart G. *Forty Years of the Public Schools in Mississippi, with Special Reference to the Education of the Negro.* New York, 1918.

15 ORFIELD, Gary. *The Reconstruction of Southern Education: The Schools and the 1964 Civil Rights Act.* New York, 1969.

16 PHILLIPS, Myrtle R. "Origin, Development, and Present Status of Public Secondary Education for Negroes in Kentucky." *J Neg Ed*, I (1932), 414-423.

17 PIERCE, Truman M., et al. *White and Negro Schools in the South: An Analysis of Biracial Education.* Englewood Cliffs, N.J., 1955.

18 PRESTON, E. Delorus, Jr. "William Syphax, a Pioneer in Negro Education in the District of Columbia." *J Neg Hist*, XX (1935), 448-476.

19 RECORD, Wilson and Jane C., eds. *Little Rock, U.S.A.* San Francisco, 1960.†

20 REDCAY, Edward E. "Pioneering in Negro Education." *J Negro Ed*, VI (1937), 38-53.

1 REDDICK, L. D. "The Education of Negroes in States Where Separate Schools Are Not Legal." *J Neg Ed*, XVI (1947), 290-300.

2 REID, Herbert O. "The Supreme Court Decision and Interposition." *J Neg Ed*, XXV (1956), 109-117.

3 ROBBINS, Gerald. "Rossa B. Cooley and Penn School: Social Dynamo in a Negro Rural Subculture, 1901-1930." *J Neg Ed*, XXXIII (1964), 43-51.

4 RUDWICK, Elliott M. "W. E. B. Du Bois and the Atlanta University Studies on the Negro." *J Neg Ed*, XXVI (1957), 466-476.

5 RUDWICK, Elliott M. *W. E. B. Du Bois, Propagandist of the Negro Protest.* New York, 1968.†

6 RUDWICK, Elliott, and August MEIER. "Early Boycotts of Segregated Schools: The Case of Springfield, Ohio, 1922-23." *Am Q*, XX(1968), 744-758.

7 SAVAGE, W. Sherman. "Legal Provision for Negro Schools in Missouri, 1865-1890." *J Neg Hist*, XVI (1931), 309-321.

8 SCOTT, Emmett J. "Twenty Years After: An Appraisal of Booker T. Washington." *J Neg Ed*, V (1936), 543-554.

9 SISK, Glenn. "Educational Awakening in Alabama and Its Effect upon the Black Belt, 1900-1917." *J Neg Ed*, XXV (1956), 191-196.

10 SISK, Glenn. "Negro Education in the Alabama Black Belt, 1875-1900." *J Neg Ed*, XXII (1953), 126-135.

11 SPENCER, Samuel R., Jr. *Booker T. Washington and the Negro's Place in American Life.* Boston, 1955.†

12 SUTTON, W. S. "The Contribution of Booker T. Washington to the Education of the Negro." *School Soc*, IV (1916), 457-463.

13 TERRELL, Mary C. "The History of the High Schools for Negroes in Washington." *J Neg Hist*, II (1917), 252-266.

14 THORNBROUGH, Emma Lou, ed. *Booker T. Washington.* Englewood Cliffs, N.J., 1969.†

15 THRASHER, Max B. *Tuskegee: Its Story and Its Work.* Boston, 1901.

16 TOPPIN, Edgar A. "Walter White and the Atlanta NAACP's Fight for Equal Schools." *Hist Ed Q*, VII (1967), 3-21.

17 WASHINGTON, Booker T. *Character Building: Being Addresses Delivered on Sunday Evenings to the Students of Tuskegee Institute.* New York, 1902.

18 WASHINGTON, Booker T. *Education of the Negro.* Butler, N.M., 1900.

19 WASHINGTON, Booker T. *My Larger Education: Being Chapters from My Experience.* New York, 1911.

20 WASHINGTON, Booker T. *Tuskeegee and Its People: Their Ideals and Achievements.* New York, 1905.

21 WASHINGTON, Booker T. *Up From Slavery; An Autobiography.* New York, 1901.†

22 WASHINGTON, Booker T. *Working with the Hands.* New York, 1904.

1 WASHINGTON, E. Davidson, ed. *Selected Speeches of Booker T. Washington.* Garden City, N.Y., 1932.

2 WEINBERG, Meyer, ed. *W. E. B. Du Bois: A Reader.* New York, 1970.

3 WINTON, Ruth M. "Negro Participation in Southern Expositions, 1881-1915." *J Neg Ed*, XVI (1947), 34-43.

4 WISH, Harvey. "Negro Education and the Progressive Movement." *J Neg Hist*, XLIX (1964), 184-200.

5 WOODSON, Carter G. "Early Negro Education in West Virginia." *J Neg Hist*, VII (1922), 23-63.

6 WOODSON, Carter G. "Negro Life and History as Presented in the Schools." *J Neg Hist*, IV (1919), 273-280.

See also 4.8, 4.18, 20.7, 74.14, 87.3, 87.5, 87.18, 90.4.

B. YOUTH AND THE DEPRESSION DECADE OF THE 1930s

7 American Council on Education. *Youth and the Future: The General Report of the American Youth Commission.* Washington, D.C., 1942.

8 BEALE, Howard K. *Are American Teachers Free? An Analysis of Restraints upon the Freedom of Teaching in American Schools.* New York, 1936.

9 BELL, Howard M. *Youth Tell Their Story.* Washington, D.C., 1938.

10 BOWERS, C. A. "Social Reconstructionism: Views from the Left and the Right, 1932-1942." *Hist Ed Q*, X (1970), 22-52.

11 BOWERS, C. A. *The Progressive Educator and the Depression: The Radical Years.* New York, 1969.†

12 BOWERS, C. A. "The *Social Frontier* Journal: A Historical Sketch." *Hist Ed Q*, IV (1964), 167-180.

13 "C. C. C. Camp Educational Activities." *U S Bur Ed, Rep Comm 1940.* Washington, D.C., 1940, pp. 73-85.

14 CAMPBELL, Doak S., Frederick H. BAIR, and Oswald L. HARVEY. *Educational Activities of the Works Progress Administration.* Washington, D.C., 1939.

15 COUNTS, George S. *Dare the School Build a New Social Order?* New York, 1932.

16 Educational Policies Commission. *Federal Activities in Education.* Washington, D.C., 1939.

17 Educational Policies Commission. *The Purposes of Education in American Democracy.* Washington, D.C., 1938.

18 Educational Policies Commission. *Research Memorandum on Education in the Depression.* Social Science Research Council Bull 28, 1937. New York, 1937.

19 Educational Policies Commission. *The Unique Function of Education in American Democracy.* Washington, D.C., 1937.

20 GOWER, Calvin W. "The Civilian Conservation Corps and American Education: Threat to Local Control." *Hist Ed Q*, VII (1967), 58-70.

1 HOLLAND, Kenneth, and Frank E. HILL. *Youth in the CCC*. Washington, D.C., 1942.

2 JOHNSON, Palmer O., and Oswald L. HARVEY. *The National Youth Administration*. Washington, D.C., 1938.

3 JONES, Harold E., et al. *Adolescence*. 43rd *Yrbk Nat Soc Stud Ed*. Pt. I. Bloomington, Ill., 1944.

4 KATZ, Michael B. "American History Textbooks and Social Reform in the 1930s." *Pae Hist*, VI (1966), 143-160.

5 KILPATRICK, William H. *Education and the Social Crisis: A Proposed Program*. New York, 1932.

6 LINDLEY, Betty G. and Ernest K. *A New Deal for Youth: The Story of the National Youth Administration*. New York, 1938.

7 LORWIN, Lewis L. *Youth Work Programs: Problems and Policies*. Washington, D.C., 1941.

8 NORTON, John K. "The Civilian Conservation Corps, The National Youth Administration, and the Public Schools." *Tchr Col Rec*, XLIII (1941), 174-182.

9 RIPPA, S. Alexander. "The Business Community and the Public Schools on the Eve of the Great Depression." *Hist Ed Q*, IV (1964), 33-43.

10 RIPPA, S. Alexander. "Retrenchment in a Period of Defensive Opposition to the New Deal: The Business Community and the Public Schools, 1932-1934." *Hist Ed Q*, II (1962), 76-82.

11 RUGG, Harold O. *American Life and the School Curriculum: Next Steps Toward Schools of Living*. Boston, 1936.

12 RUSSELL, William F. "Liberty and Learning: A Discussion of Education and the New Deal." *Tchr Col Rec*, XXXV (1933), 89-103.

13 SPIVACK, Robert G. "Growth of an American Youth Movement 1905-1941." *Am Sch*, X (1941), 352-361.

14 SUPER, Donald E., and Robert D. WRIGHT. "From School To Work in the Depression Years." *School Rev*, XLIX (1941), 17-26, 123-130.

See also 1.10, 2.5, 18.10, 27.16, 28.9, 29.19, 30.1, 48.8.

C. FROM LIFE ADJUSTMENT TO THE NEW TRADITIONALISM – THE 1940s AND 1950s

15 ALLEN, Mary L. *Education or Indoctrination*. Caldwell, Idaho, 1955.

16 BELL, Bernard I. *Crisis in Education*. New York, 1949.

17 BESTOR, Arthur E. *Educational Wastelands*. Urbana, Ill., 1953.

18 BESTOR, Arthur E. *The Restoration of Learning*. New York, 1955.

19 BRAMELD, Theodore B., ed. *The Battle for Free Schools*. Boston, 1951.

20 CALITRI, Charles J. *Strike Heaven on the Face: A Novel*. New York, 1958.

21 CONANT, James B. *The Child, the Parent, and the State*. Cambridge, Mass., 1959.†

22 COUNTS, George S. *Education and American Civilization*. New York, 1952.

1   COUNTS, George S. "The Need for a Great Education." *Tchr Col Rec*, LIII (1951), 77-88.

2   CREMIN, Lawrence A. "Toward a More Common Common School." *Tchr Col Rec*, LI (1950), 308-319.

3   DOUGLASS, Harl R. *Secondary Education for Life Adjustment of American Youth.* New York, 1952.

4   DRAKE, William E. *The American School in Transition.* Englewood Cliffs, N.J., 1955.

5   Educational Policies Commission. *Education for All American Youth.* Washington, D.C., 1944.

6   Educational Policies Commission. *Education for All American Youth: A Further Look.* Rev. ed., Washington, D.C., 1952.

7   Educational Policies Commission. *The Education of Free Men in American Democracy.* Washington, D.C., 1941.

8   Educational Policies Commission. *Policies for Education in American Democracy.* Washington, D.C., 1946.

9   First Commission on Life Adjustment Education. *Vitalizing Secondary Education.* U S Off Ed Bull 1951, no. 3. Washington, D.C., 1951.

10   FRIEDENBERG, Edgar Z. *The Vanishing Adolescent.* Boston, 1959.†

11   GARDNER, John W. *Excellence: Can We Be Equal and Excellent Too?* New York, 1961.†

12   GROSS, Neal. *Who Runs Our Schools?* New York, 1958.

13   HOLLINGSHEAD, August B. *Elmtown's Youth: The Impact of Social Classes on Adolescents.* New York, 1949.†

14   HUNT, De Witt. *Work Experience Education Programs in American Secondary Schools.* U S Dept HEW Bull 1957, no. 5. Washington, D.C., 1957.

15   HUNTER, Evan. *Blackboard Jungle: A Novel.* New York, 1954.†

16   HUTCHINS, Robert M. *The Conflict in Education in a Democratic Society.* New York, 1953.

17   KANDEL, Isaac L. *The Impact of the War upon American Education.* Chapel Hill, 1948.

18   KOERNER, James D., ed. *The Case for Basic Education.* Boston, 1959.

19   LANSNER, Kermit, ed. *Second-Rate Brains.* New York, 1958.

20   LATIMER, John F. *What's Happened to Our High Schools?* Washington, D.C., 1958.

21   *Life Adjustment Education for Every Youth.* U S Off Ed Bull 1951, no. 22. Washington, D.C., 1953.

22   LYND, Albert. *Quackery in the Public Schools.* Boston, 1953.†

23   MC GRATH, Earl J. "Sputnik and American Education." *Tchr Col Rec*, LIX (1958), 379-395.

24   MANGHAM, Iain. "Education for Autonomy: Some Comments on the Educational Thought of David Riesman." *Brit J Ed Stud*, XV (1957), 40-50.

25   MEHL, Bernard. "The Conant Report and the Committee of Ten: A Historical Appraisal." *Ed Res Bull*, XXXIX (1960), 29-38, 56.

1 MILLER, Richard L. "Admiral Rickover on American Education." *J Tchr Ed*, X (1959), 332-357.

2 NORTON, John K. "The Role of Education in a Period of Mobilization." *Tchr Col Rec*, LII (1950), 137-144.

3 PROSSER, Charles A. *Secondary Education and Life.* Cambridge, Mass., 1939.

4 REDEFER, Frederick L. "What Has Happened to Progressive Education?" *School Soc*, LXVII (1948), 345-349.

5 RICKOVER, Hyman G. *Education and Freedom.* New York, 1959.†

6 RIESMAN, David. *Constraint and Variety in American Education.* Garden City, N.Y., 1958.†

7 RIPPA, S. Alexander. "The Textbook Controversy and the Free Enterprise Campaign, 1940-1941." *Hist Ed J*, IX (1958), 49-58.

8 SCOTT, G. Winfield, and Clyde M. HILL, eds. *Public Education under Criticism.* Englewood Cliffs, N.J., 1954.

9 SCOTT, C. Winfield, Clyde M. HILL, and Hobert W. BURNS, eds. *The Great Debate: Our Schools in Crisis.* Englewood Cliffs, N.J., 1959.†

10 SEELEY, John R., et al. *Crestwood Heights: A Study of the Culture of Suburban Life.* New York, 1956.†

11 SMITH, Mortimer B. *And Madly Teach.* Chicago, 1949.

12 SMITH, Mortimer B. *The Diminished Mind: A Study of Planned Mediocrity in Our Public Schools.* Chicago, 1954.

13 SMITH, Mortimer B., ed. *The Public Schools in Crisis: Some Critical Essays.* Chicago, 1956.

14 STINNETT, T. M., ed. "A Symposium: Educationists and Other Academics." *J Tchr Ed*, X (1959), 157-210.

15 THAYER, Vivian T. *Public Education and Its Critics.* New York, 1954.

16 TYLER, Ralph W., et al. *American Education in the Postwar Period.* 44th *Yrbk Nat Soc Stud Ed*. Pts. I and II. Chicago, 1945.†

17 WARNER, W. Lloyd, Robert J. HAVIGHURST, and Martin B. LOEB. *Who Shall Be Educated? The Challenge of Unequal Opportunities.* New York, 1944.

18 WOODRING, Paul. *A Fourth of a Nation.* New York, 1957.

19 WOODRING, Paul. *Let's Talk Sense About Our Schools.* New York, 1953.

See also 26.16, 27.6, 27.7, 28.9.

D. THE CRISIS OF THE 1960s

20 ALLPORT, Gordon W. "Values and Our Youth." *Tchr Col Rec*, LXIII (1961), 211-219.

21 ALSOP, Joseph, et al. *Ghetto Schools: Problems and Panaceas.* New York, 1968.

22 BERUBE, Maurice R., and Marilyn GITTELL, eds. *Confrontation at Ocean Hill-Brownsville: The New York School Strikes of 1968.* New York, 1969.†

1 BRUNER, Jerome S. *The Process of Education.* Cambridge, Mass., 1960.†

2 CHANDLER, B.J., Lindley J. STILES, and John I. KITSUSE, eds. *Education in Urban Society.* New York, 1962.†

3 COHEN, David R. "Jurists and Educators on Urban Schools: The Wright Decision and the Passow Report." *Tchr Col Rec,* LXX (1968), 233-245. (On Negro education in Washington, D.C.)

4 COLEMAN, James S. *Adolescent Society.* Glencoe, Ill., 1969.

5 COLEMAN, James S., and Ernest Q. CAMPBELL. *Equality of Educational Opportunity.* Washington, D.C., 1966.

6 CONANT, James B. *Shaping Educational Policy.* New York, 1964.†

7 CONANT, James B. *Slums and Suburbs.* New York, 1961.†

8 CRAIN, Robert L. *The Politics of School Desegregation.* New York, 1968.

9 DEXTER, Lewis A. *The Tyranny of Schooling.* New York, 1964.

10 FRIEDENBERG, Edgar Z. *Coming of Age in America: Growth and Acquiescence.* New York, 1965.†

11 FRIEDENBERG, Edgar Z., ed. *The Anti-American Generation.* Chicago, 1970.

12 GINZBERG, Eli, ed. *The Nation's Children.* New York, 1960. (Committee on Studies for the Golden Anniversary White House Conference for Children and Youth.)

13 GINZBERG, Eli, ed. *Values and Ideals of American Youth.* New York, 1961.

14 GOODLAD, John I., et al. *The Changing American School.* 65th *Yrbk Nat Soc Stud Ed.* Pt. II. Chicago, 1966.

15 GOODMAN, Paul. *Compulsory Mis-Education and the Community of Scholars.* New York, 1966.†

16 HOLT, John C. *How Children Fail.* New York, 1964.†

17 HOLT, John C. *How Children Learn.* New York, 1967.†

18 HOLT, John C. *The Underachieving School.* New York, 1969.

19 JENCKS, Christopher. "The Future of American Education." *The Radical Papers.* Ed. by Irving Howe. New York, 1966.†

20 KERBER, August, and Barbara BOMMARITO, eds. *The Schools and the Urban Crisis: A Book of Readings.* New York, 1965.†

21 LEVINE, Daniel U. "The Integration-Compensatory Education Controversy." *Ed Forum,* XXXII (1968), 323-332.

22 LIEBERMAN, Myron. *The Future of Public Education.* Chicago, 1960.†

23 MAYER, Martin P. *The Schools.* New York, 1961.

24 MAYER, Martin P. *The Teachers Strike, New York, 1968.* New York, 1969.

25 MEAD, Margaret. *The School in American Culture.* Cambridge, Mass., 1964.

26 PASSOW, A. Harry. *Toward Creating a Model Urban School System: A Study of the Washington, D.C., Public Schools.* New York, 1967.

1 PEREL, William M., and Philip D. VAIRO. *Urban Education: Problems and Prospects.* New York, 1969.

2 POSTMAN, Neil, and Charles WEINGARTNER. *Teaching as a Subversive Activity.* New York, 1969.

3 RICKOVER, Hyman G. *American Education–A National Failure: The Problems of Our Schools and What We Can Learn from England.* New York, 1963.†

4 RICKOVER, Hyman G. *Swiss Schools and Ours: Why Theirs Are Better.* Boston, 1962.

5 ROGERS, David. *110 Livingston Street: Politics and Bureaucracy in the New York City Schools.* New York, 1968.†

6 ROSENTHAL, Robert, and Lenore JACOBSON. *Pygmalion in the Classroom: Teacher Expectation and Pupils' Intellectual Development.* New York, 1968.

7 SILBERMAN, Charles E. *Crisis in the Classroom.* New York, 1970.†

8 STINCHCOMBE, Arthur L. *Rebellion in a High School.* Chicago, 1964.†

9 STREET, David, ed. *Innovation in Mass Education.* New York, 1969.

10 THAYER, V. T., and Martin LEVIT. *The Role of the School in American Society.* 2d ed. New York, 1966.

11 TYLER, Ralph W., et al. *Social Forces Influencing American Education.* 60th *Yrbk Nat Soc Stud Ed.* Pt. II. Chicago, 1961.

12 VAN PATTEN, James. "Search for Substance in Conant's Educational Writings." *J Tchr Ed,* XVI (1965), 193-201.

13 WATTENBERG, William W., ed. *Social Deviancy Among Youth.* 65th *Yrbk Nat Soc Stud Ed.* Pt. I. Chicago, 1966.

14 WIRTH, Arthur G. "The Deweyan Tradition Revisited: Any Relevance for Our Time?" *Tchr Col Rec,* LXIX (1967), 265-269.

15 WISE, Arthur E. *Rich Schools, Poor Schools: The Promise of Equal Educational Opportunity.* Chicago, 1969.

16 WOODRING, Paul, and John SCANLON, eds. *American Education Today.* New York, 1963.†

See also 19.12, 20.10, 27.8, 27.17, 29.13.

7. Higher Education

A. GENERAL WORKS AND BIOGRAPHIES

17 ADAMS, Henry. *The Education of Henry Adams.* Boston, 1918.†

18 ANGELL, James B. *The Reminiscences of James B. Angell.* New York, 1912.

19 ANGELL, James B. "University Education in the United States." *Proc Am Philos Soc,* LXVI (1927), 645-654.

20 BALDWIN, James M. *Between Two Wars.* Boston, 1926.

1 BASKIN, Samuel, ed. *Higher Education: Some Newer Developments*. New York, 1965.

2 BECKER, Carl. "The Cornell Tradition: Freedom and Responsibility." *Bull Am Assn Univ Prof*, XXVI (1940), 509-522.

3 BEN-DAVID, Joseph, and Abraham ZLOCOWER. "Universities and Academic Systems in Modern Societies." *European Journal of Sociology*, III (1962), 45-84.

4 BERMAN, Milton. *John Fiske: The Evolution of a Popularizer*. Cambridge, Mass., 1961.

5 BOWMAN, Claude C. *The College Professor in America: An Analysis of Articles Published in the General Magazines, 1890-1938*. Philadelphia, 1938.

6 BRAGDON, Henry W. *Woodrow Wilson: The Academic Years*. Cambridge, Mass., 1967.

7 BURGESS, John W. *Reminiscences of an American Scholar: The Beginnings of Columbia University*. New York, 1934.

8 BURNS, Edward M. *David Starr Jordan*. Stanford, 1953.

9 BURRIN, Frank K. *Edward Charles Elliott, Educator*. Purdue, Ill., 1970.

10 BUTLER, Nicholas M. *Across the Busy Years; Recollections and Reflections*. 2 vols. New York, 1939-1940.

11 CAPLOW, Theodore, and Reece J. MC GEE. *The Academic Marketplace*. New York, 1958.†

12 CHUGERMAN, Samuel. *Lester F. Ward, the American Aristotle: A Summary and Interpretation of His Sociology*. New York, 1939.

13 COMMONS, John R. *Myself*. New York, 1934.†

14 COMPAYRE, Gabriel. "Higher and Secondary Education in the United States." *U S Bur Ed, Rep Comm 1895-1896*. Vol. II. Washington, D.C., 1897, pp. 1153-1174.

15 CONANT, James B. *My Several Lives: Memoirs of a Social Inventor*. New York, 1970.

16 CURTI, Merle, ed. *American Scholarship in the Twentieth Century*. Cambridge, Mass., 1953.

17 DEVANE, William C. *The American University in the Twentieth Century*. Baton Rouge, 1957.

18 DEVANE, William C. *Higher Education in Twentieth Century America*. Cambridge, Mass., 1965.

19 DUPREE, A. Hunter. *Asa Gray, 1810-1888*. Cambridge, Mass., 1959.

20 EELLS, Walter C. "The Early History of Sabbatical Leave." *Bull Am Assn Univ Prof*, XLVIII (1962), 253-256.

21 ELY, Richard T. *Ground Under Our Feet: An Autobiography*. New York, 1938.

22 FLEXNER, Abraham. *I Remember: The Autobiography of Abraham Flexner*. New York, 1940.

23 FLEXNER, Abraham. *Universities: American, English, German*. New York, 1930.†

1 GETMAN, Frederick H. *The Life of Ira Remsen.* Easton, Pa., 1940.

2 GUSTAD, John W. "They March to a Different Drummer: Another Look at College Teachers." *Ed Rec*, XL (1959), 204-212.

3 HALL, G. Stanley. *Life and Confessions of a Psychologist.* New York, 1923.

4 HARRIS, Michael R. *Five Counterrevolutionists in Higher Education.* Corvallis, Ore., 1970. (Concerns I. Babbitt, A. J. Nock, A. Flexner, R. M. Hutchins, A. Meiklejohn).

5 HARTSHORNE, E. Y. "Growth and Metabolism in the Harvard Faculty of Arts and Sciences, 1920-1940." *Har Ed Rev*, XII (1942), 143-164.

6 HOLDER, Rose H. *McIver of North Carolina.* Chapel Hill, 1957.

7 JENCKS, Christopher, and David RIESMAN. *The Academic Revolution.* Garden City, N.Y., 1968.†

8 JOHNSON, Henry. *The Other Side of Main Street.* New York, 1943.

9 JORDAN, David S. *The Days of a Man: Being Memories of a Naturalist, Teacher and Minor Prophet of Democracy.* 2 vols. New York, 1922.

10 JORDAN, David S. *The Trend of the American University.* Stanford, 1929.

11 KNAPP, Robert H. *The Origins of American Humanistic Scholars.* Englewood Cliffs, N.J., 1964.

12 KNAPP, Robert H., and H. B. GOODRICH. *The Origins of American Scientists.* Chicago, 1952.

13 KNAPP, Robert H., and Joseph J. GREENBAUM. *The Younger American Scholar: His Collegiate Origins.* Chicago, 1953.

14 LELAND, Waldo G. "The American Council of Learned Societies and Its Relation to Humanistic Studies." *Proc Am Philos Soc*, LXXI (1932), 179-189.

15 LURIE, Edward. *Louis Agassiz: A Life in Science.* Chicago, 1960.†

16 MILLER, Douglas T. "The Transformation of Higher Education in America, 1865-1875, as Reflected in *The Nation.*" *Ed Theory*, XI (1961), 186-192.

17 NEWCOMB, Simon. *The Reminiscences of an Astronomer.* Boston, 1903.

18 O'TOOLE, Simon. *Confessions of an American Scholar.* Minneapolis, 1970.†

19 PEABODY, Francis G. *Reminiscences of Present-Day Saints.* Boston, 1927.

20 PERRY, Bliss. *And Gladly Teach.* Boston, 1935.

21 PERRY, Ralph B. *The Thought and Character of William James as Revealed in Unpublished Correspondence and Notes Together with His Published Writings.* 2 vols. Boston, 1935.

22 PRUETTE, Lorine. *G. Stanley Hall: A Biography of a Mind.* New York, 1926.

23 RADER, Benjamin G. *The Academic Mind and Reform: The Influence of Richard T. Ely in American Life.* Louisville, Ky., 1966.

24 ROGERS, Walter P. *Andrew D. White and the Modern University.* Ithaca, N.Y., 1942.

1   ROSS, Edward A. *Seventy Years of It: An Autobiography.* New York, 1936.

2   ROUSMANIERE, John P. "Cultural Hybrid in the Slums: The College Woman and the Settlement House, 1889-1894." *Am Q*, XXII (1970), 45-66.

3   RUDY, S. Willis. "The 'Revolution' in American Higher Education: 1865-1900." *Har Ed Rev*, XXI (1951), 155-174.

4   SIHLER, Ernest G. *From Maumee to Thames and Tiber: The Life-Story of an American Classical Scholar.* New York, 1930.

5   SMITH, Shirley W. *James Burrill Angell: An American Influence.* Ann Arbor, 1954.

6   SOLBERG, Winton U. "The Conflict Between Religion and Secularism at the University of Illinois, 1867-1894." *Am Q*, XVIII (1966), 183-199.

7   VANDERBILT, Kermit. *Charles Eliot Norton: Apostle of Culture in a Democracy.* Cambridge, Mass., 1959.

8   VEBLEN, Thorstein. *The Higher Learning in America: A Memorandum on the Conduct of Universities by Business Men.* New York, 1918.†

9   VEYSEY, Laurence R. *The Emergence of the American University.* Chicago, 1965.†

10 WHITE, Andrew D. *Autobiography.* 2 vols. New York, 1904-1905.

11 WHITE, Morton G. "The Revolt Against Formalism in American Social Thought of the Twentieth Century." *J Hist Ideas*, VIII (1947), 131-152.

12 WHITE, Morton G. *Social Thought in America: The Revolt Against Formalism.* With a new Preface and an Epilogue. Boston, 1957.†

13 WIENER, Philip P. *Evolution and the Founders of Pragmatism.* Cambridge, Mass., 1949.

14 WILBUR, Ray L. *The Memoirs of Ray Lyman Wilbur.* Stanford, 1960.

15 YEOMANS, Henry A. *Abbott Lawrence Lowell, 1856-1943.* Cambridge, Mass., 1948.

    See also 1.12, 13.14, 14.7, 28.15, 31.5, 31.11, 42.3, 43.12, 44.12, 47.1, 48.1, 114.3, 114.6, 114.12, 114.15, 115.13, 115.21, 116.17, 117.2, 117.3, 118.8, 118.12, 118.14, 119.2, 119.3, 120.6, 120.12, 120.24, 121.2.

B. THE TRADITIONAL LIBERAL ARTS COLLEGE

16 BARNARD, John. *From Evangelicalism to Progressivism at Oberlin College, 1866-1917.* Columbus, Ohio, 1969.

17 BARNES, Sherman B. "The Entry of Science and History in the College Curriculum, 1865-1914." *Hist Ed Q*, IV (1964), 44-58.

18 BARNES, Sherman B. "Learning and Piety in Ohio Colleges, 1865-1900." *Ohio Hist Q*, LXIX (1960), 327-352.

19 BARNES, Sherman B. "Learning and Piety in Ohio Colleges, 1900-1930." *Ohio Hist Q*, LXX (1961), 214-244.

1   CHURCHILL, Alfred V. "Oberlin Students, Sinners, and Adolescents in the 1870s and 1880s." *N W Ohio Q*, XXV (1952-1953), 41-71.

2   DANIEL, W. Harrison. "Southern Baptists and Education, 1865-1900: A Case Study." *Md Hist Mag*, LXIV (1969), 218-247.

3   FULTON, John. *Memoirs of Frederick A. P. Barnard: Tenth President of Columbia College in the City of New York.* New York, 1896.

4   GETTLEMAN, Marvin E. "College President on the Prairie: John H. Finley and Knox College in the 1890s." *Hist Ed Q*, IX (1969), 129-153.

5   LE DUC, Thomas. *Piety and Intellect at Amherst College, 1865-1912.* New York, 1946.

6   LOVE, Donald M. *Henry Churchill King of Oberlin.* New Haven, 1956.

7   PETERSON, George E. *The New England College in the Age of the University.* Amherst, 1964.

8   PORTER, Noah. *The American Colleges and the American Public.* New ed. New York, 1878.

9   RUSSELL, William F., ed. *The Rise of a University: The Later Days of Old Columbia College. (From the Annual Reports of Frederick A. P. Barnard, President of Columbia College, 1864-1889.)* New York, 1937.

10 TUCKER, William J. "Administrative Problems of the Historic College." *Ed Rev*, XLIII (1912), 433-448.

    See also 11.10, 33.5, 35.2, 35.3, 35.14, 35.18, 38.16, 38.18, 38.19, 39.5, 39.10, 39.11, 39.21, 43.3, 43.4, 43.11, 43.15-17, 44.11, 47.7, 59.14, 122.19.

C. LAND GRANT AND STATE UNIVERSITIES

11 ANDREWS, Benjamin F. *The Land Grant of 1862 and the Land-Grant Colleges.* U S Bur Ed Bull 1918, no. 13. Washington, D.C., 1918.

12 BEARDSLEY, Edward H. *Harry L. Russell and Agricultural Science in Wisconsin.* Madison, 1969.

13 BROWN, Elmer E. *The Origin of American State Universities.* Berkeley, 1903.

14 BRUNNER, Henry S. *Land-Grant Colleges and Universities, 1862-1962.* U S Off Ed Bull 1962, no. 13. Washington, D.C., 1962.

15 CARRIEL, Mary T. *The Life of Jonathan Baldwin Turner.* Urbana, Ill., 1961.

16 CARSTENSEN, Vernon. "The University as Head of the Iowa Public School System." *Iowa J Hist*, LIII (1955), 213-246.

17 COFFMAN, Lotus D. *The State University: Its Work and Problems.* Minneapolis, 1934.

18 EDDY, Edward D., Jr. *Colleges for Our Land and Time: The Land-Grant Idea in American Education.* New York, 1956.

19 EVJEN, Harry. "Illinois State University, 1852-1868." *J Ill St Hist Soc*, XXXI (1938), 54-71.

1 *Federal Laws and Rulings Relating to Morrill and Supplementary Morrill Funds for Land-Grant Colleges and Universities.* U S Off Ed Pam, no. 91. Washington, D.C., 1940.

2 FLORER, John H. "Major Issues in the Congressional Debate of the Morrill Act of 1862." *Hist Ed Q*, VIII (1968), 459-478.

3 FOERSTER, Norman. *The American State University: Its Relation to Democracy.* Chapel Hill, 1937.

4 GARRISON, George P. "The First Twenty-Five Years of the University of Texas." *SW Hist Q*, LX (1956), 106-117.

5 GATES, Paul W. "Western Opposition to the Agricultural College Act." *Ind Mag Hist*, XXXVII (1941), 103-136.

6 GATES, Paul W. *The Wisconsin Pine Lands of Cornell University.* Ithaca, N.Y., 1943.

7 GEIGER, Louis G. *Higher Education in a Maturing Democracy.* Lincoln, Neb., 1963.

8 GLOVER, Wilbur H. "The Agricultural College Crisis of 1885." *Wis Mag Hist*, XXXII (1948), 17-25.

9 GOING, Allen J. "The South and the Blair Education Bill." *Miss Val Hist Rev*, LXIV (1957), 267-291.

10 HATCH, Richard A., ed. *An Early View of the Land-Grant Colleges: Convention of Friends of Agricultural Education in 1871.* Urbana, Ill., 1967. (Published for the Committee on the Centennial of the University of Illinois.)

11 HATCH, Richard A., ed. *Some Founding Papers of the University of Illinois.* Urbana, Ill., 1967.

12 JAMES, Edmund J. *The Origin of the Land Grant Act of 1862 (The So-Called Morrill Act) and Some Account of Its Author, Jonathan B. Turner.* Urbana, Ill., 1910.

13 KERSEY, Harry A., Jr. *John Milton Gregory and the University of Illinois.* Urbana, Ill., 1968.

14 KNOBLAUCH, H. C., E. M. LAW, W. P. MEYER et al. *State Agricultural Experiment Stations: A History of Research Policy and Procedure.* U S D A Misc. Pub., No. 904. Washington, D.C., 1962.

15 LEE, Gordon C. "The Morrill Act and Education." *Brit J Ed Stud*, XII (1963), 19-40.

16 MC CARTHY, Charles. *The Wisconsin Idea.* New York, 1912.

17 MARTIN, Asa E. "Pennsylvania's Land Grant Under the Morrill Act of 1862." *Pa Hist*, IX (1942), 85-117.

18 MORRILL, James L. *The Ongoing State University.* Minneapolis, 1960.

19 MUNFORD, Frederick B. *The Land Grant College Movement.* Columbia, Mo., 1940.

20 NEVINS, Allan. *The State Universities and Democracy.* Urbana, Ill., 1962.

21 PARKER, William B. *The Life and Public Service of Justin Smith Morrill.* Boston, 1924.

1 ROBERTS, O. M. "A History of the Establishment of the University of the State of Texas." *SW Hist Q*, I (1898), 233-265.

2 ROSS, Earle D. *Democracy's College: The Land-Grant Movement in the Formative Stage.* Ames, Iowa, 1942.

3 ROSS, Earle D. "The Father of the Land Grant College." *Ag Hist*, XII (1938), 151-186.

4 ROSS, Earle D. "History in the Land-Grant College." *Miss Val Hist Rev*, XXXII (1945-1946), 577-581.

5 ROSS, Earle D. *The Land-Grant Idea at Iowa State College: A Centennial Trial Balance, 1858-1958.* Ames, Iowa, 1958.

6 ROSS, Earle D. "The Manual Labor Experiment in the Land Grant College." *Miss Val Hist Rev*, XXI (1935), 513-528.

7 SIMON, John Y. "The Politics of the Morrill Act." *Ag Hist*, XXXVII (1963), 103-111.

8 TEN BROOK, Andrew. *American State Universities: Their Origin and Progress.* Cincinnati, 1875.

9 THWAITES, Reuben G., ed. *The University of Wisconsin: Its History and Its Alumni.* Madison, 1900.

10 WAHLQUIST, John T., and James W. THORNTON, Jr. *State Colleges and Universities.* Washington, D.C., 1964.

11 WHETZEL, H. H. "The History of Industrial Fellowships at the Department of Plant Pathology at Cornell University." *Ag Hist*, XIX (1945), 99-103.

12 WILSON, M. L. "Cultural Patterns in Agricultural History." *Ag Hist*, XII (1938), 3-10.

See also 16.20, 17.4, 18.13, 21.16, 26.4, 26.5, 32.16, 33.3, 33.12, 33.22, 34.1, 35.5-11, 35.15-17, 35.19, 36.1, 36.4-10, 36.13, 36.14, 36.18-21, 37.1-3, 37.7-9, 37.11, 37.12, 37.17, 38.3, 38.6, 38.8, 38.22, 38.23, 39.3, 39.12-14, 39.16, 40.4, 40.6, 44.10, 49.5, 81.13, 113.6.

D. GRADUATE AND PROFESSIONAL SCHOOLS

13 AHERN, Patrick H. "The First Faculty of the Catholic University of America." *Cath Hist Rev*, XXXIII (1947), 129-157.

14 BERELSON, Bernard. *Graduate Education in the United States.* New York, 1960.

15 CARMICHAEL, Oliver C. *Graduate Education: A Critique and a Program.* New York, 1961.

16 CARTTER, Allan M. *An Assessment of Quality in Graduate Education.* Washington, D.C., 1966.†

17 CORDASCO, Francesco. *Daniel Coit Gilman and the Protean Ph.D.* Leiden, The Netherlands, 1960.

1 ELLIOTT, Edward C., ed. *The Rise of a University: The University in Action. (From the Annual Reports, 1902-1935, of Nicholas Murray Butler, President of Columbia University.)* New York, 1937.

2 FLEXNER, Abraham. *Daniel Coit Gilman: Creator of the American Type of University.* New York, 1946.

3 FRANKLIN, Fabian. *The Life of Daniel Coit Gilman.* New York, 1910.

4 GILMAN, Daniel C. *The Launching of a University, and Other Papers.* New York, 1906.

5 GILMAN, Daniel C. *University Problems in the United States.* New York, 1898.

6 HAWKINS, Hugh D. "Sevge William Brown and His Influence on the John Hopkins University." *Md Hist Mag,* LII (1957), 173-186.

7 HAWKINS, Hugh. "Charles W. Eliot, Daniel C. Gilman, and the Nurture of American Scholarship." *N Eng Q,* XXXIX (1966), 291-308.

8 HAWKINS, Hugh. "Three University Presidents Testify." *Am Q,* XI (1959), 99-119.

9 HOLLEY, Howard L. "Medical Education in Alabama." *Ala Rev,* VII (1954), 245-263. (Concerns the years from 1852 to 1946.)

10 HOLLIS, Ernest V. "Forces That Have Shaped Doctoral Work in the United States." *Bull Am Assn Univ Prof,* XXXI (1945), 357-382.

11 HORTON, Bryne J. *The Graduate School (Its Origin and Administrative Development).* New York, 1940.

12 JOHN, Walton C. *Graduate Study in Universities and Colleges in the United States.* U S Off Ed Bull, 1934, no. 20. Washington, D.C., 1934.

13 KRAUS, Charles A. "The Evolution of the American Graduate School." *Bull Am Assn Univ Prof,* XXXVII (1951), 497-506.

14 LEFLAR, Robert A. "Legal Education in Arkansas: A Brief History of the Law School." *Ark Hist Q,* XXI (1962), 99-131. (Concerns the years from 1890 to 1957.)

15 MC GRATH, Earl J. *The Graduate School and the Decline of Liberal Education.* New York, 1959.†

16 PARKER, Franklin. "A Golden Age in American Education: Chicago in the 1890s." *School Soc,* LXXXIX (1961), 146-152.

17 PARKER, Joel. *The Law School of Harvard College.* New York, 1871.

18 PIERSON, Mary B. *Graduate Work in the South.* Chapel Hill, 1947.

19 REED, Glenn A. "Fifty Years of Conflict in the Graduate School." *Ed Rec,* XXXIII (1952), 5-23.

20 REIDLER, A. "American Technological Schools." *U S Bur Ed, Rep Comm 1892-1893.* Vol. I. Washington, D.C., 1895, pp. 657-686.

21 RUDY, Willis. "Eliot and Gilman: The History of an Academic Friendship." *Tchr Col Rec,* LIV, (1953), 307-318.

22 RYAN, W. Carson. *Studies in Early Graduate Education.* New York, 1939.

1 STORR, Richard J. *The Beginnings of Graduate Education in America.* Chicago, 1953.

2 WATRIN, Rita. *The Founding and Development of the Program of Affiliation of the Catholic University of America: 1912 to 1939.* Washington, D.C., 1966.

See also 1.4, 13.19, 14.9, 33.8-11, 33.13, 33.14, 33.16, 33.18, 33.20, 34.8, 34.15, 34.19, 34.20, 34.22, 34.23, 35.12, 35.13, 36.2, 36.16, 38.9-13, 38.20, 38.22, 38.23, 39.17, 40.13, 42.6, 44.17, 122.4.

E. FROM THE ELECTIVE SYSTEM TO THE PROGRESSIVE COLLEGE AND GENERAL EDUCATION

3 AIKIN, Wilford M. *The Story of the Eight-Year Study.* New York, 1942.

4 "Amherst Plan for Reading and Study." *Bull Am Assn Univ Prof*, IX (1923), 238-248.

5 AYDELOTTE, Frank. *Breaking the Academic Lock-Step.* New York, 1944.

6 AYDELOTTE, Frank. "Honors Work in College." *Prog Ed*, II (1925), 135-138.

7 BABBITT, Irving. "President Eliot and American Education." *Forum*, LXXXI (1929), 1-10.

8 BAKER, Ray S. *Woodrow Wilson, Life and Letters: Princeton, 1890-1910.* Garden City, N.Y., 1927.

9 BELL, Daniel. *The Reforming of General Education.* New York, 1966.†

10 BENEZET, Louis T. *General Education in the Progressive College.* New York, 1943.

11 BESTOR, Arthur. "The American University: A Historical Interpretation of Current Issues." *College and University*, XXXII (1957), 175-188.

12 BLANSHARD, Frances. *Frank Aydelotte of Swarthmore.* Middletown, Conn., 1970.

13 BOUCHER, Chauncey S. *The Chicago College Plan.* Chicago, 1936.

14 BRAGDON, Henry W. *Woodrow Wilson: The Academic Years.* Cambridge, Mass., 1967.

15 BRAMELD, Theodore B. "President Hutchins and the New Reaction." *Ed Forum*, I (1937), 271-282.

16 BREWER, Joseph, and Donald HEIGES. "The Search for Unity in Higher Education." *Har Ed Rev*, XVI (1946), 21-43.

17 CAPEN, Samuel P. "The Effect of the World War 1914-18 on American Colleges and Universities." *Ed Rec*, XXI (1940), 40-48.

18 CARPENTER, Hazen C. "Emerson, Eliot, and the Elective System." *N Eng Q*, XXIV (1951), 13-34.

19 CHASE, Harry W. "Hutchins' 'Higher Learning' Grounded." *Am Sch*, VI (1937), 236-244.

20 CITRON, Abraham F. "Experimentalism and the Classicism of President Hutchins." *Tchr Col Rec*, XLIV (1943), 544-553.

1 COOPER, Russell M. *The Two Ends of the Log; Learning and Teaching in Today's College.* Minneapolis, 1958.

2 COTTON, Edward H. *The Life of Charles W. Eliot.* Boston, 1926.

3 CRAIG, Hardin. *Woodrow Wilson at Princeton.* Norman, Okla., 1960.

4 DEMOS, Raphael, et al. "A Symposium on Educational Philosophy." *Philosophy and Phenomenological Research*, II (Dec., 1946), 187-213.

5 "Developing the Track System: Sectioning Students on the Basis of Ability." *Bull Am Assn Univ Prof*, XII (1926), 133-191.

6 DEWEY, John. "President Hutchins' Proposals to Remake Higher Education." *Social Frontier*, IV (1937), 103-166.

7 DRESSEL, Paul L., and Lewis B. MAYHEW. *General Education: Explorations in Evaluation.* Washington, D.C., 1954.

8 DUFFUS, Robert L. *Democracy Enters the College: A Study of the Rise and Decline of the Academic Lockstep.* New York, 1936.

9 ECKERT, Ruth E. *Outcomes of General Education: An Appraisal of the General College Program.* Minneapolis, 1943.

10 ELIOT, Charles W. *Educational Reform: Essays and Addresses.* New York, 1898.

11 ELIOT, Charles W. *University Administration.* Boston, 1908.

12 EURICH, Alvin C., et al. *General Education in the American College.* 38th *Yrbk Nat Soc Stud Ed.* Pt. II. Bloomington, Ill., 1939.

13 FARNSWORTH, Dana L. "Psychiatry and HigherEducation." *Am J Psy*, CIX (1952), 266-271.

14 FLEXNER, Abraham. *A Modern College and a Modern School.* Garden City, N.Y., 1923.

15 FRODIN, Reuben, et al. *The Idea and Practice of General Education: An Account of the College of the University of Chicago, by Present and Former Members of the Faculty.* Chicago, 1950.

16 *General Education in a Free Society: Report of the Harvard Committee on the Objectives of a General Education in a Free Society.* Cambridge, Mass., 1945.

17 GIDEONSE, Harry D. *The Higher Learning in a Democracy.* New York, 1937.

18 GRAY, William S., ed. *General Education: Its Nature, Scope, and Essential Elements.* Chicago, 1934.

19 HAWKINS, Hugh. "Charles W. Eliot, University Reform, and Religious Faith in America, 1869-1909." *J Am Hist*, LI (1964), 191-213.

20 HENDERSON, Algo D., and Dorothy HALL. *Antioch College: Its Design for Liberal Education.* New York, 1946.

21 HERBST, Jurgen. "Liberal Education and the Graduate Schools: An Historical View of College Reform." *Hist Ed Q*, II (1962), 244-258.

22 HOOK, Sidney. *Education for Modern Man.* New York, 1946.

23 HUTCHINS, Robert M. *The Great Conversation: The Substance of a Liberal Education.* Chicago, 1952.

24 HUTCHINS, Robert M. *The Higher Learning in America.* New Haven, 1936.†

1 HUTCHINS, Robert M. *No Friendly Voice.* Chicago, 1937.

2 HUTCHINS, Robert M. *The State of the University, 1929-1949.* Chicago, 1949.

3 HUTCHINS, Robert M. "The University of Chicago and the Bachelor's Degree." *Ed Rec*, XXIII (1942), 567-573.

4 HUTCHINS, Robert M. "The University of Chicago: Its Past Record and Its Future Mission." *School Soc*, LXII (1945), 65-69.

5 HUTCHINS, Robert M. *The University of Utopia.* Chicago, 1953.†

6 JAMES, Henry. *Charles W. Eliot: President of Harvard University, 1869-1909.* 2 vols. Boston, 1930.

7 KENNEDY, Gail, ed. *Education at Amherst, The New Program.* New York, 1955.

8 KIRKPATRICK, John E. *Academic Organization and Control.* Yellow Springs, Ohio, 1931.

9 KIRKPATRICK, John E. *The American College and Its Rulers.* New York, 1926.

10 LEWIS, Hal G. "Meiklejohn and Experimentalism." *Tchr Col Rec*, XLIV (1943), 563-571.

11 LIMBERT, Paul M. "Trends and Patterns in the Changing College Curriculum." *Tchr Col Rec*, XL (1939), 669-684.

12 LOWELL, Abbott L. *At War with Academic Traditions in America.* Cambridge, Mass., 1934.

13 MC CONN, Charles M. *College or Kindergarten?* New York, 1929.

14 MC CONNELL, T. R., et al. *General Education.* 51st *Yrbk Nat Soc Stud Ed.* Pt. I. Chicago, 1952.

15 MC GRATH, Earl J., et al. *Toward General Education.* New York, 1948.

16 MC HALE, Kathryn, et al. *Changes and Experiments in Liberal Arts Education.* 31st *Yrbk Nat Soc Stud Ed.* Pt. II. Bloomington, Ill., 1932.

17 MC LEISH, Archibald. "Professional Schools of Liberal Education." *Yale Rev*, X (1926), 362-372.

18 MAYHEW, Lewis B. *The Smaller Liberal Arts College.* Washington, D.C., 1962.

19 MEIKLEJOHN, Alexander. *Education Between Two Worlds.* New York, 1942.†

20 MEIKLEJOHN, Alexander. *The Experimental College.* New York, 1932.

21 MEIKLEJOHN, Alexander. "The Unity of the Curriculum." *New Republic*, XXXII (Oct. 25, 1922), 2-3.

22 MILLSAP, Kenneth. "Parsons College." *Palimpsest*, XXXI (1950), 281-328.

23 MORISON, Samuel E., ed. *The Development of Harvard University Since the Inauguration of President Eliot (1869-1929).* Cambridge, Mass., 1930.

24 NEILSON, William A., ed. *Charles W. Eliot: The Man and His Beliefs.* 2 vols. New York, 1926.

1 PACE, Charles R. *They Went to College: A Study of 951 Former University Students*. Minneapolis, 1941.

2 POPE, Arthur U. "Alexander Meiklejohn." *Am Sch*, XXXIV (1965), 641-645.

3 RAVI-BOOTH, Vincent. "A New College for Women." *Prog Ed*, II (1925), 138-145. (Refers to Bennington College, Vt.)

4 SPAFFORD, Ivol, et al. *Building a Curriculum for General Education: A Description of the General College Program*. Minneapolis, 1943.

5 THOMAS, Russell. *The Search for a Common Learning: General Education, 1800-1960*. New York, 1962.

6 TROWBRIDGE, Hoyt. "Forty Years of General Education." *J Gen Ed*, XI (1958), 161-169.

7 VAN DOREN, Mark. *Liberal Education*. New York, 1943.

8 VEYSEY, Laurence R. "The Academic Mind of Woodrow Wilson." *Miss Val Hist Rev*, XLIX (1963), 613-634.

9 WALTON, John. "The Apostasy of Robert M. Hutchins." *Ed Theory*, III (1953), 162-165.

10 WHIPPLE, Guy M., ed. *General Education in the American College*. 38th Yrbk Nat Soc Stud Ed. Bloomington, Ill., 1939.

11 WILLIAMS, Cornelia T. *These We Teach: A Study of General College Students*. Minneapolis, 1943.

12 WRISTON, Henry M. *Academic Procession; Reflections of a College President*. New York, 1959.

13 WRISTON, Henry M. *The Nature of a Liberal College*. Appleton, Wis., 1937.

See also 32.18, 34.20, 39.21, 41.3, 42.17.

F. BLACK AMERICANS

14 ATWOOD, Rufus B. "The Origin and Development of the Negro Public College, with Especial Reference to the Land-Grant College." *J Neg Ed*, XXXI (1962), 240-250.

15 BADGER, Henry G. "Negro Colleges and Universities: 1900-1950." *J Neg Ed*, XXI (1952), 89-93.

16 BOND, Horace M. "Evolution and Present Status of Negro Higher Education in the United States." *J Neg Ed*, XVII (1948), 224-235.

17 BOND, Horace M. "The Origin and Development of the Negro Church-Related College." *J Neg Ed*, XXIX (1960), 217-226.

18 CLARK, Felton G. "The Development and Present Status of Publicly-Supported Higher Education for Negroes." *J Neg Ed*, XXVII (1958), 221-232.

19 CLEMENT, Rufus E. "The Historical Development of Higher Education for Negro Americans." *J Neg Ed*, XXXV (1966), 299-305.

20 DYSON, Walter. *The Founding of Howard University*. Washington, D.C., 1921.

21 DYSON, Walter. *Howard University, the Capstone of Negro Education: A History, 1867-1940*. Washington, D.C., 1941.

1 EELLS, Walter C. "The Center of Population of Negro Higher Education." *J Neg Ed*, V (1936), 595-598.

2 EELLS, Walter C. "Higher Education of Negroes in the United States." *J Neg Ed*, XXIV (1955), 426-434.

3 FRANKLIN, John H. "Jim Crow Goes to College: The Genesis of Legal Segregation in Southern Schools." *S Atl Q*, LVIII (1959), 225-235.

4 FRAZIER, E. Franklin. "Graduate Education in Negro Colleges and Universities." *J Neg Ed*, II (1933), 329-341.

5 HOLMES, Dwight O. W. *The Evolution of the Negro College.* New York, 1934.

6 HOLMES, Dwight O. W. "Fifty Years of Howard University." *J Neg Hist*, III (1918), 128-138, 368-380.

7 JACKSON, L. P. "The Origin of Hampton Institute." *J Neg Hist*, X (1925), 131-149.

8 JENCKS, Christopher, and David RIESMAN. "The American Negro College." *Har Ed Rev*, XXXVII (1967), 3-60; "Four Responses and a Reply." *Ibid.*, pp. 451-468.

9 LE MELLE, Tilden J. and Wilbert J. *The Black College: A Strategy for Achieving Relevancy.* New York, 1969.

10 LOGAN, Frenise A. "The Movement in North Carolina to Establish a State Supported College for Negroes." *N C Hist Rev*, XXXV (1958), 167-180.

11 LOGAN, Rayford W. "The Evolution of Private Colleges for Negroes." *J Neg Ed*, XXVII (1958), 213-220.

12 MC LEAN, Malcolm S. "Impact of World War II upon Institutions for the Higher Education of the Negro." *J Neg Ed*, XI (1942), 338-345.

13 MARTIN, William H. "Desegregation in Higher Education." *Tchr Col Rec*, LXII (1960), 36-47.

14 NEYLAND, Leedell W. "State-Supported Higher Education Among Negroes in the State of Florida." *Fla Hist Q*, XLIII (1964), 105-122.

15 PIEDMONT, Eugene B. "Changing Racial Attitudes at a Southern University: 1947-1964." *J Neg Ed*, XXXVI (1967), 32-41.

16 SEKORA, John. "The Emergence of Negro Higher Education in America: A Review." *Race*, X (1968), 79-87.

17 SIMS, David H. "Religious Education in Negro Colleges and Universities." *J Neg Hist*, V (1920), 166-207.

18 WHITEHEAD, Matthew J. "Origin and Establishment of the Negro College Deanship." *J Neg Ed*, XIV (1945), 166-173.

19 WILSON, Ruth D. "Negro Colleges of Liberal Arts." *Am Sch*, XIX (1950), 461-470.

See also 35.1.

G. SCHOLARSHIP AND SCIENCE

20 ANDERSON, Paul R. *Platonism in the Midwest.* New York, 1963.

1 BEARDSLEY, Edward H. *The Rise of the American Chemistry Profession, 1850-1900.* Gainesville, Fla., 1964.

2 BEISNER, Robert L. "Brooks Adams and Charles Francis Adams, Jr.: Historians of Massachusetts." *N Eng Q*, XXXV (1962), 48-70.

3 BEN-DAVID, Joseph, and Randall COLLINS. "Social Factors in the Origins of a New Science: The Case of Psychology." *Am Soc Rev*, XXXI (1966), 451-465.

4 BERNARD, Luther L. and Jessie. *Origins of American Sociology: The Social Science Movement in the United States.* New York, 1965.

5 BESTOR, Arthur E., Jr. "The Transformation of American Scholarship, 1875-1917." *Libr Q*, XXIII (1953), 164-179.

6 BRYSON, Gladys. "The Comparable Interests of the Old Moral Philosophy and the Modern Social Sciences." *Social Forces*, XI (1932), 19-27.

7 BRYSON, Gladys. "The Emergence of the Social Sciences from Moral Philosophy." *Int J Ethics*, XLII (1932), 304-323.

8 BRYSON, Gladys. "Sociology Considered as Moral Philosophy." *Am Soc Rev*, XXIV (1932), 26-36.

9 BUCK, Paul, ed. *Social Sciences at Harvard: 1860-1920.* Cambridge, Mass., 1965.

10 CARMICHAEL, Leonard. "Scientific Psychology and the Schools of Psychology." *Am J Psy*, LXXXVIII (1932), 955-968.

11 COATS, A. W. "American Scholarship Comes of Age: The Louisiana Purchase Exposition of 1904." *J Hist Ideas*, XXII (1961), 404-417.

12 COATS, A. W. "Henry Carter Adams: A Case Study in the Emergence of the Social Sciences in the United States, 1850-1900." *J Am St*, II (1968), 177-197.

13 COLE, Arthur H. "Economic History in the United States: Formative Years of a Discipline." *J Econ Hist*, XXVII (1968), 556-589.

14 COPE, Jackson I. "William James's Correspondence with Daniel Coit Gilman, 1877-1881." *J Hist Ideas*, XII (1951), 609-627.

15 DONNAN, Elizabeth, and Leo F. STOCK, eds. *An Historian's World: Selections from the Correspondence of John Franklin Jameson.* Philadelphia, 1956.

16 DREEBEN, Robert. "Political and Educational Ideas in the Writing of George Herbert Mead." *Har Ed Rev*, XXV (1955), 157-168.

17 DUPREE, A. Hunter, ed. *Darwiniana.* Cambridge, Mass., 1963.†

18 EISENSTADT, Abraham S. *Charles McLean Andrews: A Study in American Historical Writing.* New York, 1956.

19 EVERETT, John R. *Religion in Economics: A Study of John Bates Clark, Richard T. Ely, and Simon N. Patten.* New York, 1946.

20 FAY, Jay W. *American Psychology Before William James.* New Brunswick, 1939.

21 FENTON, Charles A. "The Founding of the National Institute of Arts and Letters in 1898." *N Eng Q*, XXXII (1959), 435-444.

22 FISCH, Max H. "Evolution in American Philosophy." *Philos Rev*, LVI (1947), 357-373.

1 FLEXNER, Abraham. "Medical Education, 1909-1924." *Ed Rec*, V (1924), 75-91.

2 FOERSTER, Norman. *The American Scholar: A Study in Litterae Inhumaniores*. Chapel Hill, 1929.

3 GLASS, Bentley. "The Academic Scientist, 1940-1960." *Bull Am Assn Univ Prof*, XLVI (1960), 149-154.

4 HALL, G. Stanley. "Philosophy in the United States." *Mind*, IV (1879), 89-105.

5 HALL, G. Stanley. "Psychological Education." *Am J Psy*, LIII (1896), 228-241.

6 HARTER, Lafayette G. *John R. Commons: His Assault on Laissez-Faire*. Corvallis, Ore., 1962.

7 HERBST, Jurgen. "Francis Greenwood Peabody: Harvard's Theologian of the Social Gospel." *Har Theol Rev*, LIV (1961), 45-69.

8 HERBST, Jurgen. "From Moral Philosophy to Sociology: Albion W. Small." *Har Ed Rev*, XXIX (1959), 227-244.

9 HERBST, Jurgen. "Social Darwinism and the History of American Geography." *Proc Am Philos Soc*, CV (1961), 538-544.

10 HIGHAM, John. "The Schism in American Scholarship." *Am Hist Rev*, LXXII (1966), 1-21.

11 HOLT, W. Stull. "The Idea of Scientific History in America." *J Hist Ideas*, I (1940), 352-362.

12 HOLT, W. Stull, ed. *Historical Scholarship in the United States, 1876-1901: As Revealed in the Correspondence of Herbert B. Adams*. Baltimore, 1938.

13 JAMES, William. *The Principles of Psychology*. 2 vols. New York, 1890.†

14 JAMES, William. *Talks to Teachers on Psychology: And to Students on Some of Life's Ideals*. New York, 1900.†

15 JONCICH, Geraldine. "Scientists and the Schools of the Nineteenth Century: The Case of American Physicists." *Am Q*, XVIII (1966), 667-685.

16 KIMBALL, Elsa P. *Sociology and Education*. New York, 1932.

17 KNIGHT, Margaret. *William James*. London, 1950.†

18 LAZARSFELD, P. F., and Wagner THIELENS, Jr. *The Academic Mind: Social Scientists in a Time of Crisis*. Glencoe, Ill., 1958.

19 LEVERETTE, William E., Jr. "E. L. Youmans' Crusade for Scientific Autonomy and Respectability." *Am Q*, XVII (1965), 12-32.

20 MADSEN, David. "Daniel Coit Gilman at the Carnegie Institution of Washington." *Hist Ed Q*, IX (1969), 154-186.

21 MEAD, George H. "The Philosophies of Royce, James, and Dewey in Their American Setting." *Int J Ethics*, XL (1929-30), 211-31.

22 MENDELSOHN, Everett. "Science in America: The Twentieth Century." *Paths of American Thought*. Ed. by A. M. Schlesinger, Jr., and Morton White. Boston, 1963, pp. 432-445.

1 O'CONNOR, Michael J. L. *Origins of Academic Economics in the United States.* New York, 1944.

2 PAINE, N. Emmons. "Instruction in Psychiatry in American Medical Colleges." *Am J Psy*, L (1894), 372-380.

3 PATRICK, George T. W. "Founding the Psychological Laboratory of the State University of Iowa." *Iowa J Hist*, XXX (1932), 404-416.

4 PERKINS, Dexter, and John L. SNELL. *The Education of Historians in the United States.* New York, 1962.

5 ROBINSON, Elmo A. "One Hundred Years of Philosophy Teaching in California, 1857-1957." *J Hist Ideas*, XX (1959), 369-384.

6 RUCKER, Darnell. *The Chicago Pragmatists.* Minneapolis, 1969.

7 SCHUYLER, William. "The St. Louis Philosophical Movement." *Ed Rev*, XXIX (1905), 450-467.

8 SHRYOCK, Richard H. *The Unique Influence of the Johns Hopkins University on American Medicine.* Copenhagen, 1953. Also printed in *Acta Historica Scientiarum Naturalium et Medicinalium.* Copenhagen, 1953.

9 SMALL, Albion. "Fifty Years of Sociology in the United States (1865-1915)." *Am J Soc*, XXI (1916), 721-864.

10 SNIDER, Denton J. *The St. Louis Movement.* St. Louis, 1920.

11 STEPHENSON, Wendell H. "Herbert B. Adams and Southern Historical Scholarship at the Johns Hopkins University." *Md Hist Mag*, XLII (1947), 1-20.

12 STRICKLAND, Charles E., and Charles BURGESS. *Health, Growth, and Heredity: G. Stanley Hall on Natural Education.* New York, 1965.†

13 "A Study of the Medical Course: Its History and Future." *Bull Am Assn Univ Prof*, XI (1925), 354-364.

14 VISHER, Stephan S. "J. McKeen Cattell and American Science." *School Soc*, LXVI (1947), 449-452.

15 WATSON, John B. *Behaviorism.* Rev. ed. Chicago, 1930.†

16 WATSON, John B. *Psychology from the Standpoint of a Behaviorist.* 2nd ed. Philadelphia, 1924.

17 WEBB, Walter P. "The Historical Seminar: Its Outer Shell and Its Inner Spirit." *Miss Val Hist Rev*, XLII (1955), 3-23.

18 WILKINS, Burleigh T. "James, Dewey, and Hegelian Idealism." *J Hist Ideas*, XVII (1956), 332-346.

See also 12.14.

H. THE CRISIS OF THE 1960s

19 AVORN, Jerry L. et al. *Up Against the Ivy Wall.* New York, 1968.†

20 BARLOW, William, and Peter SHAPIRO. *An End to Silence: The San Francisco State Student Movement in the '60s.* New York, 1970.

21 BARZUN, Jacques. *The American University: How it Runs, Where It Is Going.* New York, 1968.

1 BAY, Christian. "Political and Apolitical Students: Facts in Search of Theory." *J Soc Iss*, XXIII (1967), 76-91.

2 BELL, Daniel, and Irving KRISTOL. *Confrontation: The Student Rebellion and the Universities.* New York, 1969.

3 BLACK, Max, ed. *The Morality of Scholarship.* Ithaca, N.Y., 1967.

4 BROWN, David G. *The Mobile Professors.* Washington, D.C., 1967.

5 BYSE, Clark. "The University and Due Process: A Somewhat Different View." *Bull Am Assn Univ Prof*, LIV (1968), 143-148.

6 CHAMBERS, Merritt M. *The Campus and the People: Organization, Support, and Control of Higher Education in the United States in the Nineteen Sixties.* Danville, Ill., 1960.

7 COCKBURN, Alexander, and Robin BLACKBURN, eds. *Student Power: Problems, Diagnosis, Action.* Baltimore, 1969.†

8 COHEN, Mitchell, and Dennis HALE, eds. *The New Student Left: An Anthology.* Boston, 1966. (2d rev. ed., 1968)†

9 *Crisis at Columbia: Report of the Fact-Finding Commission Appointed to Investigate the Disturbances at Columbia University in April and May, 1968.* New York, 1968.†

10 DENNIS, Lawrence E., and Joseph F. KAUFFMAN, eds. *The College and the Student.* Washington, D.C., 1966.

11 DRAPER, Hal. *Berkeley: The New Student Revolt.* New York, 1965.†

12 EHRENREICH, Barbara and John. *Long March, Short Spring: The Student Uprising at Home and Abroad.* New York, 1969.†

13 FEUER, Lewis S. *The Conflict of Generations.* New York, 1969.

14 FORMAN, Sidney. "Scandal Among Cadets: An Historical Verdict." *Tchr Col Rec*, LXVI (1965), 485-491.

15 FOSTER, Julian, and Durward LONG, eds. *Protest: Student Activism in America.* New York, 1970.

16 FRANKEL, Charles. *Education and the Barricades.* New York, 1968.†

17 GLAZER, Penina. "The New Left, A Style of Protest." *J High Ed*, XXXVIII (1967), 119-130.

18 GOODMAN, Paul. *The Community of Scholars.* New York, 1962.†

19 GRAUBARD, Stephen R., and Geno A. BALLOTTI, eds. *The Embattled University.* New York, 1970.

20 GROSSVOGEL, David I., and Cushing STROUT, eds. *Divided We Stand: Reflections on the Crisis at Cornell.* New York, 1970.†

21 HAVIGHURST, Robert J. *American Higher Education in the 1960s.* Columbus, Ohio, 1960.

22 HOOK, Sidney. *Academic Freedom and Academic Anarchy.* New York, 1970.

23 JACOBS, Paul and Saul LANDAU, eds. *The New Radicals.* New York, 1966.†

24 JENCKS, Christopher, and David RIESMAN. "The War Between the Generations." *Tchr Col Rec*, LXIX (1967), 1-22.

1 JOHNSON, Michael T. "Constitutional Rights of College Students." *Tex Law Rev*, XLII (1964), 344-363.

2 KATZ, Joseph. *The Student Activists*. Stanford, 1967.

3 KENISTON, Kenneth. "The Sources of Student Dissent." *J Soc Iss*, XXIII (1967), 108-137.

4 KENISTON, Kenneth. *The Uncommitted: Alienated Youth in American Society*. New York, 1960.†

5 KENISTON, Kenneth. *Young Radicals: Notes on Committed Youth*. New York, 1968.†

6 KENNAN, George. *Democracy and the Student Left*. New York, 1968.

7 KERR, Clark. *The Uses of the University*. Cambridge, Mass., 1964.†

8 LIPSET, Seymour M. "Students and Politics in Comparative Perspective." *Daedalus*, XCVII (1968), 1-28.

9 LIPSET, Seymour M., ed. *Student Politics*. New York, 1967.

10 LIPSET, Seymour M., and Philip ALTBACH, eds. *Students in Revolt*. Boston, 1970.†

11 LIPSET, Seymour M., and Sheldon S. WOLIN, eds. *The Berkeley Student Revolt: Facts and Interpretations*. Garden City, N.Y., 1965.†

12 LUNSFORD, Terry F. *The Free Speech Crisis at Berkeley, 1964-1965: Some Issues for Social and Legal Research*. Berkeley, 1965.

13 MAYHEW, Lewis B., ed. *Higher Education in the Revolutionary Decades*. Berkeley, 1967.

14 MENASHE, Louis, and Ronald RADOSH, eds. *Teach-Ins, U.S.A.: Reports, Opinions, Documents*. New York, 1967.

15 MILLER, Michael V., and Susan GILMORE, eds. *Revolution at Berkeley: The Crisis in American Education*. New York, 1965.†

16 MILTON, Ohmer, and Edward J. SHOBEN, eds. *Learning and the Professors*. Columbus, Ohio, 1968.†

17 MORISON, Robert S., ed. *The Contemporary University: USA*. Boston, 1966.†

18 MUSCATINE, Charles et al. *Education at Berkeley: Report of the Select Committee on Education, University of California, Berkeley*. Berkeley, 1966.

19 NEWFIELD, Jack. *A Prophetic Minority*. New York, 1966.

20 ORRICK, William H., Jr. *College in Crisis*. Nashville, Tenn., 1970. (Concerns San Francisco State.)

21 PERKINS, James A. *The University in Transition*. Princeton, 1966.†

22 PETERSON, Richard E. *The Scope of Organized Student Protest in 1967-1968*. Princeton, 1968.

23 PUSEY, Nathan M. *The Age of the Scholar: Observations on Education in a Troubled Decade*. Cambridge, Mass., 1964.

24 RAPOPORT, Roger, and Laurence J. KIRSHBAUM. *Is the Library Burning?* New York, 1969.†

1 RATTERMAN, P. H. *The Emerging Catholic University: With a Commentary on the Joint Statement on the Rights and Freedoms of Students.* New York, 1968.

2 RIDGEWAY, James. *The Closed Corporation: American Universities in Crisis.* New York, 1968.†

3 RIESMAN, David, and Christopher JENCKS. "A Case Study in Vignette: San Francisco State College." *Tchr Col Rec*, LXIII (1962), 233-266.

4 ROGAN, Donald L. *Campus Apocalypse.* New York, 1969.

5 ROSKENS, Ronald W., and Robert I. WHITE, eds. *Paradox, Process, and Progress: Essays on the Community of Higher Education.* Kent, Ohio, 1968.

6 ROSZAK, Theodore, ed. *The Dissenting Academy.* New York, 1968.†

7 SAMPSON, Edward E. "Student Activism and the Decade of Protest." *J Soc Iss*, XXIII (1967), 1-33.

8 SAVIO, Mario. "The Uncertain Future of the Multiversity: A Partisan Scrutiny of Berkeley's Muscatine Report." *Harper's* (Oct. 1966), pp. 88-94.

9 SCHWAB, Joseph J. *College Curriculum and Student Protest.* Chicago, 1969.

10 SEAVEY, Warren A. "Dismissal of Students: Due Process." *Har Law Rev*, LXX (1956-57), 1406-1410.

11 SELDEN, William K. "Some Observations on the Governance of the American University." *Tchr Col Rec*, LXVIII (1967), 277-288.

12 SMITH, G. Kerry, et al., eds. *Stress and Campus Response: Current Issues in Higher Education.* New York, 1968.

13 SPENDER, Stephen. *The Year of the Young Rebels.* New York, 1969.†

14 Students for a Democratic Society. *Port Huron Statement.* Chicago, 1966.

15 TAYLOR, Harold. *Students Without Teachers: The Crisis in the University.* New York, 1968.

16 TUSSMAN, Joseph. *Experiment at Berkeley.* New York, 1969.†

17 VON HOFFMAN, Nicholas. *The Multiversity. A Personal Report on What Happens to Today's Students at American Universities.* New York, 1966.

18 WALLERSTEIN, Immanuel. *University in Turmoil: The Politics of Change.* Boston, 1969.

19 WOLFF, Robert P. *The Ideal of the University.* Boston, 1969.

20 WOODRING, Paul. *The Higher Learning in America: A Reassessment.* New York, 1968.†

See also 1.8, 41.13, 44.1, 46.5-8, 46.10, 46.11, 46.13, 46.15, 47.2, 47.6, 47.8, 47.10, 47.12, 48.2, 48.9, 48.13, 49.14, 111.1, 111.18.

NOTES

INDEX

INDEX

INDEX

C

138

INDEX

INDEX

142

INDEX

INDEX

INDEX

INDEX

INDEX

S

150

INDEX